Library of
Davidson College

*The Political Philosophy
of the Frankfurt School*

The Political Philosophy of the Frankfurt School

GEORGE FRIEDMAN

Cornell University Press
ITHACA AND LONDON

Copyright © 1981 by Cornell University

All rights reserved. Except for brief quotations in a review, this book, or parts thereof, must not be reproduced in any form without permission in writing from the publisher. For information address Cornell University Press, 124 Roberts Place, Ithaca, New York 14850.

First published 1981 by Cornell University Press.
Published in the United Kingdom by Cornell University Press Ltd.
2-4 Brook Street, London W1Y 1AA.

International Standard Book Number 0-8014-1279-X
Library of Congress Catalog Card Number 80-66890
Printed in the United States of America
Librarians: Library of Congress cataloging information appears on the last page of the book.

For my parents,
Emil and Friderika Friedman

Contents

Acknowledgments	9
Introduction	13
PART I. PHILOSOPHICAL ROOTS OF THE FRANKFURT SCHOOL	
1. Introduction to Their Heritage	29
2. Marx	33
3. Hegel and Hegelianism	50
4. Nietzsche	62
5. Heidegger	71
6. Spengler	79
7. Freud	87
8. Judaism	92
9. Conclusion	103
PART II. POSING THE PROBLEM OF MODERNITY	
10. The Crisis of the Enlightenment	111
11. The Crisis of Art and Culture	136
12. The Crisis of the Human Psyche	168
13. The Crisis of History	186
PART III. THE SEARCH FOR THE SOLUTION	
14. The Exegetical Solution	207
15. The Political Solution	226
16. The Transfiguration of Being	248
Conclusion. The Frankfurt School and the Failure of Modernity: A Critique	279
Bibliography of Cited Works	303
Index	309

Acknowledgments

Many institutions and people have been generous and helpful during the writing of this book. The Cornell University Program in the Humanities and Social Sciences and the New York State Regents' Fellowship Program funded the research, and Dickinson College was generous in its support while the various drafts and revisions were being prepared. I thank the many people who read and criticized the manuscript and encouraged me. George Allan, Isaac Kramnick, David Mozingo, William Riggins, and Myron Rush were thoughtful and helpful critics. Victoria Kuhn and Jane Krebs typed tirelessly, and Agnes Fine typed and tried to explain the rules of punctuation to me. Bill Hervey and William Shapiro directed my attention to the Frankfurt School at a time when I was interested in things far less important. Without them this book would not exist, and to them I am eternally indebted. More than to anyone else, I am grateful to Werner J. Dannhauser, my adviser and friend, who guided this work with wisdom and humor. He was my teacher in the fullest sense of that term. Finally, I thank my wife, Dorothy, who remained remarkably pleasant through the preparation of this book.

GEORGE FRIEDMAN

Carlisle, Pennsylvania

*The Political Philosophy
of the Frankfurt School*

Introduction

The Frankfurt School was both an institution and a mode of thought. The Institute of Social Research was founded in Frankfurt, Germany, in 1923, and it reached maturity in 1931 when Max Horkheimer became its director. The Institute continued its work in exile in the United States following Hitler's rise to power and did not return to Germany until 1950.

During this time, the Institute's members developed a unique and powerful critique of modern life. This critique served as a basis for much of the student movement of the 1960s and thus had consequences beyond academe, where the Frankfurt School's brilliance and erudition made a lasting and powerful impression.

This book is dedicated to explicating the thought of the Frankfurt School and to understanding the significance of that thought. I have chosen to study four men who were instrumental in developing the mode of thought known collectively as the Frankfurt School: Walter Benjamin, Theodor W. Adorno, Max Horkheimer, and Herbert Marcuse. My hope in carrying out this study was to learn more about the nature of the modern crisis. I have not been disappointed. The Frankfurt School proved to be among its supreme explicators.

It is difficult to speak of the crisis of modernity, since it is difficult to speak of ourselves. To describe modernity's crisis is even more challenging. Still we all seem to know that there is something seriously wrong with our time and we know as well that not all epochs have felt such an odd lack of self-confidence. Perhaps we might start by considering the origins of modernity's lack of self-confidence.

We moderns have felt our greatest pride in our reason and in the attendant triumphs of our sciences. From the Enlightenment onward we had the firm belief that reason and science were paths to redemption. Now, in our time, we have discovered the darker side of reason. We have found that along with great triumphs, reason has also brought great brutality. The Frankfurt School set itself the task of defining the relationship between reason and brutality.

Leo Strauss teaches us that modernity began with Machiavelli, who made the first argument against a transcendent philosophy. In doing so, he also made the argument for reason as an instrument in service to the interests of humanity. Machiavelli was in part attempting to abolish the estrangement between philosophy and existence, between reason and reality.

Hegel brought Machiavelli's project to fruition. When he argued that the real and rational had become one, he claimed that humanity had triumphed over the depredations of reality. Karl Marx affirmed the essence of Hegel's position, while substituting the proletariat for the German Civil Service as the solution to the riddle of history. Marx shared Hegel's confidence that there was such a thing as history, that history possessed a riddle, and that the riddle could be solved.

Modern philosophy, therefore, is marked by a radical self-confidence. It believes it possible that all things could be as they ought to be. The outward signs of modernity—its technologies, both industrial and social—are testimonies to this self-confidence. What binds together medicine, civil engineering, city planning, and the disparate other sciences that rule us today is their confidence that they have a wisdom sufficient and proper to the task of remaking nature in the image of their imaginings.

Modern thought is paradoxical, however. As the sciences it created triumph, its sensibilities rebel. The question is this: if the real has become rational and the rational real, then what is there left for men to do? Philosophy, poetry, war, and politics—their greatness was rooted in the tragic opposition between the ideal and real. With that tension abolished, the abysmal question must be faced: is there a place left in this world for man? Or is man, the great critic of the world and of mankind, to be reduced, with his philosophy and art, to a mere instrument supporting a world at peace with itself?

The triumph of modern reason leaves us, as Nietzsche and Dostoevsky show, with the problem of the function and limits of man in a world in which man's function as a critic has been abolished and in which limits that were thought to be natural and eternal have been overcome. We late moderns, who live after the triumph of

Introduction

reason, face the problem of creating—or, more precisely, resurrecting—a critical theory that will tell us once more about those things that ought to be as well as about administering things as they already are.

In short, the modern sensibility faces a crisis of success. Reason has given us that which it promised, power over nature. The question that remains, the abysmal question, is what it is that it is now proper to wish for. To be human we must want something, but what are the grounds upon which we are now to make our choice?

It is perhaps easier to begin with what we would not wish to choose. For this a single name sufficed for the Frankfurt School: Auschwitz. At Auschwitz the awful problem of modernity made itself evident. If modernity reached its most extreme and self-confident point when Hegel declared that the real had become rational and the rational real, Auschwitz revealed the emptiness of that claim.

At Auschwitz, the alliance between the peculiarly modern vision of reason as primarily an instrument of administration and the brutality that sprang from such reason was revealed. Hegel's own countrymen had demonstrated reason's potential for evil when it became a tool of rulers in a world that had banished critical reason. The terrible novelty of Auschwitz was that passionless slaughter became an end in itself. Always before, men had killed as a means to an end or as an end in itself when they were moved by passion. Only at Auschwitz—that is, only with the Nazis—did the slaughter of innocents become both an end in itself and a matter of detached, reasoned, and authoritative state policy. The death of children has always been incidental to war. With the Nazis, the death of children became war's end, its justification. Thus, Auschwitz is the appropriate symbol for modernity because it combined reason and madness in such a way as to make it impossible to separate them.

Auschwitz was a rational place, but it was not a reasonable one. It was rational in that it was efficient and sophisticated for its given task. It would not have been practical or even seriously conceivable except for the technologies of modern science. Furthermore, except for the modern belief that thought and practice can be identical (a belief that is the basis of technology), the translation of Hitler's nightmare image into practical reality would have been inconceivable.

The power of modern reason is that it feels itself honor bound to take everything seriously. This openness to everything is the result of our peculiar skepticism, in which we are reverent about nothing. The modern feels not only that everything is possible but also that all things possible are practical. The destruction of the Jews had always been imaginable. With Hitler it became practical. The skepticism of scientific reason sapped our critical reason. Our obligation to take the awful seriously meant that we were not free simply to condemn. Our social scientists and philosophers felt that there was something terribly wrong at Auschwitz, but their methodologies, their rational procedures, did not allow their personal revulsion to be turned into scientific principle. Their methods required neutrality. Revulsion was reduced to value judgments. Since moral values were viewed as irrational, and the irrational has no place in the scientific mode of thought, our social scientists had to be open to the suspicion that there was nothing demonstrably wrong with Auschwitz.

Not only was nothing sacred, but all things had possible merit. Reason denied itself the right to an a priori revulsion at Auschwitz. Modernity's reason led us into a fully unreasonable condition in which the common sense of the humane tradition had to be denied. It was this unreasonable rationality, this modern paradox, that was the great concern of the Frankfurt School.

The project of the Frankfurt School centered on a question that Theodor Adorno and Max Horkheimer posed for themselves at the beginning of the *Dialectic of Enlightenment* (1944), "why mankind, instead of entering into a truly human condition, is sinking into a new kind of barbarism."[1] For Adorno and Horkheimer, the reason for the descent into barbarism was shrouded in mystery, but the barbarism was not accidental. The fundamental assumption of the Frankfurt School was that all things had causes and that things human had an order and thus a meaning. The Frankfurt School denied modernity's complacent certainty of its progressive excellence but affirmed modernity's confidence that all things human could be known, or at least sensed, however dark their origins.

This is the paradoxical power of the Frankfurt School. It lay in denying the superficial in modernity while affirming its essence. Over and over again, the Frankfurt School condemned modernity's

---

1. Adorno and Horkheimer, *Dialectic of Enlightenment*, p. xi. Full citation for this and other works is given in the Bibliography. The dates in the text are those of the original German publications.

Introduction

sense of itself without denying its project. The concerns of the Frankfurt School were not reason as such but the rationality of the twentieth century, not equality but mass society, not the conquest of nature but its rape. This attempt to draw a distinction between a thing and its aura was the essential problematic of the Frankfurt School. This effort involved the School in an assault on philistinism.

Modern radicalism in the West appears to us a movement of intellectuals, both within and without the university. These intellectuals have been perpetually bemused at the indifference of the mass to its importunements. No amount of complex theorizing can conceal the fact that it is the intellectual and not the working class which resonates to the critique of bourgeois life. Workers have no quarrel, in principle, with the bourgeois. Theirs is a debate between people of the same sort. Wealth and comfort motivate both; the issue between them is the technical one of distribution and, as such, is soluble.

Between bourgeois and intellectual there yawns an abyss, however, for their debate is between kinds of men. The bourgeois is obsessed with use and ornamentation and cares little for reflection. The intellectual is obsessed with a graceful and reflective ornamentation, which is appreciated for its useless beauty. The intellectual looks upon the bourgeois with contempt and fear because the dull bourgeois, buttressed by the unassailable standard of usefulness and bolstered by the strength of an unreflected life, is impregnable. His children, however, are not. Without reflection, the bourgeois trains his children to be ornaments to his life. As ornaments, the children, are, by their nature, graceful and useless. They become intellectuals, finding personal affirmation in the vivid contempt they feel for their fathers.

Thus, bourgeois and intellectual engage in an ongoing and utterly unequal struggle. Each triumphs absolutely. In generation after generation of modernity—Voltaire, Flaubert, Marx—the intellectuals absolutely reject the bourgeois. In graceful theory, they lay bare the emptiness of bourgeois life. Alas, aside from a mild unease or a titillating self-loathing, the bourgeois is unaware of defeat. By nature, they do rather than reflect. Their victory is absolute in their own realm. They look on the intellectuals now with benign contempt, now with a savage fury. The worker, who used to deal with whichever side promised more, now deals with whichever side delivers the goods. The triumph of the bourgeoisie is that they deliver.

that they deliver and no more condemns the bourgeois in the eyes of the intellectual. What the intellectual loathes far more than human suffering is human indifference to it. The philistinism of the bourgeois sensibility and not bourgeois practice itself is what nauseates intellectuals and drives them to their radicalism.

This repugnance lies at the heart of the Frankfurt School. Their project, in part, was to teach the children of the bourgeoisie, sent to them to become ornaments to their dull fathers' lives, to take arms against the emptiness of those lives. As the true progenitors of the children's revolt of the 1960s, the Frankfurt School took on as its political project an attack on bourgeois philistinism. Their loathing was not for poverty but for the affluent society, not for brute suffering but for subliminal dehumanization. Aesthetics and not economics was their political arena. This is not said to denigrate the Frankfurt School. On the contrary, it is praise for their singular insight into the true rather than mythical functioning of politics in the twentieth century.

The essence of bourgeois hubris is in its assumption that nothing is beyond the reach of bourgeois reason. The bourgeois thus attempt to administer the very souls of men, molding them to their standards. Without reflecting on what it does, bourgeois reason acts to distort men, making them less than they could be. To the Frankfurt School, bourgeois unreflectiveness and bourgeois pride are one, rendering bourgeois life horrible as well as contemptible. Without thought, the bourgeois attacks the sacred and conquers it for the profane. The Frankfurt School meant to resurrect the sacred, keep it from being sullied by the profane, and arm it to triumph over the profane.

This was their great gamble. That their understanding of the notion 'bourgeois' was primarily aesthetic rather than social or economic can be seen in their treatment of orothodox Marxism. Both Social Democracy and the Soviet model were criticized by the Frankfurt School for failing to liberate man authentically and radically. Their failures had to do not so much with their concrete political understandings as with the sensibilities they engendered. Both movements elevated the prosaic above the sacred. Both had the idea of consequential effort at their heart. This notion of consequentiality, the desperate desire to have an impact upon the concrete substance of history, led them to compromise. Both were willing to defeat the bourgeois as men but at the price of allowing the bourgeoisie to triumph over them in principle. As Blum and Stalin prevailed politically, they succumbed to the bourgeois theory of consequential and unreflected activity. Work as an end in itself, indifference to the renewed sensibility of being human, and rejection of authentic liberation of the senses as infantile romanticism—these formed the historic compromise between the bourgoisie and its orthodox socialist opponents. Thus part of the Frankfurt School's project against the bourgeoisie was to undermine the Old Left. A merely political triumph was intolerable and, indeed, was a more radical evil as it robbed the opposition of its angry strength. The triumph needed to be an aesthetic one; the bourgeois practice of being unreflectively human had to be replaced by a humane understanding of humanity itself.

Thus the Frankfurt School must be understood as the most radical and thoroughgoing instance of the intellectuals' struggle against the bourgeoisie. Although they appropriated Marxism as the most explicit critique of bourgeois life, almost any antibourgeois aspect of twentieth-century intellectual thought was apt to be pressed into service. Nietzsche, Heidegger, and Spengler were as much part of the artillery of the Frankfurt School as Marx or Hegel. Even such an extreme bourgeois as Freud was not beyond appropriation, as long as one of his ideas could be turned against his kind. Judaism, the most extreme instance of antimodernity in the Western tradition, was appropriated as the ground from which to resurrect the sacred in order to undermine the profanity of bourgeois life.

Since the project of the Frankfurt School so largely involved appropriation rather than creation, we must ask of them the question that Nietzsche made salient concerning all thought: were they philosophers or scholars? This is not a trivial distinction, for how the question is answered determines in part how seriously the Frankfurt School is to be taken. But it is not an easy question to answer, inasmuch as it is not clear whether philosophy is any longer possible.[2]

I would say that the Frankfurt School was not a philosophic movement but a scholarly one. Whether or not a new transcendental philosophy was possible, a retroactive act was possible:

---

2. The distinction between philosophy and scholarship was one that the Frankfurt School clearly recognized. See Horkheimer's Postscript to *Critical Theory*. That philosophy was higher than scholarship is evident elsewhere in Horkheimer; see for example *Eclipse of Reason*, p. 162.

the realm of the transcendental could be resurrected. To effect this resurrection, those who had rendered philosophy problematic would first have to be enlisted in the enterprise. The Frankfurt School recognized that it is necessary to know philosophy in order to become philosophic. Thus a philosophic insight into the nature of the historical crisis led them to undertake the highest task of scholarship: explication.

Critical Theory, the method of the Frankfurt School, was first concerned with the explication of the text. But the purpose of explication was not profane; it did not represent a surrender to the preceding and existent moments but rather was intended to defy them. Its task was nothing less than to comprehend the crisis of modernity from every perspective and to appropriate the soul of modernity, as that soul was congealed in the philosophic language of the age. Much that was written by the Frankfurt School thus appears distant and unengaged, the work of disinterested scholars. Under the apparently dispassionate exegesis moved a radical purpose: to comprehend modernity in order to undermine it. Behind the Frankfurt aestheticism lurked true politics, a politics of principle rather than of mere effectiveness.

We can see, therefore, two separate if related causes that brought the Frankfurt School to disengage from conventional political life and to engage in a life of scholarship. The first was the recoil of the fastidious intellectual against the profane activity of bourgeois life. This first motive is important in understanding the social forces that created a class of men such as the Frankfurt School. The second motive for the entry into scholarship was the desire to resurrect philosophy. Only an act of will, directed in the only direction that history seemed to have left open to the will, the past, seemed effective. Those of the Frankfurt School became scholars in order to use the philosophic strength of the past dialectically in order to destroy the past that had destroyed philosophy and, with it, justice. This second reason explains further the strange alliance that the Frankfurt School forged between such disparate thinkers as Marx and Nietzsche. In part, the perceived commonality was the shared loathing of bourgeois life, but in greater part the appeal to them came from the desire to appropriate the strength of all who had created the crisis discovered at Auschwitz.

Before turning to examine the nature and the genesis of the thought of the Frankfurt School, we should address the methodological question raised in a study of this sort: is it legitimate to treat a number of men, each a discrete scholar in his own right, as a collectivity? Were this study intended primarily as a work of intellectual history, this would be a relatively unimportant question; intellectual history, properly concerned with the flow of ideas, can legitimately deal with groups of people united institutionally or personally, demonstrating their relationships. The Frankfurt School members' institutional and personal affinities would be, to the intellectual historian, prima facie justification for treating them as a group. Since intellectual history is primarily concerned not with the idea itself but with the genesis, relationship, and impact of the idea, any violence done to the idea itself, while discomforting, is not fatal to the study. The idea is secondary to the event of the idea.

This book, however, does not intend to be intellectual history.[3] It is concerned primarily with the ideas of the Frankfurt School and with their moment in intellectual history primarily as the ideas themselves are revealed and clarified. This book is intended as a systematic treatment of the thought of the Frankfurt School. Melding discrete elements into one intellectual event would here be illegitimate if the idea itself were damaged; although manipulation of an idea—its abstracted deformation—might serve to clarify its external relationships, manipulation would clearly not aid in understanding the idea itself. Thus a defense must be made of a work entitled "The Political Philosophy of the Frankfurt School," as opposed to one called "The Political Philosophies of Marcuse, Adorno, et al."

This defense is doubly important because this book will continually assume mutual support and mutual responsibility among the various figures of the School. It will use the position of one thinker to clarify the position of another and, more dangerously, hold one thinker (at times and with great caution) responsible for the thoughts of another. A defense of collectivity, then, is crucial and must preface this book.

The first ground of justification is also the simplest. Those associated with the Frankfurt School shared long-term memberships in a formal institution as well as lifelong friendships. Each of those discussed, with the exception of Walter Benjamin, had a formal

---

3. Two such histories already exist and are together quite enough. One is Martin Jay, *The Dialectical Imagination*; the other is Susan Buck-Morss, *The Origins of Negative Dialectics*, pp. 238–42.

relationship with the Institute, sharing its declared commonality of purpose. By itself, however, this relationship is not enough to justify treating them as a whole.

The avowed purpose of the Frankfurt Institute made it different from other institutions. It was not merely a refuge for scholars. Rather, it was a systematic project of scholars from diverse disciplines united by the intention of creating an authentically critical theory. The Frankfurt School comprised a core of men involved in a systematic effort to formulate a theoretical exegesis of the sociocultural crisis of the contemporary world and to prepare the theoretical ground for practical activity.

The Frankfurt Institute saw its project as a shared and collaborative one. Aside from a number of studies around which the School organized itself and which gave them a formal collaborative unity, there was collaboration on the formulation of the tenets of Critical Theory. For example, the opening statements concerning Critical Theory were written jointly in two successive articles by Max Horkheimer and Herbert Marcuse. Even more significantly, Horkheimer and Theodor Adorno together wrote the seminal work of the School, *The Dialectic of Enlightenment,* which sets forth the problematic that served as the basis of the School's enterprises. Finally, Walter Benjamin was closely linked to the Institute although he never formally joined it; he published a number of articles in the *Zeitschrift* and selected Adorno to serve as his literary executor, along with Gershom Scholem.

More important than either institutional or obvious links such as the joint authorship of books was the open and continual interchange of ideas. Horkheimer's cultural criticism showed up consistently in Marcuse's work; Benjamin's analysis of the structure of art in mass society was replicated by Adorno; Marcuse's Freudianism was later reflected in both Adorno and Horkheimer. The examples are numerous and are explicated later in this book. What is important here is that the School shared a sense of joint scholarship, engaged in joint projects, and consistently transferred insights and ideas to the point that considering any member alone would do graver damage to the integrity of this book than treating the members as a whole.

Clearly, each served distinct functions; also, at certain points, they disagreed, although more usually there was disagreement on degree or emphasis rather than on any substantive element. Dif-

Introduction

ferences are dealt with as necessary. But what is of first significance in a study of the Frankfurt School is not their disagreements but their profound unities. These scholars were craftsmen engaged in an enormous and workmanlike project; they and their work must be treated as a whole because the parts derive their greatest meaning from the whole.

A more important issue than commonality might be selecting whom to include and whom to exclude. The chief figures included are Walter Benjamin, Theodor W. Adorno, Max Horkheimer, and Herbert Marcuse. Excluded are Karl Mannheim, Karl Wittfogel, and Erich Fromm. An argument could be made for the exclusion of some of the first group (particularly Benjamin) and the inclusion of some from the second group (particularly Fromm). I have, however, reasons for my selection.

An exegesis of the texts of political theory (as opposed to a work of primarily intellectual history, such as that of Martin Jay) requires some limit. Careful treatment of the work of all of the members associated at one time or another would result in a bulk that would make a systematic treatment of the Frankfurt School impossible. Some associates had to be included and some excluded lest violence be done to all their work.

The problem was to select those with the greatest bearing on the political philosophy of the School over the longest time. Wittfogel and Mannheim, therefore, are not included for two reasons. First, these men dealt with political things, sometimes on a highly abstract level, but neither their intention nor method was philosophic. They were almost exclusively sociological in method and descriptive in intent. Each of them (and others like them) did address the general question of Critical Theory; each was influenced by and in turn influenced the founders of Critical Theory; but each in the end was peripheral to the formulation of the general critique of modern society. Neither was fundamentally involved in the search for a historical solution to that society. Second, the relationships of Wittfogel and Mannheim to the Institute were shorter than those of people selected for intense study. Wittfogel formally broke with the school (he ultimately became a witness for Joseph McCarthy) and Mannheim also left, although in a less dramatic way. Like others not treated here, they were peripheral to the School's main work.

Fromm was one of those who ultimately drifted away from the

group and so is excluded here. The causes of his break were complex. The immediate occasion was a disagreement concerning a theory of Freud on patriarchy, that Fromm included in his patriarchical/matriarchical dichotomy.[4] In the end, the Frankfurt School lumped Fromm with the neo-Freudian revisionists.[5] The true reason for the split, however, is best described by Jay: "From his writings alone, it seems evident that Fromm's sensibility was less ironic than that of the other members of the inner circle, his approach to life less colored by the aesthetic nuances shared by both Horkheimer and Adorno."[6] Quite simply, Fromm's work was too leaden and unsubtle to be truly appreciated by or included in the work of the Frankfurt School. His treatment of Marx was too cavalier and his handling of Freud too unimaginative to serve in the synthetic creation of a Freudian Marxism, one that would go beyond popular appeal to achieve scholarly propriety.

Those included in this study had both a lifelong relationship with one another and an overriding concern with the formulation of a political philosophy (to the extent that such a thing was possible to them at that time). Horkheimer was the second head of the Frankfurt Institute. As such, he defined its goals and wrote its manifesto: "Traditional and Critical Theory." Adorno's intimate relationship with Horkheimer is demonstrated by their coauthorship of the *Dialectic of Enlightenment*. Marcuse was associated with all of them throughout his life. Moreover, his work in synthesizing Marx and Freud, along with his popularized critiques of modern society (which took their bearing from the work of the others), demands that he be included.

The most problematic inclusion is that of Benjamin. As I have noted, he never had a formal relationship with the Frankfurt Institute, nor did he ever formally embrace Critical Theory. I include him because certain elements of his thought had a profound impact on the formulations and developments of the Frankfurt School and, in particular, on Adorno. Benjamin's Marxism and effective cultural criticism affected the aesthetic sensibilities of the group. His turn to cultural criticism as a primary enterprise while he maintained the stance of a committed Marxist strongly influenced the cultural focus of Adorno and Horkheimer. Benjamin was central in

4. Jay, *Dialectical Imagination,* p. 101.
5. See Marcuse, *Eros and Civilization,* pp. 238–43.
6. Jay, *Dialectical Imagination,* p. 101.

Introduction

elevating the importance of the cultural realm in Critical Theory. Moreover, his "Theses on the Philosophy of History" gave the Frankfurt School a metaphysical dimension that complemented their thought. Also, his sheer brilliance demands that he be discussed here. His friendship with Adorno and acquaintance with Marcuse and Horkheimer reinforce this decision. What makes his inclusion imperative, however, despite his formal distance from the School, is the manner in which the School subtly absorbed both the specifics and the flavor of his teachings. To the Frankfurt School, Benjamin's metaphysical sensibility was the buttress of their vision of the problems and possibilities of the world.

Indeed, Benjamin's sensibilities provide the ground for a study of the Frankfurt School. Benjamin concluded his "Theses on the Philosophy of History" with the following:

> We know that the Jews were prohibited from investigating the future. The Torah and the prayers instruct them to remembrance, however. This stripped the future of its magic, to which all those succumb who turn to soothsayers for enlightenment. This does not imply, however, that for the Jews the future turned into homogeneous empty time. For every second of time was the strait gate through which the Messiah might enter.[7]

Marx, in a way, had been a soothsayer. For those who consulted him, the historical had turned into magic. When history turned against man, in an age of which Auschwitz was the towering symbol, Marx remained magical and his historical magic, black. His students became impotent against Auschwitz, for history was their totem and Auschwitz was irretrievably historical. Only in a turning backward, in a nostalgia for things that had been properly lost and in a reverence for the past's suffering, which had been righteously annihilated, could the magic be stripped away. With the resurrection of mankind's autonomy, the formula (magical only in format, coldly rational in ritual) could be found for the invocation of the Messiah, who might, even without human aid, still come in any fragment of time.

This was the sensibility that informed the project of the Frankfurt School. Marx had become totemic. He had imbued theory with an inhuman magic. This inhuman certainty about the esoteric gave

---

7. Benjamin, *Illuminations*, p. 264.

Marxism a terrifying self-confidence, which led to brutal catastrophe. All looked to the future, ignoring the dead and the dying. The Frankfurt School resurrected nostalgia. It longed for the delicate aesthetic sensibilities of times well rid of. Its task was to create a paradoxical time in which those sensibilities could flourish and yet be bearable. Thus, it searched for a means to force the coming of the Messiah.

We study the Frankfurt School's thought, therefore, because those associated with it resurrected an inkling of the Messianic promise and power. And we study them because they craved the Messianic from the bitterest roots of historical despair. Beyond their other synthetic accomplishments, beyond their critique of inhuman times, the Frankfurt School must be studied as the response of humans to the inhuman and as the search for the divine within both.

PART I
PHILOSOPHICAL ROOTS OF THE FRANKFURT SCHOOL

1. Introduction to Their Heritage

It is an intellectual convention that the Frankfurt School was Marxist. This understanding is not altogether incorrect, but it is superficial to the point of being misleading. The true roots of the Frankfurt School are to be found in the complex of antibourgeois thought that emerged from the nineteenth century. To the extent that Karl Marx was an antibourgeois, that is, an enemy of philistinism, the Frankfurt School is Marxist. But as we shall see, the Frankfurt School finally breaks with Marx on issues central to his system of thought.

The heart of the man of the Left must be committed to the notion that men are by nature equal. In this sense the Frankfurt School was of the Left—but only as far as the equality at issue was natural. The Frankfurt School was revolted at the quality in modernity that resulted in a leveling of men, in the attainment of a conventional equality, which was mistaken by the Left for a true and natural equality. The Frankfurt School rejected mass culture, and with it, the mass itself. It believed that contemporary mass egalitarianism was flawed by nature. The idea of natural equality has as its esoteric and radical side the idea of an equality that conforms to nature, that fulfills not only the formal requirements of equality but the concrete requirement that those who are equal should conform to their natures—that is, be as good as it is proper for all men to be.

The notion of an equality of excellence is not at all alien to Marx, but in the intellectual history of the late nineteenth and early twentieth centuries, it was not this side of Marx that held sway. Both the Second and Third Internationals were exercises in philistinism. The pedestrian prudence of such men as Kautsky and Bebel and the militant commitment to first things of men like Lenin and Trotsky led them to denigrate culture and to be indifferent to that which was excellent by nature. Thus, the egalitarianism of the Left came to mean formal equality, a leveling of men rather than a striving to render all men good by nature.

It was their concern for the collapse of the highest things in human life that was the ground of the Frankfurt School's project. Marxism, particularly as it was manifested under Blum and Stalin, was not adequate to deal with this concern. Marxism failed to grasp that its obsession with deprivation of material things represented just as much a fetishization of commodities as any bourgeois concern for status. Indeed, the abolition of gross scarcity in the West gave the illusion that the relative equality of men in the possession of goods constituted the realization of the condition that was naturally good for men.

The Frankfurt School's critique of bourgeois culture had to be inspired by figures other than Marx. The critique of mass culture did not, until the work of Georg Lukács and of the Frankfurt School itself, come from the Left. The Left was either indifferent to high culture or actually hostile. The common notion of equality left little room for a theory of universal cultural excellence. To raise the issue was considered traitorous indifference to the pressing needs of the mass or an implicit criticism of the popular mind. It was the Right, the Right being understood as the denial of equality, that criticized the mass. Men like Nietzsche, Heidegger, and Spengler were the great critics of the mass. At the same time they criticized what they regarded as the ground of the mass: the assumption of the equality of man.

To understand the Frankfurt School, therefore, one must recognize that its roots were in the Right as well as in the Left. The Frankfurt School's contribution to intellectual history was to appropriate the criticism of the mass for the Left. This course was not without its difficulties. The charge of elitism, the antithesis of the Left's self-image, was regularly hurled at Marcuse and Adorno. But as equality shows itself in our age as a phenomenon bound up with the mass, a critique of mass culture could not avoid elitism. The Frankfurt School thus continually faced the problem of how to reconcile the concept of high culture with that of the equality of men.

This tension is always on the surface of their thought. Beneath the surface were other, related ambivalences. As heirs to the French

Revolution and to the modern Enlightenment, the Left was committed to support the virtue of reason. It was the Right that doubted reason's goodness. Such thinkers as Freud demonstrated the dark, indeed uncanny, origins of reason. Others, including Heidegger and Nietzsche, demonstrated the problematic quality of reason, showing how it displayed destructive as well as redemptive powers. The Right was concerned both with the problem of reason, its enfeeblement of the human being, and with its maculate origins. The Frankfurt School was not simply of the Left, because it also doubted the virtue of reason, brooding over both its method of operation and those whom it came to serve.

Doubting reason leads to doubting reason's workbench: history. The notion of progress is the practical outcome of a belief in reason. Whether of dialectical necessity or as a profound hope, the Left must maintain the idea that the unfolding of reason is superior to the darkness of myth. The Right, doubting both the efficacy of reason and the virtue of its unfolding, doubts progress as well. The question of history, brought to the fore by the Enlightenment, concerns the possibilities inherent in mankind. To deny progress is to deny the potential excellence of men in general. When the Frankfurt School, along with men of the Right such as Nietzsche, Freud, and Spengler, raised questions concerning progress and the ultimate potential of man, it was breaking with the Left. Ultimately, as Peter Gay put it, they sprang from a soil in which "the philosophical irrationalism of Bergson and the brooding poetic irrationalism of Dostoevsky appealed to sensitive spirits from the extreme left to the extreme right, who could no longer bear the shape of modernity and were sickened by Wilhelminian culture"[1] Their own project was shaped by the tendency of Weimar Culture to force together all those who stood against bourgeois life.

Although I will contend in this book that it is necessary to understand the Frankfurt School as being in some sense a part of the Marxist camp, simply to consider them as Marxists is woefully insufficient and even misleading. They did not share Marx's idea that the perpetual rationalization of the human condition is a good and inevitable thing. Further, they believed that the equality of men must come through the realization of their nature. They were not

---

1. Gay, *Weimar Culture*, p. 7.

certain this nature was realizable—a pessimistic concept incompatible with the socialist reality of equality of condition.

In short, it is far more useful and evocative to regard the members of the Frankfurt School as men of the Right than of the Left. As we shall see, their movement away from the Left was so radical that they can finally be understood only through metaphors deriving from Judaism, the movement that Karl Marx regarded as the mortal enemy of progress and equality.

2. Marx

If the Marxist label was to prove inadequate for an understanding of the Frankfurt School, it was one that the School itself embraced at its beginning. Carl Grünberg[1] made clear in his inaugural address at the 1923 founding of the Institut für Sozialforschung that Marxism was to be the official perspective of the Institute and that the Institute was to be considered part of the Marxist project.[2] Although this Marxism was to be undogmatic it was still to determine the general commitment of the Institute.

At the same time, the chosen name betrayed a certain ambivalence. An Institute for Social Research is a rather neutral appellation for an ideological project, particularly one that formally denied the possibility of value neutrality. The choice of such a name reveals much about the intellectual ground of the Institute.

First, the choice was a prudent one. It had been suggested that the name should be "Institut für Marxismus," but that was abandoned as being too provocative.[3] Peter Gay, writing less than charitably, compared the Frankfurt School's histories, written in the 1930s for American consumption, to Brechtian characters telling their audience only what they wanted to hear and were capable of absorbing.[4] Such circumspection was not peculiar only to the School's American interlude, but was typical of their approach even during the Weimar period.

Obviously, an open avowal of Marxism would have been imprudent either in a Germany just recovering from the trauma of revolt and counterrevolution or in an America where they were only tolerated guests. Of course, on a scale of cynicism displayed by twentieth-century thinkers, this particular manifestation would scarcely register.

1. Grünberg was the first head of the Institute.
2. Grünberg, *Festrede*, pp. 10–12.
3. Jay, *Dialectical Imagination*, p. 8.
4. Gay, *Weimar Culture*, p. 8.

However, prudence is not a sufficient answer to the problem of the name. As Weimar Germany moved to its close, the Institute could have abandoned its neutral stand without any great danger. The novel and the outrageous were praised, not condemned, in Weimar. But rather than becoming progressively more radical, the Frankfurt School kept both their name and their rhetoric moderate, refusing to employ Marxist terminology. Even in the 1930s, when many of its members were in France and the popular front made open Marxism possible, the Institute's rhetoric remained detached and neutral. George Lichtheim wrote:

> No reader of the *Zeitschrift für Sozialforschung* could for a moment be in doubt as to the Marxian inspiration of the critical essays on contemporary philosophy and sociology contributed by the Institute's director [Horkheimer]. But, and this constituted the peculiar fascination of the journal in the 1930's—the Marxism was not that of Moscow. Indeed, Marx was rarely mentioned, Lenin, never.[5]

Why this was so is not a matter of antiquarian interest, but a question which may reveal the essence of the Frankfurt School's intellectual stance.

After the Russian revolution and the domestication of the German Social Democrats, Marxism presented two political alternatives—both distasteful to the Frankfurt School. On the one hand, there was the orthodoxy of Marxism-Leninism, very quickly to come into the hands of Stalin. On the other hand, there were the Social Democrats: successful, bureaucratic, and philistine. To be thoroughly Marxist meant, in the world's eyes, to be objectively aligned with Moscow. To use Marx while making certain revisions in his thought meant to appear to be allied with the tradition of Bernstein and Kautsky. The other alternatives were dead or not yet born. For the Frankfurt School, then, it was politically wise to avoid overt Marxism. The reason was not to placate the bourgeoisie but to work for the salvation of Marxism, to see it reborn into a humane political act. This purpose required that the institute keep its distance from Marxism, at least for the time being.

However, this distance from Marx lasted into the 1960s when new varieties of Marxism had been developed (indeed, when the Frankfurt School's own Marxism had become almost a new Marxist orthodoxy). Why the Frankfurt School (Marcuse is a very mild

---

5. Lichtheim, *Marx to Hegel*, p. 129.

exception to this) did not return to a more distinctly explicit Marxism requires explanation on a level deeper than either personal prudence or political strategy.

Far from being an accident, the omission of the name of Marx from the title of the Institute, the failure to adhere to either Marxist canons or style, and the devotion of the bulk of time to matters other than the Marxist texts can be seen as an intended message. The Frankfurt School wanted to make clear that their project was more than a simple restatement or even reexamination of the Marxist problematic. It was instead a movement to a new problematic, in the tradition of Marx and in his spirit, but not of his word.

The official name, which announced an institute intended for social research, could certainly be in the Marxist tradition. As early as the preface to the *1844 Manuscripts,* Marx had declared his intention to move into the realm of empirical social research (as opposed to the supposedly speculative realm of philosophy). The difficulty was that Marxist social research became inextricably tied up with the dogma of Marxism. At the same time, the mantle of social science, which Marx had attempted to claim for himself, was claimed by the heirs of Comte and Durkheim in France and of Weber in Germany (with a strange and at times indiscriminate melange of the two in the English-speaking world). Social science took a stance of value freedom, and so followed an imperative of being uncommitted, unrooted in social issues except as observer.

The Frankfurt School, then, had two intentions: to rescue Marxist social research from the hands of the vulgar Marxists and to rescue social science from the Weberians. The title *Institut für Sozialforschung* positioned them well for both projects. They could claim to be Marxists, fulfilling the imperatives of Marx himself, and to be social scientists as well, engaged in social research. Their work would give them credentials as Marxists, while Weberians could not accuse them, simply on the basis of their name, of being mere polemicists.

Their name made clear that their fundamental commitment was to social research and that their Marxism was an adjunct. Personally, they could be committed Marxists, but their professional commitment was to social research. This stance gave them the theoretical freedom of eclecticism. As social scientists, they could claim the right to select their intellectual baggage from wherever necessary, a right denied to rigid Marxists.

Behind this, however, there was something more basic at work.

Their name was an admission that it was no longer sufficient to be simply Marxist. It has by now reached the point of cliché to observe that Marxism is not a single system but an evolving and dynamic method through which to view the world (a statement also useful to Marxists attempting to explain away Marx's abysmal predictive record). In the 1920s, despite Lenin's proclamations on the subject, this stance had not yet become orthodoxy; it needed to be stated and the Frankfurt School did so. Retrospectively, Horkheimer said, "The doctrine of Marx and Engels, though still indispensable for understanding the dynamics of society, can no longer explain the domestic development and foreign relations of the nations."[6] The point was to use Marx to explain the world, even if that explanation made Marx himself problematic.

Too much had happened (and would continue to happen); too many crucial concepts had been called into question on profoundly disturbing levels to allow the Frankfurt School to remain simply Marxist. Reason, progress, industrialism, even the possibility of human comprehension of human things, had been brought into question both by thought and by history. Even those who remained committed to the Marxist project had to avoid becoming a prisoner of Marxism.

Moreover, Marxism had lost its status as an observer, which Marx had been able to claim by virtue of his personal ineffectiveness. Marxism had moved too deeply into the world, making itself an event and hence an object of study. As part of the real, it neccessarily made itself the object of the perpetual criticism of its antipode, reason. The dialectical method required dialectical criticism. With Marxism becoming official, an unofficial Marxism was required; and this unofficial Marxism, by the logic of the moment, had to draw its strength both from Marx and from Marx's enemies. The enemies' criticisms had to incorporated into the structure of Marxism in order to strengthen Marxism while pacifying its opposition. The Marxist perspective and intent of the Frankfurt School were precisely what impelled it to move toward its enemies.

The name of Marx had been omitted from the title at least in part because the members of the Frankfurt School had come to hold suspect both the truth and the virtue of Marx. It is easy to dispute the truth of Marx on numerous levels. However, the Frankfurt School did not question Marx on his most obviously vulnerable

---

6. Horkheimer, *Critical Theory*, p. vi.

points, such as his faulty predictions, but rather they questioned the essence of his doctrine. They had read Nietzsche, so they knew that adherence to reason was no longer an easy thing. They had read Heidegger, so they had to question the simple identity that Marx had developed between the ontic and ontological. They had read Freud, so they knew the difference between political and psychic liberation. Moreover, they had seen Lenin, suspected Stalin, and loathed the philistinism of Social Democracy. They excluded Marx's name from the title of their Institute, finally, not because they feared for their safety, nor to make fine political distinctions, nor from methodological necessity. They excluded his name because they simply were no longer Marxists in any ordinary sense. It is from this perspective that the origins of their project must be viewed.

None of this is to say that they were not in profound agreement with certain areas of Marxism. Whatever the precise formulation of their position, it is clear that an essentially Marxist problematic formed their understanding of the relation of man's free and autonomous action. The poles that comprised the causal possibilities of human practice are Marxist: at one pole is individual man and at the other are the material forces of production. Moreover, the Frankfurt School was committed to the primacy of the material over the individual will in determining action. Marcuse makes this explicit, even while refusing to commit himself to its perpetual and exhaustive conclusiveness: "the philosophical contents relevant to the theory are to be educed from the economic structure. They refer to conditions that, when forgotten, threaten the theory as a whole. In the conviction of its founders the critical theory of society is essentially linked with materialism."[7] This is a limited, but not insignificant, statement. In it Marcuse is acknowledging the intimate connection of philosophy and economic structure. But it is then made clear that the connection is not in the formative strength of material condition but in the necessity of philosophy being concerned with those conditions. Material factors are not the sole determinant of consciousness, but they are never insignificant. In other words, if philosophy is to represent a will that is both autonomous and significant in its effect, then philosophy must concern itself with matters of economic significance. The shift from the vulgarly Marxist formulation is crucial, for it demonstrated both

---

7. Marcuse, "Philosophy and Critical Theory," in *Negations*, p. 135.

the genetic source of the thought of the Frankfurt School and the need to adjust it subtly.

Horkheimer does something similar:

> The concept of the dependence of the cultural on the economic has thus changed. With the destruction of the classically typical individual, the concept has as it were become more materialistic, in the popular sense of the term, than before. The explanation of social phenomena has become simpler yet also more complicated. Simpler, because economic factors more directly and consciously determine men and because the solidity and relative capacity for resistance of the cultural spheres are disappearing. More complicated, because the economic dynamism which has been set in motion and in relation to which most individuals have been reduced to simple means, quickly brings ever new visions and portents. Even advanced sectors of society are discouraged and gripped by the general sense of helplessness.[8]

Here, the polarity between material conditions and philosophy is replaced by one between those conditions and culture or individuals. The essential polarity between matter and will is maintained, but a strange twist in the classical Marxist formulation takes place. Rather than an acceptance of economic determinism as the essence of historical truth, radical determinism is seen as a product of late capitalism. As such, it is not an insight into the nature of human history but rather is an attitude of a corrupted age. Hence, historical determinism is presented as temporally true but humanly false and evil.

Marx, who intended to solve the riddle of history through a Communism that was the necessarily ordained outcome of radically determined man, is instead seen as the explicator of the riddle—a riddle not fully posed until late capitalism and one that, outside of portents and visions, may have no solution. The determination of man, human objectivity, has its solution in the creation of its opposite, the indeterminate subject. The riddle of history is the manner in which radical determination might yield freedom. It is a riddle that might yield no dialectical solution but can only be resolved through the catastrophic shattering of the historical itself, as well as of a moment of history. As Benjamin puts it: "The conformism which has been part and parcel of Social Democracy from the beginning attaches not only to its political tactics but to its economic

---

8. Horkheimer, "Traditional and Critical Theory," in *Critical Theory*, p. 237.

Marx 39

views as well. It is one reason for its later breakdown. Nothing has corrupted the German working class so much as the notion that it was moving with the current."[9] By moving with history, man moved toward slavery and unnaturalness rather than toward the solution of history's riddle. The Frankfurt School had no faith that out of objectivity would come subjectivity.

Thus the influence of Marx on the Frankfurt School in this area is a subtle one. They are most certainly Marxists in the way that they express their concerns. The actual formulations of the relationships, the structures of the historical equations that are their prime concern, however, takes them unto strange and subtle paths, ones that Marx may have touched on but which were not central to his thought. The School was Marxist in that it faced the problematic of the relationship between materialism and freedom. This concern conditioned much of its thought, but only to the extent of constituting an ongoing problematic.

A similar perspective is revealed by their general sociology. In this century, for scholars to begin a project concerning society with a class analysis, which predicates classes on their relationship to the means of production, is to owe a conscious debt to some element of Marx, for few know of other serious theoreticians of class. Thus their starting point showed a commitment by the Frankfurt School to Marxism. Their Marxism had deeper roots than this, however, for not only did they view the world through the prism of classes, they were also committed to the oppressed class, and, in particular, to the potentially progressive and redemptive qualities of the proletariat. Most important, they were committed to fomenting the class struggle. It was within the context of this struggle that Horkheimer intended to place the Frankfurt School:

> If, however, the theoretician and his specific objective are seen as forming a dynamic unity with the oppressed class, so that his presentation of the societal contradictions is not merely an expression of the concrete historical situation but also a force within it to stimulate change, then his real function emerges.[10]

And, as he makes clear before this passage, the oppressed class with which unity must be created is the proletariat.[11]

---

9. Benjamin, "Theses on the Philosophy of History," in *Illuminations*, p. 258.
10. Horkheimer, "Traditional and Critical Theory," in *Critical Theory*, p. 215.
11. Ibid., p. 213.

However, the School's commitment was to the ends of the proletariat, its objective needs and not the proletariat as it existed:

> ... it must be added that even the situation of the proletariat is, in this society, no guarantee of correct knowledge. The proletariat may indeed have experience of meaninglessness in the form of continuing and increasing wretchedness and injustice in its own life. Yet, this awareness is prevented from becoming a social force.... Even to the proletariat the world superficially seems quite different than it really is.[12]

When the ability of the proletariat to carry out its historical task is called into question,[13] the conception of the proletariat becomes a strangely metaphysical one. It is not the proletariat itself but the possibilities inherent within the proletariat, the traits that may not even be present in its actual practice but may exist simply as an unrealized and even unrealizable potential, that are of concern to the Frankfurt School. Indeed, the proletariat may not even act as its own agent. Thus, the commitment of the Frankfurt School to the outlines of Marx's class conception, and indeed to some of its specifics, takes a strange twist. It separates the proletarian principle from the actual proletarian.

The Frankfurt School's opposition to capitalism and commitment to socialism both derived in large part from Marx. The opposition to capitalism appears in many places, expressed in the harshest of tones. Thus Marcuse says:

> In the affluent society, capitalism comes into its own. The two mainsprings of its dynamic... permeate all dimensions of private and public existence. The available material and intellectual resource have so much outgrown the established institutions that only the systematic increase in waste, destruction and management keeps the system going.[14]

A commitment to socialism can be illustrated with equal ease from numerous other works.[15]

---

12. Ibid., pp. 213–14.
13. Marcuse, *Negations,* p. xix; Horkheimer, *Critical Theory,* p. vi.
14. Marcuse, *Essay on Liberation,* p. 7. Similar attacks can be found in virtually all works by all members of Frankfurt School.
15. See Marcuse, "A Biological Foundation for Socialism," ibid., pp. 7–22;

It is, however, an unorthodox socialism, one that stands in opposition to both varieties of official Marxism. It is contemptuous of the philistinism of the Social Democrats, who, by concerning themselves with political reform and moderate social gains, are accused, in effect, of adopting the stance and concerns of the bourgeoisie.[16] This criticism of Social Democracy, of course, merely repeats the standard Leninist critique of reformism. What is somewhat more interesting is how the critique is extended to the other variant of official Marxism, the Soviet. The Frankfurt School argued that the Soviets also emulated the affirmative, commodity-centered culture of the capitalist states.[17] Of course, this simply develops the general criticism begun by anti-Stalinists in the days of rapid industrialization and Socialist Realism. What made the Frankfurt School's criticisms of orthodox socialism radical was their concern with the inner, psychic form of existence rather than with the social. This is certainly not in utter opposition to Marx. But the Frankfurt School, in accepting the idea of socialism, goes beyond psychic transformation as the *outcome* of social change to psychic transformation as the *essence* of social change.[18]

Concern for life style (particularly in the late works of Marcuse) is not mere foppish affectation. It is a serious attempt to penetrate the realm of sensibility. Sensibility and sensitivity, which are crucial to Marx historically and humanly but which are continually on the periphery of both his theoretical concern and practical activity, become for the Frankfurt School the centerpiece of their project. Far from doing violence to Marx, this shift could be said simply to explicate things implicit in Marx and, as such, to serve as an ornament to Marx's own words. Yet, it signifies the importance of their loathing for bourgeoise insensitivity, a loathing that derives as much from the aesthetics of Flaubert or of Matthew Arnold as from Marx. For the Frankfurt School, capitalism was refuted by the affluent shallowness of bourgeois life far more than by the grinding

---

Benjamin, "Theses on the Philosophy of History," in *Illuminations,* pp. 262-64; Horkheimer, *Eclipse of Reason,* pp. 160-61.

16. This can be seen in both Benjamin's XI and XII "Theses on the Philosophy of History," in *Illuminations,* pp. 258-60 and in Marcuse's *Essay on Liberation,* p. 10.

17. Marcuse, *Soviet Marxism,* p. 66.

18. See Marcuse, *Eros and Civilization,* pp. 118-56. Also Benjamin's mysterious statement of the problem in "Theologisch-politisches Fragment," in *Zur Kritik der Gewalt,* pp. 95-96. See Adorno and Horkheimer, *Dialectic of Enlightenment,* pp. 231-36, on the need for sensual transformation.

poverty of its proletarian victims. The poverty they saw in modern life was of the soul and not of the body.

In crucial matters, however, the Frankfurt School takes its essential bearings from Marx. It sees men as being formed through the impact of the material conditions under which they live. It views society through the prism of class analysis and has a general commitment to the proletariat. When all is said and done, members of the Frankfurt School are socialists.

These are not trivial points. The Frankfurt School's general metaphysical view, their perspective on the structure and the function of society, and their solution to the problem of society come from their awareness of Marx. But neither are they Marxists in any conventional sense of the term. There are simply too many subtle ways in which they transfigure Marx's teachings in these areas. What is more, they simply disagree with Marx on too many crucial issues and doubt him too seriously on other points.

The simplest difference has already been touched on, but the simplest may also be the most profound. This is the question of the status of the proletariat. To Marx, the proletariat was not merely one class among many. It was the class that offered the authentic solution to the human condition and riddle. Moreover, it carried this solution within itself. That is, it required no external intervention but, left to its own devices and its own suffering, would transform society and itself in such a way as to make history's solution manifest and complete. The proletariat was the answer, and it was an answer which would explicate itself. To question the status of the proletariat, therefore, was to strike at the heart of Marx.

This was precisely what the Frankfurt School did, both out of necessity and choice. The necessity was imposed by brute reality. Rather than becoming progressively radicalized by their existence under capitalism, the proletariat became, in a process noted well before the Frankfurt School, progressively more complacent and even reactionary. Horkheimer notes this event, saying:

> Since the years after World War II the idea of the growing wretchedness of the workers, out of which Marx saw rebellion and revolution emerging as a transitional step to the reign of freedom, has for long periods become abstract and illusory, and at least as out of date as the ideologies despised by the young. The living conditions of laborers and employees at the time of THE COMMUNIST MANIFESTO were the outcome of open oppression. Today, they are, instead, motives for trade union organization and for discussion between dominant eco-

nomic and political groups. The revolutionary thrust of the proletariat has long since become realistic action within the framework of society. In the minds of men at least, the proletariat has been integrated into society.[19]

Thus, rather than serving as the negation of capitalism, the proletariat had become its bulwark.

The Frankfurt School abandoned the proletariat as the revolutionary subject by choice, as well. To be an advocate and spokesman for the proletariat in an age in which the proletariat is profoundly conservative places the socialist in one of two positions. The socialist is either impotent, an empty posturer on a stage watched only by other pretenders, or becomes as conservative as the proletariat. If one retains a commitment to the transformation of human existence, one abandons the proletariat by choice, Resurrecting the distinction between subjective and objective happiness, the Frankfurt School discounted the subjective feelings of satisfaction enjoyed by the proletariat and criticized their objective misery. Thus both observation and theory led the members of the Frankfurt School, while retaining their conviction concerning the desirability of socialism, to question the efficacy of the proletariat as an agent of transformation.[20]

The dull complacency of proletarian life, its embourgeoisement, refuted the proletarian as the revolutionary subject. The Frankfurt School, having lost its historical basis, retained only the residue, an antibourgeois sentiment. It was to validate this sentiment that the School recalled the distinction between objective and subjective states of mind as a crucial historical determinant. Out of this distinction, which Marx had labored to demonstrate could not maintain itself for long in historical practice, came the Frankfurt School's substitute for Marx's progressive impoverishment of the proletariat: false consciousness. In this way, the antibourgeoise sentiment of the Frankfurt School could be transferred to the proletariat while the proletarian soul was exempted from eternal damnation. Opposition to capitalism was thus uncoupled from Marx's overt teleology.

19. Horkheimer, *Critical Theory*, p. vi.
20. Adorno comments on the inability and unwillingness of official Marxism to perceive the changing position of the proletariat in *Minima Moralia*, p. 113, comparing Marxist pronouncements on the revolutionary will of the proletariat to Kaiser Wilhelm's dictum, "I will tolerate no Jeremiahs." Also see Marcuse, *One-Dimensional Man*, p. 31.

The problematic character of the proletariat raised a more serious question: if capitalism was still objectively destructive, and if those who bore its brunt were unable subjectively to appreciate this fact, did any solution exist to capitalism in its latest form or would capitalism maintain itself indefinitely? The Frankfurt School brought the very rigor of Marx's historicist contribution to political economy into question. As Marcuse puts it:

> To be sure, Marx held that organization and direction of the productive apparatus by the 'immediate producers' would introduce a qualitative change in the technical continuity: namely, production toward the satisfaction of freely developing individual needs. However, to the degree to which the established technical apparatus engulfs the public and private existence in all spheres of society—that is, becomes the medium of control and cohesion in a political universe which incorporates the laboring classes—to that degree would the qualitative change involve a change in the technological structure itself. And such change would presuppose that the laboring classes are alienated from this universe in their very existence, that their consciousness is that of the total impossibility to continue to exist in this universe.... Thus, the negation exists prior to the change itself, the notion that the liberating historical forces develop within the established society is a cornerstone of Marxian theory. Now, it is precisely this new consciousness, this 'space within' the space for the transcending historical practice, which is being barred by a society in which subjects as well as objects constitute instrumentalities in a whole.... Its supreme promise is an ever-more-comfortable life for an ever-growing number of people who, in a strict sense, cannot imagine a qualitatively different universe.[21]

Thus, the reasons behind the growing conservatism of the proletariat cast doubt upon the possibility that capitalist society could ever be transcended. A problem has been posed by history to which history in practice might have no solution. Marcuse thus faced a crisis in Marx's central article of faith: that man does not pose problems for himself for which there are no solutions.

The break with Marx on the question of the future of capitalism and the status of the proletariat are serious but further point to a break with Marx on the most basic level, that of empirical projections into the future, the inevitability of history. The obvious question is whether Marx himself saw history as inevitable. A number of scholars (most notably Marxists embarrassed by the

---

21. Marcuse, ibid., p. 23.

Marx

failure of their teacher's apparent predictions) have argued in recent years that Marx regarded the rise of Communism as an 'existential gamble'[22] or that he regarded it as an inevitable event following certain necessary paths only within a limited number of western European countries.[23] It is no argument to be entered into lightly.

Crucial for our discussion, however, is that the Frankfurt School regarded Marx as an historical determinist. Marcuse puts it most clearly and bluntly:

> The concept that definitely connects Marx's dialectic with the history of class society is the concept of *necessity*. The dialectical laws are necessary laws; the various forms of class society necessarily perish from their inner contradictions. The laws of capitalism work with 'iron necessity toward inevitable results.'[24]

There might be exceptions to this in certain contingent areas, but according to Marcuse, Marx regarded the general path of history as something determined because of man's objective needs and desires. Thus, in criticizing the notion of historical necessity, the Frankfurt School saw themselves as breaking with Marx.

And criticize they did. Benjamin began his enigmatic "Thesis on the History of Philosophy" with the following aphorism:

> The story is told of an automaton constructed in such a way that it could play a winning game of chess, answering each move of an opponent with a countermove. A puppet in Turkish attire and with a hookah in its mouth sat before a chessboard placed on a large table. A system of mirrors created the illusion that this table was transparent from all sides. Actually, a little hunchback who was an expert chess player sat inside and guided the puppet's hands by means of strings. One can imagine a philosophical counterpart to this device. The puppet called 'historical materialism' is to win all the time. It can easily be a match for anyone if it enlists the services of theology, which today, as we know, is wizened and has to keep out of sight.[25]

There is much present in this *Thesis* and it is a preface for much more. But as a preface, it demonstrates that for the effective formulation of any "Theses on the Philosophy of History" the current

---

22. This argument is most clearly made by Lichtheim, *From Marx to Hegel*, pp. 67–69.
23. This and a number of related arguments are made by Avineri, *Social and Political Thought of Karl Marx*, pp. 151–62.
24. Marcuse, *Reason and Revolution*, p. 317.
25. Benjamin, "Thesis on the Philosophy of History," in *Illuminations*, p. 253.

dogma must first be scrutinized in order to reveal its illusions. Marx's (or at least Marxism's) concept of history—a lovely machine that will flawlessly and (like all machines) of necessity emerge victorious in history's dialectical chess game—is shown to be only an illusion conjured by mirrors. The wondrous, seemingly infallible machine has a shriveled and cynical man inside. The machine always wins. Only on the surface is the wonder of the machine dispelled, however. After all, as we know too well, a wondrous machine soon becomes commonplace; one expects it to function flawlessly. This particular machine is even more wondrous: it is no machine and yet it consistently wins! The illusion of a miraculous thing is ripped away, only to reveal an even more marvelous miracle: a figure who cannot be defeated, yet who is human. A human who is divine. The marvelous machine of historical materialism, which foretells and creates, has within it the last withered dreg of its archrival: theology. But how does it win? In the end, historical materialism, like theology, must always refuse to play. It declares itself to be an act of faith, a logical necessity, which it is, if one begins with the axioms yielded by faith. It wins by declaring itself the winner, thus bursting the bonds of dialectical logic that held the game together. The little hunchback, so long as he employs theology, cannot lose.

It must be added that this is by no means a condemnation either of historical materialism or theology. To Benjamin, there is clearly something miraculous in the act of faith. Magical things, far from being refutations, are the confirmation of lives that are at root magical in very practical ways. But neither is this a simple acceptance of the notion of the inevitability of history. On a certain level, historical materialism remains a profound illusion. It believes itself to be true, in a simpleminded, empirical way. Its truth, however, is of much more mysterious sort, and the idea that history possesses the type of necessity that a Kautsky, a Plekhanov, an Engels, or even a Marx would ascribe to it is clearly alien to Benjamin's thought.[26]

Others in the Frankfurt School paralleled this doubt about the inevitability of Marx's historical conception. The two chief works produced by the Frankfurt School concerning the status and future of modern society both begin with the images of doubt and fear.

26. See also Tiedeman, *Studien zur Philosophie Walter Benjamins,* pp. 133-36, where it is claimed, with only limited justification, that this is primarily a critique of the Second International. Also, for a much too limited analysis, see Weber, "Walter Benjamin," in *Unknown Dimension,* p. 253.

Marx

The general fear concerning the times are best seen in the following passages that Adorno wrote in 1951:

> The constantly enforced insistence that everybody should admit that everything will turn out well, places those who do not under suspicion of being defeatists and deserters.[27]

and:

> How far progress and regression are intertwined today can be seen in the notion of technical possibilities. Mechanical processes of reproduction have developed independently of what they reproduce and become autonomous. They are considered progressive and anything that has no part in them, reactionary and quaint.[28]

Significantly, there are no promises made following these passages that out of the darkness would come light.[29]

Something important happens in the final passage quoted. Until now, only the possibility of progress was in question. Here, its very virtue is in doubt. It is not that they regarded the conquest of nature as inconceivable: on the contrary, they declared it to be an accomplished fact.[30] But the price paid to the social organization that made this conquest possible becomes the problem:

> What is retrogressive is not mechanization and standardization but their containment, not the universal co-ordination but its concealment under spurious liberties, choices, and individualities. The high standard of living in the domain of the great corporations is restrictive in a concrete sociological sense: the goods and services that the individuals buy control their needs and petrify their faculties.... The better living is offset by an all-pervasive control over living.[31]

This would appear to be the standard critique of the bourgeois form of the conquest of nature, but it emerges that the bourgeois form, as long as it is tied to the logic of the machine (something to which socialism itself is linked)[32] will remain and become more and more

---

27. Adorno, *Minima Moralia*, p. 114.
28. Ibid., p. 118.
29. A curious sidelight is that one of the few places where hope becomes a dominant motif is in an article on Schopenhauer (Horkheimer, "Schopenhauer Today," in *Critique of Instrumental Reason*, p. 71), where his only source of hope is in the ability to face hopelessness.
30. Marcuse, *Eros and Civilization*, p. 90.
31. Ibid., pp. 90–91.
32. Marcuse, *Soviet Marxism*, pp. 63–76.

repressive. The conquest of nature becomes the ratification of repression rather than the preface to liberation.

The conquest of nature through labor is the triumph of reason. Reason's demystification is the abstract side of labor's orderliness. When reason acts upon nature, it can only proceed through the rigors of labor and the discipline of the machine. As the triumph over unruly nature proceeds, so does the triumph over unruly man. The repression of man, his denaturalization, is the counterpart of the conquest of nature. There is no obvious escape. One cannot conquer nature except through reason. One cannot maintain the conquest without remaining rational. But, to the Frankfurt School, a rationalized existence is antithetical to a free one. Thus the problem of capitalism is not its inefficient irrationality but, on the contrary, its absolutely efficient rationality. To break with reason means to lose affluence; to maintain affluence means to be unfree.

At the precise moment when nature is most radically conquered, first, in the sense of being brought under human control and, second, in the sense of being thoroughly demystified, the agent of liberation becomes an oppressor. This, by becoming oppressive, calls the totality of the dialectic into question, first, by raising the question of whether reason is an effective agent for the liberation of man, and second, by raising the possibility that man has posed a problem for himself to which there is no solution. The agency of solution becomes the problem.

This is the most profound break with Marx. To Marx, reason could never lose its subjective nature and its critical dimension. It could turn itself into the opposite, but it could not then maintain itself in the face of the withdrawn and hostile authentic rationality. Capitalism might turn its rationality into an oppressive form, and this form might even retain some internal rationality, but in the end its universal irrationality would be abolished by the agent of reason, the proletariat. The possibility that the rational would turn itself into object and oppressor and, at the same time, maintain itself without the possibility of dialectical opposition was inconceivable. Reason, by its nature, was both critical and cunning. But it was precisely this that the Frankfurt School had come to doubt. To the Frankfurt School, reason had become affirmative and seemed to have lost its cunning. Therefore, progress, while still being possible in the formal sense of expanding the domain of reason, had ceased to be liberating.

The dialectical necessity of liberation had been called into doubt. With this, the political act that confirmed what had already taken place in the subterranean realm of the economic (and hence in the struggle between reason and nature) became insufficient. The revolutionary act remained important but not in the elegantly clear manner of Marx. Revolution had to penetrate beyond the political to become a revolution of the psyche and of the sensibility of being. To Marx also this was necessary, but as such, it was beyond willing; it was part of a dialectical process. To the Frankfurt School, the dialectic had become doubtful and so the transformation of the human soul had to become both conscious and willed. With this, the revolutionary act became more profound than Marx had envisioned it and more subjectively free than he thought was possible within the realm of bourgeois existence. As it became more profoundly problematic, the stakes and risks were both multiplied.[33]

In sum, the Frankfurt School is ambivalent toward Marx and the tradition of Marxism. In any number of distinct and overlapping areas, the Frankfurt School found it necessary either to break with or to modify Marx's position. They began with doubts about the proletariat as the revolutionary subject and from this moved to question the inevitability of a fatal crisis in capitalism. Thus, they doubted the teleological component of Marx's historical conception. Finally, doubting the virtue of both progress and social rationalization (and, thus, of reason itself), the Frankfurt School broke radically and profoundly with Marx.

In the final analysis, of course, the Frankfurt School was inextricably bound to Marxism as a tradition. But, to see the School as simply Marxist or even, in certain instances, as primarily Marxist, is to understand only one rather limited aspect of a complex genesis. Now in this century, another sectarian reinterpretation of the Marxist texts has an aura of sterility about it. There is little left to be said. But a vision of Marx mediated through a complex of non- and anti-Marxist perspectives holds the fascination of a tension between things that are both seductive and in opposition. What makes the Frankfurt School interesting is the non-Marxist origins of its thought.

---

33. Adorno, *Minima Moralia*, pp. 145–56; Marcuse, *Essay on Liberation*, pp. 23–48. Each discusses the primacy of the aesthetic and sensible over the political as an act of liberation.

3. Hegel and Hegelianism

Geographers of Marxism who see ambivalence within a Marxist, turn, as if drawn by magnetism, to Hegel. Things that cannot be explained in the thought of a twentieth-century Marxist by simple reference to the Marxist text are immediately attributed to Hegel, and all proclaim (or sigh at) the birth of another Hegelian Marxist. Behind this process is usually an inadequate perception of both Marx and Hegel. People hold an image of Marx in which he appears shallow and mechanistic. When a Marxist displays qualities other than these, the critics turn to Hegel, whose image seems deep and subtle.[1]

Seeing the Frankfurt School as Hegelians, however, is no more satisfactory than viewing them as Marxists. The Frankfurt School did indeed stand in the tradition that grew out of Hegel. But, in a sense, all German thought can be seen in that light. We are all Young Hegelians. This is argued most cogently by Karl Löwith:

> In 1931, there were three congresses on the occasion of the centenary of Hegel's death: one in Moscow and the others in Rome and Berlin. In spite of their mutual antipathy, they belonged together as had the Hegelian right and left of the previous century. As then, the greater degree of culture belonged to the epigones. . . . . But the real sundering of what Hegel's mediation had joined together has already been accomplished, in opposite directions, by Marx and by Kierkegaard. These two dogmatic and mutually opposed critics of Hegel were both

---

1. This attitude is taken by many interpreters of the Frankfurt School and its members: Marks, *Meaning of Marcuse,* p. 5; MacIntyre, *Herbert Marcuse,* pp. 34–41; Cohen, "Critical Theory," in *New Left Review* 57 (Sept.–Oct. 1969): 42–43; Bernstein, "Herbert Marcuse," in *Social Theory and Practice* 1 (Fall 1971): 98–99; Lichtheim, *From Marx to Hegel,* pp. 21–23; Gay, *Weimar Germany,* pp. 30–31.

under the spell of his concepts. This demonstrated the power of the spirit which could produce such extremes.[2]

Hegel had set the terms of philosophical discourse; all that came after had to settle accounts with him. If this is true, then calling somebody Hegelian tells little in any particular case. The purpose of a name is to distinguish. The term "Hegelian" unifies.

Although the Frankfurt School differed profoundly with the positive positions and the sensibilities of Hegel, there is no question that Hegel had hegemony over their thought. They were obsessed with the problems of history and reason. The crises in each, the possibility for the rationalization of history and the problem of the historicity of reason served as the ground of their work. It was a ground to which they returned continually. But so did all thought after Hegel. This quality of the Frankfurt School reveals only that their thought was bound to its time.

The Frankfurt School's critique of Hegel consists of four overlapping parts. First is the critique of Hegel's theory of identity, in which the Hegelian dialectic is attacked as consisting, in the end, of positivity and unity rather than of radical negativity and disharmony. Hegel is perceived as essentially positivist and affirmative in relation to the prevailing social order. Second is a critique of the use by Hegel of the concept of reason, in which Hegel's treatment of reason as instrumentality and as cunning instrumentality, is criticized. Out of this comes, third, a criticism of Hegel's positive faith in the dialectical certainty of history, bringing the idea of an end to history into question. Finally, and to some extent independently of the other three divisions, the Frankfurt School criticizes Hegel's vision of the historical solution, his actual social and political prescriptions. This critique, made on primarily Marxist grounds, questions the validity of the historical end envisioned in the *Philosophy of Right*.

To Hegel, the world is divided between subject and object, the concept and the thing conceived. The relationship between these two elements is essentially historical; it develops over time.[3] Subject and object begin radically estranged from one another. They conclude by becoming identical; the thing becomes the substance of the

2. Löwith, *Hegel to Nietzsche*, p. 134.
3. Hegel, *Philosophy of History*, pp. 9–10.

thought, the thought transfigures the thing into its image. The end of this process is thus identity. The procedure whereby this identity is attained is negativity, the continual mutual criticism and transformation of subject and object. The problem is, however, the potentially irreconcilable opposition between the process of negation and the end of identity. Negation is inherently critical, identity is affirmative. The former condemns existence, the latter affirms it.[4]

To the Frankfurt School, Hegel had understood properly that the process of history and reason was negation. In so doing, Hegel had established the role of criticism in saving man from an affirmation of the inhuman. But, in allowing the negative only as a mediating step, allowing it only partial legitimacy, Hegel, they argued, did an injustice to his own insight and thereby denied the revolutionary significance of his own vision.[5] Hegel, they argue, introduced the concept of negativity and nonidentity only to move toward a reconciliation—that is, in order to abolish negativity as quickly as possible. Thus, having arrived at the solution to the real problem—which is, in a sense, not the particular positivity negated but the category of positivity itself—Hegel quickly abandoned the solution in favor of the reaffirmation of the problem.

All this leads the Frankfurt School to break with Hegel. In Adorno's words:

> What is negated is negated until it has passed. This is the decisive break with Hegel. To use identity as a palliative for dialectic contradiction, for the expression of the insolubly nonidentical, is to ignore what the contradictions mean. It is a return to purely consequential thinking. The thesis that the negation of a negation is something positive can only be upheld by one who presupposes positivity—as all-conceptuality—from the beginning. He reaps the benefit of the primacy of logic over the metalogical, of abstract philosophy's idealistic delusion, of vindication as such. The negation of the negation would be another identity, a new delusion, a projection of consequential logic—and ultimately of the principle of subjectivity—upon the absolute.[6]

Thus Hegel, who postulates negativity, fails to allow it free rein: he fails to allow negation to be authentic. He allows negativity to be

---

4. Hegel, *Phenomenology*, pp. 96–99.
5. Adorno, *Negative Dialectics*, p. 120; Horkheimer, *Hegel und das Problem der Metaphysik*, p. 86.
6. Adorno, *Negative Dialectics*, p. 160.

bought off. Negativity is really not in opposition to the real but actually wants to affirm reality's essence. Adorno here breaks with Hegel on two grounds. First, he rejects the logical limitation placed upon negativity, in that it is forced into fundamental identity with positivity. Second, he breaks with the affirmative *intention* of identity. Identity seeks to defang the dialectical possibilities of negation and, by so doing, deny the social threat that it poses. What this leads to is stated by Marcuse:

> It is precisely this absorption of all particular individuality and restriction by the will in its state of self-identity which constitutes 'universality' into which Hegel's theory of freedom debouches.[7]

Identity theory within the social context results in what Marcuse will later refer to as 'one-dimensionality'. It allows only one-sided existence; and that side is the one that affirms what already is. Its danger is that it does this while giving the illusion of freedom through the formal affirmation of negativity. It allows subjectivity a formal, although never substantial, existence and therefore allows only the affirmative side to rule.

The critique of Hegel's notion of identity brought the formal structure of Hegel's notion of reason into doubt, for Hegel's concept of identity constitutes the essence of his concept of reason.[8] Identity would be unacceptable for two reasons. It would be unacceptable because in its final moment reason would no longer be transcendentally critical, ceasing to stand in opposition to the world. Reason would thus be transformed into an instrument of the *status quo* where it had once been an opponent. Second, identity would be unacceptable because Hegel's notion of logical identity presupposes that reason has a cunning. This the Frankfurt School finds historically problematic.

To Hegel, the opposition between subjectivity (the freedom of reason) and objectivity (the unfreedom of the concrete world) would be resolved. In the end, the State would come to embody both reality and rationality.[9] Under that circumstance, reason would abandon the cast of pure subjectivity in order to take its

---

7. Marcuse, "A Study on Authority," *Studies in Critical Philosophy*, p. 102.
8. Stace, *The Philosophy of Hegel*, pp. 135–37, on identity as the essence of Hegel's ontology. Also see Rosen, *Hegel*, p. 42, where he implies the centrality of identity; also see pp. 114–21.
9. Hegel, *Philosophy of Right*, p. 10.

rightful place as the essence of the State. At the same time, the State would abandon its fundamental objectivity, by allowing reason to rule it. Reason would thereby become the State's principle.[10] It would rule the State; at the same moment it would serve the State, becoming its instrument.

For Hegel, this notion of reason as objectivity is embodied in Germany—to be more precise, as the Prussian Civil Service.[11] In other words, reason would become manifested in the administrative forms of a rational and objective civil service. This is so much the case that Hegel can write:

> The security of the State and its subjects, against the misuse of power by ministers and their officials, lies directly in the authority given to societies and Corporations, because in itself this is a barrier against the intrusion of subjective caprice into the power entrusted to a civil servant.[12]

Thus, the essence of the State (and the dominant class of civil society) becomes the civil servant.[13] Bureaucracy, whose prime virtue is that it objectifies reason in concretely useful forms, becomes the dominant mode of social organization. Indeed, bureaucracy is the only conceivable form of governance for Hegel. Thus, reason becomes an instrument at the end of history[14] and history ceases to be the autonomous unfolding of reason.

This concept is unacceptable to the Frankfurt School on simply Marxist grounds. Marx objected that this notion of Hegel is an illusory reconciliation; Marx held that bureaucracy represents a formal concretization of reason, without allowing for a more general and thoroughgoing liberation.[15] As such, bureaucracy is doubly oppressive. First, it is authentically oppressive in its social reality. Second, it is oppressive because it gives the illusion of objectifying reason instead of actually realizing it. The Frankfurt School has no trouble with either of these objections. Clearly, bourgeois no-

---

10. Thus uniting freedom and necessity in one structure.
11. Hegel, *Philosophy of History*, pp. 46–47; *Philosophy of Right*, pp. 152–53, 188–93.
12. Hegel, *Philosophy of Right*, p. 192.
13. Ibid., p. 193.
14. On this I take my bearings from Kojève, *On Reading Hegel*, pp. 97–99.
15. Marx, *Critique of Hegel's "Philosophy of Right,"* pp. 46–48.

tions of bureaucracy and the use of reason in bourgeois society fail in their promise.[16]

The Frankfurt School's critique of instrumental reason and of bureaucracy is, however, more radical and thoroughgoing than would be a simple recapitulation of Marx's *Critique of Hegel's "Philosophy of Right."* It is more radical in raising the possibility that *all reason* must in the end become instrumental.[17] The suspicion is raised that reason does obey the law of identity. If that is the case, then reason can never escape turning into its opposite. Therefore, reason can never avoid the final abandonment of its subjectivity; it will inevitably realize itself and at that moment of its realization make itself and what it rules unfree by forcing them into its necessarily formal confines. Horkheimer writes:

> Having given up autonomy, reason has become an instrument. In the formalistic aspect of subjective reason, stressed by positivism, its unrelatedness to objective content is emphasized; in its instrumental aspect, stressed by pragmatism, its surrender to heteronomous contents is emphasized. Reason has become completely harnessed to the social process. Its operational value, its role in the domination of men and nature, has been made the sole criterion.[18]

Reason becomes, in other words, a prisoner of forces beyond its control. The problem is not simply that in this particular moment reason has become instrumentalized. The difficulty is that the instrumentalization of reason may be intrinsic to both reason and to the process of historical rationalization.[19] Reason itself may have turned into its own enemy—into "absurdly rational product."[20] The Frankfurt School holds open the possibility that reason might not have been able to avoid this fate. Hegel, after all, regarded becoming an instrument as reason's and the world's proper end. The Frankfurt School tended to take Hegel at his word, and regarded instrumental reason as a fearsome possibility.

From this, it becomes necessary to doubt the cunning of reason.

16. Marcuse, "Industrialization and Capitalism in Max Weber," in *Negations*, p. 208; Horkheimer, *Eclipse of Reason*, p. 22.
17. The theme of Adorno and Horkheimer's *Dialectic of Enlightenment*.
18. Horkheimer, *Eclipse of Reason*, p. 21.
19. Marcuse, "Industrialization and Capitalism in Max Weber," in *Negations*, p. 225; Adorno and Horkheimer, *Dialectic of Enlightenment*, p. xiii.
20. Adorno, *Negative Dialectic*, p. 21.

One can postulate a historical working out of reason that simultaneously fulfills its formal promise and concretely turns into its opposite: an insoluble problematic. Reason can come to rule the world but rule badly. The Frankfurt School raises the possibility that reason and history have joined to propose a problem for which there is no solution, precisely because the triumph of reason in history is the problem.[21]

One need not follow the Frankfurt School's analysis in all its complexity in order to see the disagreement between them and Hegel, for their objection may be simply stated in this way: that reason cannot realize itself. The Frankfurt School, while consistently moving toward the view that the problem of modernity was reason's realization and then subtly backing off from a final, Nietzschean acceptance of it, explicitly and fully accepts the idea that reason couldn't be realized. This position also constitutes a serious break with Hegel. Horkheimer writes:

> Hegel's teaching shows that the positivity that distinguishes him from Schopenhauer cannot ultimately stand up. The failure of a logically stringent system in its highest form in Hegel, means the logical end of attempts at a philosophic justification of the world, the end of the claim of philosophy to emulate positive theology.[22]

Horkheimer, in the face of the failure of systematic philosophy, is even willing to adopt Schopenhauer's philosophical pessimism. This is an explicit attack on the central element of Hegel—systematic philosophy as the abstract solution to an unsystematic world. If systematic philosophy fails, then for Hegel, history has failed.

From Schopenhauer, Adorno's turn toward Spengler and a more concrete pessimism is a small step:

> There is good reason to raise the question of the truth and untruth of Spengler's work again. It would be conceding him too much to look to world history, which passed him by on its way to the new order, for the last judgment on the value of his ideas. And there is all the less

---

21. Horkheimer, *Zum Begriff der Vernunft*, pp. 15–16.
22. Horkheimer, "Schopenhauer Today," in *Critique of Instrumental Reason*, p. 78.

Hegel and Hegelianism

reason to do so, considering that the course of world history vindicated his immediate prognoses to an extent that would astonish if they were still remembered. Forgotten, Spengler takes his revenge by threatening to be right.[23]

No simple Hegelian can write about the possibility that Spengler was correct. Clearly, to the Frankfurt School, something has gone profoundly wrong with history. History has lost its cunning. And what cunning it retained, it turned toward brutish oppression.

Thus, the concept of identity was inadequate. Moreover, it resulted in an oppressive concept of reason, an oppression that might have been inherent in the structure of reason itself. In any event, it was still clear to the Frankfurt School that history had lost its way, whatever the cause.

The issue for them was whether there existed a way out of the historical cul-de-sac of the twentieth century. To one such as Hegel, the existence of a cul-de-sac, particularly one with no exit, was literally unthinkable. Men who could think such thoughts were not Hegelians. When one adds to this un-Hegelian thought the obvious fact of the Frankfurt School's socialism and their rejection of the positive social intentions of Hegel, a simple conclusion is inescapable: contrary to popular opinion, the Frankfurt School is not Hegelian, except as we are all Hegelians.

It might still be argued that, if the Frankfurt School was not Hegelian, it could be counted among the Young Hegelians. Each of the Young Hegelians chose to argue with the Master, even while intending to extend and radicalize his basic project. They applied his legacy rather than breaking new ground.[24] The Frankfurt School, however, broke with Hegel on grounds not worked by Hegel. This point distinguishes them most radically from the Young Hegelians, who developed their views strictly from antinomies implicit in Hegel. This is illustrated by an issue with which both the Young Hegelians and the Frankfurt School were obsessed but which the Frankfurt School radicalized: the issue of the death of God.[25]

This issue was one that each of the members of the Frankfurt School knew of and agonized over. Each faced the problem as if it

23. Adorno, "Spengler after the Decline," in *Prisms*, pp. 53–54.
24. Brazill, *Young Hegelians*, p. 11.
25. Ibid., pp. 23–26.

were the critical moment of contemporary existence. Each sought somehow to come to grips with the social and psychological implications of the abolition of divinity.[26] What was the possibility of redemption in an age in which metaphysics had reduced itself to either Positivism or Heideggerianism? Each in turn searched for the Messianic; each was afraid that it could not be found in the form required: human activity. They sought urgently for the possibility of true and human things in an age in which the truth had been reduced to the sensual and the human to the merely human. Thus, according to Brazill's definition of the critical significance of the Young Hegelians, the Frankfurt School can be seen either as the last of the old or the first of the new Young Hegelians.

It is, however, insufficient to call them this. First, their experience of the death of God was mediated through Nietzsche, a richer and more immediate source. Second, the Young Hegelians greeted atheism with a sense of liberation.[27] History did not permit the Frankfurt School such shallowness. Both before and after Auschwitz they met atheism with a growing sense of its implicit horror. Thus this aspect of their 'Young Hegelianism' was also abolished.

There was more similarity between their respective methodologies: the School's Critical Theory and the Young Hegelians' criticism. To the Young Hegelians, criticism was the essence of historical movement.[28] But Hegel had rooted the critical act in the necessity of praxis; the Young Hegelians were content, as Marx caricatured, to allow criticism to remain in its abstract moment.[29] Thus Strauss could critically interpret Christ's life and be content.

Although the Frankfurt School has been accused of fostering such abstracted contentedness,[30] their own intention was quite different. They consciously attempted to distance themselves from the one-sided idealism of which Marx accused the Young Hegelians and of which the orthodox Marxists were all too ready to accuse them.

26. A few examples are Horkheimer, "Theism and Atheism," *Critique of Instrumental Reason*, pp. 35–50; Marcuse, *Eros and Civilization*, pp. 107–12; Benjamin, "Theologisch-politisches Fragment," in *Zur Kritik der Gewalt*, pp. 95–96; and the entire *Dialectic of Enlightenment*.
27. Brazill, *The Young Hegelians*, p. 24.
28. Ibid., p. 37.
29. Marx, *German Ideology*, pp. 3–4.
30. Marks, *Meaning of Marcuse*, pp. 3–4; Therborn, Göran, "The Frankfurt School," in *New Left Review* 63 (Sept.–Oct. 1970): 85–87.

Hegel and Hegelianism

Critical Theory was never intended to remain theoretical. It was seen as a base from which to launch practical activity, however distant or improbable that activity might be.

Nevertheless, the superficial resemblance of the two methodologies with their central concept of criticism, does reflect an underlying unity. Both intended to perform a transformative criticism that, using the existent intellectual materials, would overthrow the prevailing system of thought and practice in a revolutionary surge. Feuerbach criticized Christianity in order to abolish it; Stirner criticized the Enlightenment in order to transcend it. Adorno criticized Kierkegaard while Horkheimer wrote on Schopenhauer for similar reasons. But, once more, an important distinction must be made. The intention of the Young Hegelians was to abolish the mystical bonds of Christianity and later those of Enlightenment. The Frankfurt School had more complex designs. They wanted authentic transcendence in the Hegelian sense of *Aufhebung,* that is, to transcend by absorbing within one's own structure of thought. The Frankfurt School didn't simply subject their objects of study to withering criticism; Adorno knew that Spengler had to be so understood that his teaching would form part of the edifice that transcended him, if ever such a thing could be constructed.

What finally distinguished the Frankfurt School from the Young Hegelians is its lack of certainty and optimism. The Frankfurt School saw the entire critical project as too difficult and, in the end, the enemy as always too powerful and able to absorb and transcend the critics. This danger was inconceivable to the Young Hegelians with their historical and hermeneutical optimism.

Furthermore, there existed a certain clarity in the organization of the Young Hegelians; they organized the factions of their party scrupulously along a line laid down by Hegel. Hegel had said, "What is rational is actual and what is actual rational."[31] The Young Hegelians had divided this unified dictum and organized themselves along the fragments. The Right Hegelians argued that the actual was the rational; the Left Hegelians argued that the rational was the actual.[32] Thus the Right accepted the argument for the teleological completion of history; the world had been made

---

31. Hegel, *Philosophy of Right,* p. 10.
32. Löwith, *From Hegel to Nietzsche,* p. 68.

rational, or, at the very least, whatever took place in the world was rational in the sense of being historically necessary. The Left, on the other hand, accepted only the primacy of reason. That which did not conform to reason was unreal—that is, theoretically abolished and awaiting historical confirmation as to its absence. Each of the Young Hegelians was affiliated with one camp or another. Those who could not be so easily categorized (Kierkegaard, Marx, Schopenhauer) could not be considered Young Hegelians. The Frankfurt School could never fit within the confines of such a neat schema.

There were two sides to the Left Hegelians' doctrine that the rational was the actual. There was a faith in the virtue of the rational becoming the actual and there was also the certainty that such an event would take place. The Frankfurt School found both assertions problematic. The triump of rationality over reality did not seem to them an unmitigated blessing. Reason itself troubled them. It constituted a sort of mythology that destroyed all other mythology without properly fulfilling the humanly necessary role of myth.[33] At the same time, rather than serving human liberation, reason came to oppress men, turning them into instruments and denying them their freedom. Further, as I have discussed before, they no longer accepted even a limited rationalization of the world as historically certain. Thus, they cannot simply be seen as Left Hegelians.

The Right Hegelians, on the other hand, had argued for the world: they saw it as already being rational. In a strange way, the Frankfurt School has a greater affinity with the positive position of the Right Hegelians (although certainly not with the spirit in which they made the claim). At certain points the Frankfurt School accepted that the actual had become rational; this constituted the problem that they faced. For them, the rationalized world constituted the gravest threat to authentic being. They were not concerned with the relationship of reason to the world at any given historical moment. The problem, rather, had become one of reason itself: should the rational become the actual; could the actual ever be authentically rationalized.[34] Lacking the historical optimism that

---

33. Adorno and Horkheimer, *Dialectic of Enlightenment*, pp. 8–13.
34. On the real being rational, the rational being real, see Horkheimer, *Hegel und das Problem der Metaphysik*, pp. 84–85.

marked both the Left and Right they could not be organized into either camp of the Hegelian party.

They were neither Hegelian nor Young Hegelian because they lacked the simple hope that the Young Hegelians certainly had, which was the core of Hegel himself. History—the redemptive hope and certainty of humanity to Hegel and his followers—had played too many tricks on the Frankfurt School. More than that, the dialectical kernel of history, reason, had become damaged and deranged for them. Rather than liberating men, it had become an instrument of enslavement. Enlightenment had not driven away the darkness; it had caused the darkness to descend more thoroughly than ever. Worse, the darkness masqueraded as light. The Frankfurt School's thoughts, if not more profound, were certainly darker than those Hegel allowed himself to entertain publicly. For the origins of the Frankfurt School, we must trace its roots into darker and more dangerous veins than either Marxism or Hegelianism.

4. Nietzsche

One could not be a student of philosophy in Germany during the first half of this century and be unaware of Nietzsche. More importantly, one could not speculate on the problems of philosophy without speculating on the problems that Nietzsche had created or discovered. Even Marxism came under the influence of Nietzsche's thought.[1] The fundamental problem has already been touched upon—the problem of the death of God. To the Frankfurt School, this was not a problem of formal theology, any more than it was to Nietzsche. Rather it was a crisis of horizons; the West had lost itself amid inhuman and unlivable boundaries. Reason, which had existed to discover authentically true horizons, had succeeded only in abolishing the old and false ones. Reason had become its own horizon, and the formal and objective requirements of the logic of reason had supplanted an authentically useful horizon. The instrumentalization of reason meant that one could opt either for the sterile logic of positivism or for the stifling morality and metaphysics of the past.

The result was a universally mediocre culture, providing a ceaseless diet of facts for mass man and serving his needs by means of a relentlessly rational structure, that came to dominate authentic creativity. Creativity was replaced by the culture industry and the mass market. The Frankfurt School saw that there was no going back. The only possibility of escape was to create theoretical and aesthetic structures within the small pits and cracks that existed in the general seamlessness of contemporary culture. The Frankfurt School searched for a prismatic truth rather than for a systematic truth. In this they leaned more heavily on Nietzsche than on anyone else.

---

1. Lichtheim, *Marx to Hegel*, pp. 47–48; on Marcuse and Lukács. Deutscher discusses the influence of Nietzsche on Trotsky in *Prophet Armed*, pp. 48–49; also see Jay, *Dialectical Imagination*, p. 43.

Nietzsche

As did Nietzsche, they took a certain joy in what Enlightenment made possible—the attack on sterile moralities and metaphysics.[2] As Marcuse puts it:

> Nietzsche exposes the gigantic fallacy on which Western Philosophy and morality were built—namely, the transformation of facts into essences, of historical into metaphysical conditions.[3]

Nietzsche repudiated the attempt to turn transitory events into metaphysics. In this repudiation of metaphysics, Nietzsche simply announced what had already taken place with the very process of Enlightenment. Enlightenment's task was to abolish the illusions of permanence. Similarly, the Enlightenment created the basis for assaulting the transcendental and antisensual moralities that were predicated upon a transcendental metaphysics. This assault, too, Nietzsche hailed, and this too was praised by the Frankfurt School, which officially acknowledged and praised Nietzsche's role in the project.[4] This attack made real the possibility of the sensually erotic life, which was the true intention of the Frankfurt School.

Yet, just as Enlightenment makes an objective sensuality possible, it creates conditions that render its realization impossible. Enlightenment intends to destroy false gods and substitute the authentic god of reason. Reason, however, constitutes its own mythology, as Nietzsche knew, and as such becomes as illusory as the old myth.[5] Worse, while reason destroys the old myths, it is only a formal structure that is devoid of positive instructions. While liberating man from the illusions of the past, it denies to humanity authentically needed values, because it is incapable of supplying anything beyond facticity and doubt.[6] Thus reason becomes a myth itself, promising solutions and failing to supply them, all the while masquerading as something utterly antimythological. It abolishes myths that remain, in a human sense, useful.

---

2. Nietzsche, *Use and Abuse of History*, pp. 7–11, on knowledge undermining standards; Marcuse, *Eros and Civilization*, pp. 109–10; Adorno, *Minima Moralia*, pp. 96–99.
3. Marcuse, *Eros and Civilization*, p. 109.
4. Nietzsche, "On the Despisers of the Body" and "On Enjoying and Suffering Passions," *Zarathustra*, in *The Portable Nietzsche*, pp. 146–49; Horkheimer, "Zum Rationalmusstreit in der gegenwärtigen Philosophie," *Zeitschrift für Sozialforschung*, III, 44.
5. Nietzsche, "Twilight of the Idols," in *The Portable Nietzsche*, pp. 479–85.
6. Nietzsche, *Use and Abuse of History*, pp. 42–46.

This empty remythologization of the world by reason is the core of the Frankfurt School's understanding of the crisis of modernity:

> Ultimately, the Enlightenment consumed not just the symbols but their successors, universal concepts, and spared no remnant of metaphysics apart from the abstract fear of the collective from which it arose.

and:

> As the organ of this kind of adaptation, as a mere construction of means, the Enlightenment is as destructive as its romantic enemies accuse it of being.[7]

Reason becomes myth by claiming that metaphysics are unnecessary and by, therefore, claiming that it has made its own highest moment possible. It begins by denying man the ancient myths and then moves to deny him the concepts that were embedded in the myth, all the while creating the illusion that it has made man the ruler of the world. What it has actually done is to turn Enlightenment into the ruler of the world, with an instrumentalized reason as its principle—and man as its object. The instrumentalization of reason was already implicit in Plato.[8] But when reason finally collapsed into instrumentalization, it moved to an intention opposite that of Plato:

> The force of consciousness extends to the delusion of consciousness. It is rationally knowable where an unleashed, self-escaping rationality goes wrong, where it becomes true mythology. The ratio recoils into irrationality as soon as in its necessary course it fails to grasp that the disappearance of its substrate—however diluted—is its own work, the product of its own abstraction. . . . Regression of consciousness is a product of its lack of self-reflection.[9]

Yet reason, in its final moment concluding its dominance over the world, must deny the autonomy of any part excluded from its reality. It must deny autonomous will; and the denial of autonomous will must have its ground in an attack upon self-consciousness, since it is only from this ground that will can operate

---

7. Adorno and Horkheimer, *Dialectic of Enlightenment*, pp. 23, 42.
8. Ibid., p. 7.
9. Adorno, *Negative Dialectics*, pp. 148–49.

Nietzsche

effectively. Reason, in order to conclude its own conquest must regress, since it must deny the one thing that would allow will: consciousness. This is also the one thing which could save reason from regression. Thus, the conquest of the world by reason has as its final moment Positivism, which also represents the triumph over man by brute facticity.

Reason, therefore, must deny what it had initially promised: freely realized humanity. This final act requires a moment of will that reason cannot allow. The similarities between the Frankfurt School's analysis and that of Nietzsche are obvious on this level. While both must accept the virtue of the initial movement of modernity's reason toward the abolition of archaic and inhuman morality and metaphysics, the movement of reason necessarily turns modernity toward a reaffirmation of human unfreedom. This reaffirmation is all the more pernicious in that it denies its nature outright and in that it fails to allow room for its own refutation. Reason is the sole ground of criticism. Modernity is catastrophic for man; creating manifold possibilities, it simultaneously denies man the possibility of realizing those possibilities by denying him autonomy. The social manifestation of this unfreedom is what both Nietzsche and the Frankfurt School despise: mass culture. Mass culture gives the illusion of autonomy although it is actually its diametrical opposite. Mass culture is unfree and without the possibility of freedom.

The formulation of the rational affects the structure of the aesthetic; and with the aesthetic, the cultural structure of modern society is transformed. This event, which has its origins in a reason that compels all events to demonstrate a socially legitimate causation, forces culture to submit to the demands of the social mechanism.[10] The effect of this is a philistinism that reduces culture to a commodity and at the same time makes it mediocre. This argument concerning the status of culture is central to the analysis of all of the members of the Frankfurt School.[11] It is the cutting edge for their critique of modern society. It must be, for with the collapse of the

---

10. Which brings to mind Nietzsche's discussion of the arbitrariness of causality in "Twilight of the Idols," in *The Portable Nietzsche*, pp. 494-97; *Gay Science*, pp. 157-59.

11. See Adorno and Horkheimer, *Dialectic of Enlightenment*, pp. 120-67; Marcuse, *One-Dimensional Man*, pp. 56-83; Benjamin, "Work of Art in an Age of Mechanical Reproduction," in *Illuminations*, pp. 218-42.

argument that capitalism will end in the impoverishment of the proletariat, the critique of capitalism (and what they perceive as the socialist variants upon capitalism's theme) depends on the cultural argument—the impact of capitalism upon the structure of the human mind. The argument concerning the status of reason, therefore, has its effective outcome at the point at which the rational structure affects the cultural makeup of society. The argument against philistinism is not tangential to the argument of the Frankfurt School concerning the crisis of modernity but is at its core.

The roots of this critique are to be found in Nietzsche and in the impact on European thought in the twentieth century of Nietzsche's conception of culture in the bourgeois era. Europe, and even a great part of the Left of Europe, learned of the decline of culture from Nietzsche. They believed Nietzsche when he wrote: "Historical culture is really a kind of inherited grayness and those who have borne its mark from childhood, must believe, instinctively, in the old age of mankind."[12] And when Nietzsche wrote of the overall degeneration of modern man,[13] he meant not only the degeneration of men, but the degeneration of culture: "To the artist of decadence: there we have the crucial words. And here my seriousness begins. I am far from looking guilelessly on while this decadent corrupts our health—and music as well. Is Wagner a human being at all? Isn't he rather a sickness? He makes sick whatever he touches... That people in Germany should deceive themselves about Wagner does not surprise me. The opposite would surprise me."[14] Just as the Frankfurt School saw the self-annihilation of Enlightenment as inevitable from its very origins in Plato, so to Nietzsche the decadence of the West had been inevitable since Socrates. The final manifestation of the historical outcome to both Nietzsche and the Frankfurt School was the unhealthy culture that repelled humans but attracted the epigone.

Adorno, learning from Nietzsche, suggests a strange solution; strange, at least, for a Marxist:

> The best mode of conduct, in the face of all this [the decline of human architecture] still seems an uncommitted, suspended one: to lead a

12. Nietzsche, *Use and Abuse of History*, p. 49.
13. Nietzsche, *Beyond Good and Evil*, p. 118.
14. Nietzsche, *The Case of Wagner*, pp. 164–65.

Nietzsche

private life, as far as the social order and one's own needs will tolerate nothing else, but not to attach weight to it as to something still socially substantial and individually appropriate. 'It is even part of my good fortune not to be a house-owner', Nietzsche already wrote in the GAY SCIENCE. Today we should have to add: it is part of morality not to be at home in one's home.[15]

The solution, if there is such a thing as a solution any longer, is for man to withdraw into himself; to be more precise, to withdraw from the culture that makes one ill—which is illness. The illness of culture is the critical concern of the Frankfurt School and what distinguishes their Marxism from that of others.[16] The crisis to the Frankfurt School, on this level, is a crisis of aesthetic sensibility.

Yet, again with Nietzsche, they knew that despite their contempt for modern mass culture, there was no going back. The Frankfurt School viewed the past with a melancholy nostalgia.[17] There were things there that were worth having; the past possessed a sensibility and a sensuality that modernity had abolished. However, both Nietzsche and the Frankfurt School hold forth the possibility that there is nothing to go forward to, or worse still, if there is something there, it may be impossible to reach.

From such a standpoint, the Frankfurt School might easily have slipped into an empty and impossible romanticism. Three factors stopped them. First, they stood on the ground of Marxism; a move into formal romanticism would have been a complete repudiation. Second, they had the example of Stefan George and his circle; the hopelessness of George's aestheticized and romanticized politics and its undesirable social consequences were apparent. Yet, these two things were not enough to explain how they clung to some hope. The real answer is the third element—Nietzsche.

Nietzsche had written a warning against romantic conservatism that would attempt to return to the mythic image of a lost age: "Whispered to conservatives: What was not known formally, what is known or might be known, today: a reversion, a return in any

---

15. Adorno, *Minima Moralia*, p. 39.
16. On the withdrawal from culture see Marcuse, *Essay on Liberation*, pp. 39–45; Horkheimer, "Art and Mass Culture," in *Critical Theory*, p. 289; Benjamin, "Wissenschaft nach der Mode," in *Stratege im Literaturkampf*, pp. 70–71.
17. Jameson, *Marxism and Form*, pp. 60–93, uses this phrase in relation to Benjamin. It is equally applicable to the others.

sense or degree is simply not possible."[18] Where their contempt for Marxist progressivism or for Hegel's forced identity theory would not have barred their way to romanticism (they perpetually toyed with its possibility), this passage cut off retreat for them. Nietzsche, having understood the historical roots of the crisis in culture, knew just as well that the crisis had exhausted history. This time, history could not move forward. The Frankfurt School's analysis agreed: they knew full well that one could never go back. Horkheimer writes:

> We are the heirs, for better or for worse, of the Enlightenment and technological progress. To oppose these by regressing to more primitive stages does not alleviate the permanent crisis they have brought about. On the contrary, such expedients lead from historically reasonable to utterly barbaric forms of social domination. The sole way of assisting nature is to unshackle its seeming opposite, independent thought.[19]

Horkheimer and the Frankfurt School learned the necessity of finding the key to the problem of the Enlightenment more from Nietzsche than from Marx. Marx's optimism would no longer bear up under historical scrutiny. A faith in teleology offered no way out of the predicament.

Certainly, neither Nietzsche's teaching of the superman, nor of the will to power, nor of the eternal return of the same, was the key to their problem (although all of these crop up in strange forms in their thought). Critical Theory, which was to become their methodology, originated structurally in another teaching of Nietzsche: "I mistrust all systematizers and I avoid them. The will to a system is a lack of integrity."[20] To Nietzsche, systems offered a false unity. They gave the illusion of completeness without touching the essence of the unruly world. More than that, the will to a system revealed a soul too pedantic to be capable of living well, let alone of willing an understanding of the world.

To the Frankfurt School, the possibilities of history were to be found outside of the systems. Both Nietzsche and the Frankfurt School believed that the Enlightenment had exhausted itself. To

---

18. Nietzsche, "Twilight of the Idols," in *The Portable Nietzsche*, p. 546.
19. Horkheimer, *Eclipse of Reason*, p. 127.
20. Nietzsche, "Twilight of the Idols," in *The Portable Nietzsche*, p. 470.

Nietzsche things exhausted loomed small. For the Frankfurt School, however (being epigone?), the Enlightenment loomed large. Positivism had come to occupy the space of systems, sharing that space only with Heideggerian ontology. The world had no more room for systems. Indeed, attempting systematic thought would put one in the camp of the Enlightenment. Thus for reasons derived from Nietzsche, but in a sense beneath him, the Frankfurt School approached the possibility of a solution to the problem of the enlightenment by shunning the type of systems expected of teleologists. Adorno writes:

> Philosophy retains respect for systems to the extent to which things heterogeneous to it face it in the form of a system. The administered world moves in this direction. It is the negative objectivity that is a system, not the positive subject. In a historical phase in which systems—insofar as they deal seriously with contents—have been relegated to the ominous realm of conceptual poetry and nothing but the pale outline of their schematic order has been retained, it is difficult to imagine vividly what used to attract philosophers to the system.[21]

For this reason, Adorno declares *Negative Dialectics* to be an antisystem. The Frankfurt School's methodology employed prismatics (*Prisms* is a title of a collection of Adorno's essays) in order to escape the systematics that had become the essence of the utterly administered society. Prismatics enabled the School to comprehend a shifting reality, so that it could conduct guerrilla warfare in the gaps of a seemingly seamless system and stand in opposition to the false and repressive systematics of modernity. The first and last reasons are arguments against systems that they learned from Nietzsche.

The Frankfurt School learned an enormous amount from Nietzsche. In the first place, they took their understanding on the crisis of modernity from Nietzsche's conception of the collapse of myth and horizons. From this they shared with Nietzsche a certain joy at the liberation afforded by the collapse of traditional metaphysics and morality. They moved, with Nietzsche, to a critique of the structure of reason as the residue of the process of Enlightenment; along with Nietzsche, they stood appalled at the mass culture that this notion of reason had wrought. And finally,

---

21. Adorno, *Negative Dialectics*, p. 20.

along with Nietzsche, they learned that there was no going back. They would have to stand their ground, yielding neither to teleology or romanticism. Finally, the method that they developed in response to this problematic, Critical Theory, took its bearings formally from Nietzsche's argument against system.

Despite Nietzsche's clear influence on the Frankfurt School, however, it is essential to recognize that their intentions were never Nietzsche's. They intended the revolution and not the proclamation of the superman. While frequently praising and occasionally defending Nietzsche, they were never truly at peace with him. Adorno warns: "Ideology lies in wait for the mind which delights in itself like Nietzsche's Zarathustra, for the mind which all but irresistibly becomes an absolute in itself."[22] In the end, the Frankfurt School could not live with the individuation implicit in Nietzsche. At the same time, Adorno and Horkheimer could write the following: " 'Where do your greatest dangers lie?' was the question Nietzsche once posed himself, and answered thus: 'In compassion.' With his denial he redeemed the unshakable confidence in man that is constantly betrayed by every form of assurance that seeks only to console."[23] The Frankfurt School took its bearings from Nietzsche, even as they tried to remain Marxist. They were impelled to move toward him, for they were wise enough to realize that the crisis of modernity rested at least as much in the knowledge he had made available as it did with Marx and that Nietzsche had understood this problem better than anyone. Also, they had little choice in being influenced by Nietzsche, since they were Germans, whose teacher, for better or worse, had been Nietzsche's finest heir: Martin Heidegger.

22. Ibid., p. 30.
23. Adorno and Horkheimer, *Dialectic of Enlightenment,* p. 119.

5. Heidegger

One could not study philosophy in Germany at the time of the Frankfurt School and avoid the influence of Martin Heidegger. Certainly, the Frankfurt School could not and did not. Marcuse had studied under him and Benjamin had read him at an early age. Adorno had constructed an elaborate critique of his position. Each had to come to terms with him in some way.[1] But, in coming to terms with him, they absorbed his concerns more than they would admit. There are those who claim that Heidegger's only influence on the Frankfurt School was through the young Marcuse.[2] This influence, however, was deeper and broader.

Adorno saw authenticity as the fundamental category underlying Heidegger's ontology.[3] Murky at best, the concept served as a mechanism in Heidegger's attempt to establish the distinction between the ontic and ontological. Only through distinguishing between these categories and through eliminating the ephemera of the ontic could authentic Being be reached. The intention behind this was to distill an essence of Being that was simultaneously substance, to abolish in Being both brute facticity and transcendent metaphysics.[4]

There is in this quest for authenticity a strange parallel with Marx's concern for the abolition of the alienation of man in the world. Heidegger himself acknowledged this positive element in Marx, writing in a famous passage, "Because Marx, in experiencing alienation, descends into an important dimension of history, the

---

1. Gay, *Weimar Culture*, pp. 81–82; Piccone and Delfini, "Marcuse's Heideggerian Marxism," pp. 42–43; Benjamin, *Briefe*, p. 252; Adorno, *Negative Dialectics* and *Jargon of Authenticity*, which was intended as an afterword to *Negative Dialectics*.
2. Jay in particular underestimated Heidegger's impact; see pp. 71–74.
3. Adorno, *Negative Dialectics*, p. 112.
4. Heidegger, *Being and Time*, pp. 267–69; also see *End of Philosophy*, pp. 1–4.

Marxist view of history is superior to all others."⁵ Heidegger praised Marx for elevating the concept of alienation to the center of history because the converse of alienation is authenticity. Both Marx and Heidegger may be said to have derived their concepts from the historical nature of Hegel's ontology but each takes a different turn. On the simplest level, Marx's unalienated authenticity is rooted in the category of species-being, while Heidegger's is to be found in a lonely being-in-itself.⁶

For our purposes it is important to note that the apparent gap between Marxism and Heidegger's ontology is subtly bridged by the concept of authenticity, at least when it is considered outside the standpoint of practice.⁷ The Frankfurt School occupies the nexus connecting the two giants. They praise the Heideggerian insight into the significance of the category, while distancing themselves from both his concrete intention and his historical practice. However, their emphasis on authenticity, even though it is not incompatible with Marx's teaching, is derived from Heidegger.

The late Heidegger had turned away from the concept of authenticity. Those of his followers who retained the notion allowed it to degenerate into a type of self-indulgence and obfuscation. This degeneration of the concept was held in contempt by the Frankfurt School. One might speculate that their later coolness toward Eric Fromm had to do with his own sentimental self-indulgences. Adorno certainly had no use for the emptiness found in many treatments of the notion of authenticity. Indeed, he entitled a companion volume to *Negative Dialectics, The Jargon of Authenticity*.

Notice, however, that Adorno's critique was not directed against the concept of authenticity but against the jargon. He opposed the practice and political function to which it was put. In a sense, it was inevitable that the notion of authenticity as developed by Heidegger would come to no good end. Heidegger's distinction between the ontological and the ontical meant that authenticity, which pertains to the ontological, would recoil from the ontic and, hence, from

5. Heidegger, "Letter on Humanism," in *Basic Writings*, p. 219.
6. Dasein does not in itself bridge the gap between Being-in-itself and species-being, insofar as Dasein is a denial of the universal category of man (see *Being and Time*, p. 171) which is crucial for Marx. Following this, Dasein is only a preface to ontology and not the ontological itself (*Being and Time*, p. 35).
7. Along these lines, Lucien Goldmann in *Lukács and Heidegger* makes a convincing argument for the compatibility of Marxist and Heideggerian categories; see pp. 40–45 in particular.

Heidegger

social and political practice. The failure was not in Heidegger's concept of authenticity but in what the Frankfurt School saw as Heidegger's ultimate inability to abolish the distinction between things and essences. This meant that authenticity would remain separate from social reality. It would remain jargon. The point was to rescue authenticity from mere language.

Indeed, the Frankfurt School praised Heidegger's intent even as they criticized his failure. His attempt to abolish the opposition between the thing and the essence of the thing was seen as the problem of philosophy since Plato. Adorno writes:

> If Heidegger, in the later phase of his philosophy, claims to rise above the traditional distinction between essence and fact, he is reflecting a justified irritation at the divergence of the essential and factual sciences.[8]

Adorno recognizes as does Heidegger, that the beginning of a critique of alienation must reside in a critique of the metaphysic that rips the world into two realms. This metaphysic shatters cognition by forcing a disjunction between modes of human thought. Marcuse goes further in this vein:

> The meaning of philosophical existentialism lay in regaining the full concretion of the historical subject in opposition to the abstract 'logical' subject of rational idealism, i.e. eliminating the domination unshaken from Descartes to Husserl, of the ego cogito. Heidegger's position before his SEIN UND ZEIT was philosophy's furthest advance in this direction.[9]

Heidegger's role, then, was twofold. In the first place, he, along with Nietzsche, attacked the opposition between thing and essence. In the second place, he attacked the epistemological outcome of such a position—the division of cognition into distinct and opposed modes. The distinction between perception of things and contemplation of essences led reason into a self-opposed and self-denying stance. In both the metaphysical and epistemological case, then, the virtue of Heidegger was his unwillingness to tolerate the fragmenta-

---

8. Adorno, *Negative Dialectics*, p. 73.
9. Marcuse, "Struggle against Liberalism in Totalitarianism," in *Negations*, p. 32.

tion of existence. His search for Being was the search for an authentic whole.

According to the Frankfurt School, the category of authenticity denotes a real longing for wholeness on the part of man.[10] What is unacceptable is the practical outcome of Heidegger's particular use of authenticity. Adorno writes:

> Heidegger did sense some of this mechanism (of negativity). But the authenticity he misses will promptly recoil into positivity, into authenticity as a posture of consciousness—a posture whose emigration from the profane powerlessly imitates the theological habit of the old doctrine of essence.[11]

Heidegger's unwillingness to allow Being to become identical with a being in the world that, at the same time, would be against the world, his unwillingness to allow the ontological category to be sullied by the ontic, forces him, according to Adorno, into one of two roles—either that of a metaphysician postulating abstract essences or that of a positivist allowing being in practice to become the brute being in the world. In either case, Heidegger's notion of authenticity becomes positive, affirming existence as it stands. If it is the first case, then it affirms the *status quo* by presenting the illusion of escape into a quasi-metaphysical realm. If it is the second case, then the ontological, without our realizing it, becomes indistinguishable from the ontical, and by so doing, falls into the positivistic affirmation of the fact. The outcome is political reaction:

> To the converted and unconverted philosophers of fascism, finally value; like authenticity, heroic endurance of the 'being-in-the-world' of individual existence, frontier-situations, becomes a means of usurping religious-authoritarian pathos without the least religious content. They lead to the denunciation of anything that is not sufficiently sterling worth, sound to the core, that is, the Jews: did not Richard Wagner already play off genuine German metal against foreign dross and thus misuse criticism of the culture market as an apology for barbarism? Such abuse, however, is not extrinsic to the concept of genuineness.[12]

10. Adorno, *Jargon of Authenticity*, pp. 107–8.
11. Adorno, *Negative Dialectics*, p. 113; also *Jargon of Authenticity*, p. 121.
12. Adorno, *Minima Moralia*, p. 152.

Heidegger

Genuineness, rooted as it is in Heidegger in the concept of the individual, is by its nature inauthentic, since it grasps at an illusion—a Being radically free of its social context.

The use of the concept and not the concept itself is what repels Adorno. Its use is repulsive, first, because it cloaks the positivism hidden within it. But it is also repulsive because of the shallowness with which it treats a critical category:

> What Hegel and Marx in their youth condemned as alienation and reification, and against which all are spontaneously united today, is what Heidegger interprets ontologically, as well as unhistorically and in its function as a being-form of Dasein, as something bodily.... That throws light on the artsy-craftsy element in the jargon. It provides a refuge for the stale notion that art should be brought back into life and that there should be more than art, but also more than mere usage.[13]

There is something odd about this criticism. At least one member of the Frankfurt School, Marcuse, had argued for just this stale notion, of art being brought into life. In his *An Essay on Liberation,* Marcuse says, "... art would be an integral factor in shaping the quality and 'appearance' of things, in shaping the reality, the way of life."[14] Marcuse's political project, as presented in *An Essay on Liberation,* was an argument for art's power over life. Adorno here is criticizing the cheapness of the jargon as being willfully unaware of the political realities separating art from life. His attack is on the trivialization of the notion and not on the notion itself.

In a way, Heidegger's project parallelled that of the Frankfurt School. The problem of history was such that we were presented with the end of metaphysics. The fall of metaphysics meant the emptiness of the critical faculty. Neither party was certain that a critical philosophy could be resurrected. Assuredly, none could be resurrected that did not, in some way, resurrect the relationship between truth and beauty that Plato had forged, this time with beauty gaining sovereignty over truth. Thus both Heidegger and Marcuse subjected politics to art. Although, as we will see later, Benjamin regarded this as fascistic, Marcuse could not help adopting this stance; reification left only the beautiful as autonomous—

---

13. Adorno, *Jargon of Authenticity,* pp. 107–8.
14. Marcuse, *Essay on Liberation,* p. 32; also, see below, Chapter 16.

even as it destroyed the capacity for enjoying beauty. Marcuse, in a way, and by Benjamin's standards, continued to work with Heidegger and to even risk fascism, for he had few alternatives. The Frankfurt School thus sought only to abolish the *staleness* of life over art; it seemed compelled to risk its practice. Adorno sought to vitiate the cheapness, the falsification of authenticity and aesthetics. But nowhere, not even in *The Jargon of Authenticity,* does he repudiate them in and of themselves.

What was unsatisfactory about Heidegger was the historical intention behind the suggested aesthetic practice. Rather than serving to negate the inauthentic conditions of existence in modern society, this intention served to affirm those conditions while projecting the illusion of negating them. The notion of an authentic negation of positivity, nonetheless, appealed to Adorno. Only Heidegger's use of the concept and the linkage of the concept to a radically privatized being is unacceptable: "Heidegger's approach is true, insofar as he accepts that and denies traditional metaphysics; he becomes untrue where—not unlike Hegel—he talks as if the contents we want to rescue were thus directly in our minds."[15] The failure of Heidegger is profound: he fails to place Being into practice. But this was Heidegger's failure and not the failure of the category of authenticity.

This ambivalence toward the authenticity of Heidegger is reflected in the political practice of the students of Marcuse. It is frequently noted that Marcuse was influenced early in his career by Heidegger but rejected his influence after joining the Institute. What is much more interesting, however, is the manner in which, despite the dissolution of a formal link, Heidegger (and Nietzsche) continued to affect Marcuse's theses on political activity for the rest of his life.[16]

The demand of the student movement of the 1960s was never really concerned with the abolition of surplus-value nor did it appeal for an end to the crisis of underconsumption. The jargon of the student movement was, on the contrary, what Adorno referred to as the jargon of authenticity. Authentic existence, commitment, aesthetic immediacy, self-realization, the catch-phrases of existen-

15. Adorno, *Negative Dialectics*, p. 98.
16. For a critical acknowledgment of Heidegger's influence on Marcuse's political practice, see Piccone and Delfini, "Marcuse's Heideggerian Marxism," pp. 44–46.

Heidegger

tialism (and of the Right before 1945) were the battle cries. It seems odd that a leading figure of the Frankfurt School should have emerged as their chief ideologue—until one considers the jargon of authenticity employed by Marcuse. Consider the following:

> Socialist solidarity is autonomy: self-determination begins at home—and that is with every I and the We, whom the I chooses. And this end must indeed appear in the means to attain it, that is to say, in the strategy of those, who within the existing society, work for the new one. If the socialist relationships of production are to be a new way of life, a new Form of life, then their existential quality must show forth, anticipated and demonstrated in the fight for their realization.[17]

The goal of the revolution is not the realization of an utterly bound together species-being but rather the primary moment, the I. The I, as an existential form, is the beginning of change and is, in the end, the object of that change as well. The revolution begins with the individual and ends with his transformation. Narcissism, a movement out of the I only in order to return to it, becomes the governing principle; self-realization becomes the only rationale. Practice, within the social world, constitutes merely an intermediate moment.

Indeed, Marcuse made Narcissism the co-ruling principle (along with the Orphic) of the post-revolutionary era.[18] The ability of man to appreciate himself as an end in himself, to relate to himself as something other than labor, is represented in the self-gratification of Narcissus. Narcissus represents the aestheticization/eroticization of being. Thus, the solipsism of which Adorno accuses Heidegger comes to rest in Marcuse's symbol of the end of things.

Along with this symbol, Marcuse becomes concerned with death, a concern that follows from any rendering of the individual as an end. Heidegger and Marcuse both face the radicalized problem of death because both render the individual radically important. As neither retains the solace of metaphysics, both must grapple directly with the problem of death where the finitude of the one comes to be identical with the totality of Being. Thus, Marcuse's *Eros and Civilization* ends with the problem of death, perhaps as unsatisfac-

---

17. Marcuse, *Essay on Liberation*, p. 89. Piccone and Delfini find similar examples in *One-Dimensional Man*, pp. 45–46.

18. The acknowledged principle of the new age, Marcuse, *Eros and Civilization*, p. 146. See below, Chapter 16 and Conclusion.

torily as does Heidegger's *Being and Time.* Again, the parallel concerns lead in similar directions, albeit for different reasons and different ends. Nonetheless, it is no accident that Marcuse, decades after his break with Heidegger, should return over and over to Heidegger's themes. His project was Heidegger's—a life without metaphysical solace.

Heidegger's influence can thus be seen on three levels. In the first place, the Frankfurt School accepts and praises his attack upon traditional metaphysics and epistemology. Second, Heidegger focused their attention upon the category of authentic being, as both a goad and supplement to Marx's species-being and alienation. Finally, the jargon emerges as the formal rhetoric of the praxis that Critical Theory promises and tried to deliver to the 1960s.

It is, of course, absolutely true that the Frankfurt School broke with Heidegger. His positive political positions were utterly repugnant to them. But their concern with him was unavoidable. Adorno was obsessed with refuting him; Marcuse had never forgotten him and always fought him. Philosophical influence is never simple, however, and the first word is usually misleading. Heidegger gave the Frankfurt School a subtle turn toward things that were important to them: art and death. The Frankfurt School cannot be understood without these issues. They would not have come to these ideas in the way that they did without Heidegger.

6. Spengler

Oswald Spengler's case is similar to Heidegger's. The Frankfurt School is officially antagonistic toward both. It explicitly excoriates both on many occasions. But for both it also has moments of praise and feels for both an unofficial and usually unacknowledged attraction. Of the two, Spengler exercises a stronger influence, both overt and covert, than does Heidegger. Only Adorno wrote extensively and explicitly on Spengler, but his spirit permeates all of their work.[1]

Spengler, of course, has long been in disrepute among intellectuals of all varieties. Even before Hitler, his lack of academic standing together with his popularity made official academia suspect him of shallow trivialization. To be sure, this suspicion may have been true. After Hitler, a taint of Spengler came to be considered a stench. The Frankfurt School, on the surface at least, has always held him to be a petit-bourgeois, shallow apologist for Naziism.[2]

However, beneath this overall contempt, Spengler was seen as a great, if limited, prophet. To Adorno, in particular, the catalogue of Spengler's insights was astounding.[3] Adorno specifies seven particular areas in which Spengler saw events in Western history and culture more clearly than did most others: "The course of world history vindicated his immediate prognoses to the extent that would astonish if they were still remembered. Forgotten, Spengler takes his

---

1. Lichtheim actually claims that Spengler's greatest influence was on Horkheimer. *From Marx to Hegel*, pp. 162–63.
2. See, for example, Marcuse, "Struggle against Liberalism in Totalitarianism," *Negations*, p. 5; Adorno, *Minima Moralia*, p. 44.
3. See Adorno, "Spengler after the Decline," in *Prisms*, pp. 53–72; and Adorno, "Wird Spengler rechtbehalten," in *Kritik, Kleine Schriften zur Gesellschaft*, pp. 94–104.

revenge by threatening to be right."⁴ First, Adorno praised Spengler's insight into the rise of Caesarism as the political culmination to Europe's struggles.⁵ Second, he praised Spengler's apprehension of the atomization and nomadization of the urban-dweller, the archetypical social type of the twentieth century.⁶ Third, he praised Spengler's understanding of the dual character of Enlightenment in its final moment.⁷ Fourth, he agrees with Spengler's view of the future of warfare, praising both his insight into war's coming universality and into the social and military structure supporting it.⁸ Fifth, Adorno praises Spengler for foreseeing the growth of a new political party, which would consist of a cult of followers rather than a group of members.⁹ Sixth, he finds parallels between his own ideas and Spengler's notion of the decline of dynamic culture and the growth of a static one.¹⁰ Finally, and perhaps most significantly, he sees power in Spengler's vision of the growth of a new barbarism in the cultural and political life of the West.¹¹

Each of these notions of Spengler find echoes in the writing of the Frankfurt School. Either they saw these as the critical problems of modern society (as opposed to Spengler, who saw them as pointing in some cases to the solution of history) or else they incorporated Spengler's criticism into their own. Of course, not all of Spengler's insights were equally significant. The most important for Critical Theory were Spengler's understandings of the dual character of the Enlightenment, his notion of the growth of a static culture, and his argument that the West would necessarily revert to a barbarism. These three insights formed the crux of the Frankfurt School's vision of the West in late modernity.

To Spengler, the Enlightenment has two aspects. The first occurs when a culture realizes its given particular end. The self-fulfillment of a culture raises the question of a future. If a culture is an action and there are no further ends toward which to act, what then is the status of culture? Having fulfilled itself, the culture must decline

---

4. Adorno, "Spengler after the Decline," in *Prisms*, p. 54.
5. Ibid., p. 55. Adorno, "Wird Spengler rechtbehalten," pp. 97–99.
6. Adorno, "Spengler after the Decline," p. 56.
7. Ibid., p. 57.
8. Ibid., p. 58.
9. Ibid., p. 59.
10. Ibid., pp. 56–58.
11. Ibid., p. 65; Adorno, "Wird Spengler rechtbehalten," p. 102.

Spengler

into pale classicism or self-pitying romanticism.[12] As fulfillment for the organism is the prelude to its death, so Enlightenment (seen as culture fulfilling itself) undermines the basis for the culture's existence. The rationalization of the world removes reason from its function. Thus, if reason is one side of Enlightenment, exhausted unreason is the other.

The second aspect is noted by Adorno, who quotes the following passage by Spengler:

> The need for universal education, which was totally lacking in the ancient world, is bound up with the political press. In it is a completely unconscious urge to bring the masses, as the objects of party politics, under the control of the newspapers. To the idealist of early democracy, universal education seemed enlightenment as such, free of ulterior motives and even today one finds here and there weak minds which become enthusiastic about the idea of freedom of the press, but it is precisely this that smooths the way for the coming of Caesars of world-journalism. Those who have learned to read succumb to their power and the anticipated self-determination to late democracy turns into radical determination of the people by the powers behind the printed word.[13]

This side of the Enlightenment is manifested as a social phenomenon. The universalization of knowledge, which appears to be a movement into liberation as the masses attain the formal requirements of Enlightenment, in fact, turns into its opposite, the unfreedom of domination by Caesarism.

Clearly, this dual character of the Enlightenment is the explicit theme of the entire Frankfurt School.[14] Adorno acknowledges the importance of Spengler in promulgating this doctrine.[15] This idea—that the Enlightenment exhausts itself through its own realization and thereby becomes unfreedom—is critical to their entire notion of the dialectic of modernity although certainly they did not perceive the movement precisely as Spengler did. The notion of organicism is anathema to them. Still, they paralleled Spengler's

---

12. Spengler, *Decline of the West*, pp. 107–8.
13. Adorno, "Spengler after the Decline," p. 57.
14. See Adorno and Horkheimer, *Dialectic of Enlightenment;* Benjamin, "Work of Art in an Age of Mechanical Reproduction," in *Illuminations*.
15. Adorno, "Spengler after the Decline," pp. 57–58; "Wird Spengler rechtbehalten," pp. 99–100.

formulations in two significant ways. First, they clearly had profound sympathies with Spengler's emphasis on the cultural event as the ground of historical being.[16] Even while they protested that there always existed a subterranean realm of the sociomaterial in which the historical actually worked itself out, they turned their primary attention to the problem of cultures. This is shown both in their active concerns and explicit statements. Spengler, of course, did not initiate the notion of the cultural as the historical, but it was Spengler who made it popular again, and it was Spengler who attempted to systematize it.

Second, there was a parallel between the Frankfurt School's notion of the precise status of modern culture and Spengler's concept. Adorno writes:

> His prediction is fulfilled even more strikingly in the static state of culture, the most advanced efforts of which have been denied understanding and a genuine reception by society since the nineteenth century. This static state compels the incessant and deadly repetition of what has already been accepted, and at the same time standardized art for the masses, with its petrified formulas, excludes history. All specifically modern art can be regarded as an attempt to keep the dynamic of history alive through magic, or to increase the horror at the stasis to shock, to portray the catastrophe in which the ahistorical suddenly begins to look archaic. Spengler's prophecy for the smaller states is beginning to be fulfilled in men themselves, even in the citizens of the largest and most powerful states. Thus, history seems to have been extinguished.[17]

Spengler had argued that the penultimate moment of the West, before its rebirth in a kind of barbarism, was a cultural enervation in which the creativity of the past would be replaced by a false and shallow re-creation of the greatness of the past or by the shallow formalism of an empty classicism.[18] This position was consistently upheld by the Frankfurt School.[19]

The Frankfurt School saw the origin of this depletion of culture

---

16. See Adorno and Horkheimer, *Dialectic of Enlightenment*, pp. 120–67; Benjamin, "Literaturgeschichte und Literaturwissenschaft," in *Der Strategie in Literaturkampf*, pp. 7–9. In this, both Spengler and the Frankfurt School are rooted in Nietzsche.
17. Adorno, "Spengler after the Decline," pp. 58–59.
18. Spengler, *Decline of the West*, 2:108.
19. See Marcuse, *One-Dimensional Man*, p. xv; Horkheimer, "Art as Mass Culture," *Critical Theory*, pp. 286–88.

Spengler

in the objectification of man by the machine.[20] This theme is also found in the writings of Spengler:

> And these machines become in their forms less and ever less human, more ascetic, mystic, esoteric: they weave the earth over with an infinite web of subtle forces, currents, and tensions. Their bodies become ever more and more immaterial ever less noisy.... Man has felt the machine to be devilish, and rightly. It signifies in the eyes of the believer the deposition of God. It delivers sacred Causality over to man and by him, with a sort of foreseeing omniscience is set in motion, silent and irresistible.[21]

As with Marx, the functioning of the machine, because of the manner in which man relates to it, makes man into its object and the machine into subject. Since the machine rules over man absolutely and controls his activity, it stands in relation to man as does God.

To Marx, of course, this situation reflected not the universal and intrinsic nature of the machine but the social structure that historically created and ruled that machine—a social structure subject to abolition. To Spengler, however, this objectification of man, and with it the remystification of the world, is bound up with the machine itself. If the cause was anything external to the machine, it was the immanent and organic movement of a Faustian culture. But the machine was really the material embodiment of such a culture. Hence, one cannot conceive of any other outcome for the machine.

The parallel between this position and the position of the Frankfurt School is haunting. Both take the machine out of the particular context of the social organization and discover causation in the very nature of the machine. Clearly, Spengler is willing to project causation farther outside of the socioeconomic context than is the Frankfurt School. Nonetheless, the Frankfurt School does see the machine itself as a problem of a radical sort, transcending even the particular social organization. They hold out the possibility of the creation of a new social order that would demystify and desubjectify the machine, but they never present this outcome as a certainty.[22]

The Frankfurt School's critique of technology may have other

---

20. Marcuse, *One-Dimensional Man*, pp. 144–46; Benjamin, "Work of Art in an Age of Mechanical Reproduction," in *Illuminations*, pp. 241–42; Adorno and Horkheimer, *Dialectic of Enlightenment*, pp. 122–31.
21. Spengler, *Decline of the West*, 2:503–4.
22. Marcuse, *One-Dimensional Man*, pp. 203–46.

sources, but its precise formulation coupled with Adorno's explicit praise of Spengler points to Spengler as the origin of their critique of technology and the culture begotten by technology. According to Spengler, the civilization of the machine comes to overwhelm the possibility of a freely created culture outside this civilization. To the Frankfurt School, a creativity outside the cultural epoch is difficult if not impossible to imagine.

To both Spengler and the School, there are only two possibilities: either an utterly administered and deadened world will collapse into epigonal tedium or the cataclysmic collapse of world culture will rend the bourgeois world asunder. As Spengler concludes in the second volume of *The Decline of the West:*

> The dictature of money marches on, tending to its material peak, in the Faustian Civilization as in every other. And now something happens that is intelligible only to one who has penetrated to the essence of money. If it were anything tangible, then its existence would be forever—but, as it is a form of thought, it fades out as soon as it has thought its economic world to finality, and has no more material upon which to feed.... But with this, money, too, is at the end of its success, and the last conflict is at hand in which the Civilization receives its conclusive form—the conflict between money and blood.[23]

For Spengler as for Marx, capital has exhausted itself. There remain only two possibilities. One is the continuation of capitalism as a static and endless prison. The other is a collapse into the barbarism of the blood: fascism.

To Spengler, the lapse into barbarism is historically ordained, the recapitulation of capitalism merely a dreadful and never acknowledged possibility. To the Frankfurt School, both are possibilities and both are dreadful. The lapse into barbarism is the motif of the *Dialectic of Enlightenment;* the perpetuation of the machine-God is the theme of *One-Dimensional Man.* It is conceivable that in the struggle between blood and money, money will win, perpetuating the endless stasis of the machine. Or it is possible that blood will win, creating an era of bloody horror. Or there is always the most horrible possibility, that blood and money will join forces, each serving the other in a static horror. Adorno writes:

> He [Spengler] demonstrates more strikingly than almost anyone else

---

23. Spengler, *The Decline of the West,* 2:506.

the way the primitive nature of culture always impels it towards decay and the way culture itself, as form and order, is in complicity with blind domination, which, forever in crisis, is always prone to annihilate itself and its victims. Culture bears the mark of death; to deny this could be to remain impotent before Spengler, who betrayed as many of the secrets of culture, as did Hitler, those of propaganda.

To escape the charmed circle of Spengler's morphology it is not enough to defame barbarism and rely on the health of culture.[24]

To Adorno the most powerful insight is that of the two possibilities. The crisis is whether any way to break out can be found.

Spengler's most direct influence on the Frankfurt School, then, was through his concept that culture (in this case, Enlightenment) moves decadently toward its own annihilation and comes to rest in its antipode: barbarism. His influence conditioned their vision of the historical possibilities. Spengler, more than Marx, created and nurtured the School's historical vision. They opposed his socioeconomic blindness, his unwillingness to root the historical possibilities in the material;[25] yet even those relatively mild protestations against him sound hollow. It is not entirely clear in the final chapter of *The Decline of the West* that Spengler ignored or misunderstood the socioeconomic roots of the crisis; indeed, it is not entirely clear that the Frankfurt School itself saw the crisis as having primarily socioeconomic roots.

It was Spengler, more than Marx, who gave the School their sense of the future. They approached history with more dread than hope. To Marx, whatever turns the dialectic took, the movement toward a resolution was inevitable. He did not consider that history might pose an insoluble problem or that the exhaustion of economic possibilities through the exhaustion of economic problems would lead to barbarism. It was Spengler, preceding the fascism that would make these the realities of history, who raised this specter. The possibility of barbarism or one-dimensional society had its roots in Spengler and not in Hegel or Marx. The Frankfurt School's historical pessimism finds its most powerful progenitor in Spengler, although to him it would have seemed a perverse optimism. Even their vision and hope for a solution, a Messianic break with the past, carries a faint aura of Spengler's cataclysmic struggle of blood against money. For Spengler, only the exogenous intervention of

---

24. Adorno, "Spengler after the Decline," in *Prisms*, p. 71.
25. Ibid., pp. 54–56.

the antipode to money gave hope; to the Frankfurt School, only the intervention of the nameless thing outside of history, in an aesthetic orgy of recreated sensibilities, offered serious possibilities. Only Adorno recognized Spengler in his writing, but the work of the Frankfurt School, individually and collectively, bears the mark of a man who was officially their enemy: Oswald Spengler.

7. Freud

The movement toward Freud by the Frankfurt School must be seen as a direct response to the insufficiency of Marxism as a mode of historical and psychological analyses. It is not by itself a movement into utter subjectivity or simply a surrender to bourgeois individuation and self-indulgence, as some charge. The turn to Freud is motivated by the School's understanding that a purely Marxist analysis of the world does not go deep enough and that a singularly Marxist revolution is not radical enough. As Adorno puts it:

> Rigorous psychoanalytic theory, alive to the clash of psychic forces, can better drive home the objective character, especially of economic laws as against subjective impulses, than theories which, in order at all costs to establish a continuum between society and psyche, deny the fundamental axiom of analytic theory, the conflict between id and ego.[1]

Psychoanalytic theory, by acknowledging the opposition between desire and reason and by comprehending how the scarcity of the world creates this opposition, offers a more profound understanding of the human condition than does the simplistic substructure/superstructure harmony of vulgar Marxism.

It is not what Marx said but what he failed to say that is important to the Frankfurt School. Marx, in all his complex analysis of the ramifications of alienation, left only the barest outline of a conception of the human psyche. He moved without pause between the utterly abstracted category of species-being to a reified causality between consciousness and material activity.[2] Missing was an

---

1. Adorno, "Sociology and Psychology," *New Left Review* 46 (Nov.–Dec., 1967):75.
2. See Marx, *German Ideology*, p. 7.

analysis of the structure of the psyche as it re-created itself in socialist practice. This had two results. First, it left open the way for contemptuous treatments of psychologism by later Marxists, thereby allowing the field to be taken by behaviorism. Marxism was thus enthralled by a mechanistic and dehumanized conception of the human mind. The second result was the failure of socialism, on its initial coming to power, to consider seriously undertaking the reformation of the human mind as it sought the restructuring of the social and political realms. The Leninist and Stalinist concern for restructuring the ideological function of men stood as the sole and sufficient solution to the problem of creating a new and human form of existence. Marx's failure to consider psychology in a way paved the way for the Russian terror. Failing to consider subjectivity in a revolution opens the door to reification and tyranny.

The failure of Marx was twofold. First, he moved too quickly from the utterly abstract to the utterly concrete and did not give sufficient and thorough consideration to the problem of the structure of the human mind. Inasmuch as Marx's thought emphasized the primacy of the economic substructure over the superstructure of consciousness, it created the illusion that socioeconomic analysis and socioeconomic transformation were sufficient in themselves. Lenin and then Lukács extended the distinction between the social condition and the consciousness of the social condition already present in Marx, but neither, except in the most rudimentary form of ideological agitation, put any emphasis on psychic practice. The economic was the ground of the psychic. Thus economic considerations could take precedence over psychological ones. Indeed, one could ignore psychology if one mastered political economy.

This led the revolution to be too shallow. Both among the Social Democrats and among the Communists, the revolution perpetually stopped short of recreating the forms of psychic existence that formed the substance of being. The possibilities of Eros, first in its sexual and then in its broader connotations, remained outside the purview of the revolution. The conquest of nature meant only the abstract liberation of the repressed. Concretely, Marxists refused to go beyond the reified and repressed practice of the bourgeoisie. Indeed, Marxism was more firmly philistine than the most thoroughgoing bourgeois could be.

Revulsion at the philistine analysis of the human condition, of which the Social Democrats and Communists were guilty, and disgust at the political practice of both parties led the Frankfurt School to Freud. Official Marxism, and even Marx himself, had failed to consider thoroughly the substance of the ontological resolution that the revolution was to represent.

Marcuse was the most effective analyst of the problem. He did the most to provide Marxism with a psychic component via Freud and to provide Freud with a historical dimension via Marx. In so doing, he intended to use the psychic liberation possibilities implicit in Freud as the basis for deepening the revolutionary possibilities of Marx; at the same time, he would use Marx's certainty concerning the conquest of nature as the basis for opening historical possibilities for the resolution of Freud's perpetual opposition between ego and id. While Marcuse wrote most consistently and extensively in this area, the whole Frankfurt School was permeated with the thought of Freud. Horkheimer, for example, underwent psychoanalysis[3] and wrote the first essay in the newly founded *Zeitschrift für Sozialforschung* on the problem of history and psychology.[4] Similarly, Adorno used Freud as a significant base for his entry into the group working on *The Authoritarian Personality*. Benjamin alone did not integrate Freud explicitly into his work, although the problem of psychic liberation was certainly crucial to him as well.

To Freud, the conflict in the human psyche is rooted in the niggardliness of the world. His vision of the world is rooted in suffering: "Life as we find it is too hard for us; it brings us too many pains, disappointments and impossible tasks. In order to bear it, we cannot dispense with palliative measures."[5] Life wants satisfaction; in its undifferentiated form, life consists purely of this demand. The world, however, is quite simply insufficient for our needs. From the simplest material deficiencies to the most profound cruelties of time and biology, the world conspires to deny the id what it demands. The pleasure principle gives way to the reality principle, in order that the organism may simply survive. Libido, which is finite, is redirected from gratification to simple survival through necessarily painful labor.[6] Pain becomes the principle of existence. For early

---

3. Jay, *Dialectical Imagination*, p. 87.
4. Horkheimer, "Geschichte und Psychologie," in *Zeitschrift für Sozialforschung* 1 (1932).
5. Freud, *Civilization and Its Discontents*, p. 22.
6. Freud, *Outline of Psychoanalysis*, pp. 13–24.

Freud, the perpetually suffering organism seeks surcease in death; for late Freud, the thanatotic principle becomes hypostasized as an autonomous motive in its own right. However one takes it, the movement to death and self-destruction has its origin in man. But, to the early (unembittered or perhaps only naïve) Freud, this cycle toward self-destruction and this perpetual warfare within the psyche between autonomous and antinomious principles (pleasure and reality) originates not in the instincts themselves but in the relationship of those instincts to a hostile world. As such, even if permanent, the conflict is potentially historical.

Marcuse intervenes at this point. To Freud, the scarcity of nature constituted a permanent and transhistorical reality. One simply could never abolish the reality that perpetually denies man those things that man craves the most. Marcuse, reading Marx, raised the possibility and the reality of conquering nature.[7] This world-historical, and to Freud inconceivable, reality is the starting point for Marcuse. With a new historical moment, radical possibilities open in the Freudian system.[8] As Marcuse puts it:

> The performance principle enforces an integrated repressive organization of sexuality and of the destruction instinct. Therefore, if the historical process tended to make obsolete the institutions of the performance principle, it would also tend to make obsolete the organization of the instincts—that is to say, to release the instincts from the constraints and diversions required by the performance principle.[9]

In essence, this would mean a circumstance in which the hitherto necessary redirection of libidinous energy, from immediate gratification to painful labor, could be abolished. Eros could become the sole principle of civilization. The conquest of nature would make possible a reorganization not simply of the social world but also of the psychic world.

Marx envisioned such a possibility but failed to give it substance. The abolition of alienation from oneself carried with it nothing beyond the formal imperative. As such, it was easily lost in the more substantial working out of the other notions of alienation (alienation from what is produced and alienation from fellow producers).

7. Marcuse, *Eros and Civilization*, p. 3.
8. Ibid., pp. 121–23.
9. Ibid., p. 119.

Freud

These required social transformations, but the social transformations could take place without psychic liberation. Indeed, they could take place in the face of profound psychic repression. Marcuse, by historicizing and radicalizing Freud, creates a dimension for resurrecting what was implicit in Marx. In so doing, he goes far beyond Marx.

First, he and the Frankfurt School pick up and employ terminology and intellectual constructs alien to Marx. Second, they moved Marx into a much more private realm than he was willing to enter. To Marx, authentic being was available only when linked to species. Freudianism accepts the species character of being in general but roots its practice (analysis) within the discrete being of the subject. To adhere to Freudianism is to turn the revolution inward. This is so both because analysis itself is a private event and because Freudianism turns the revolution into a psychological phenomenon, which may be worked out concretely in the political realm but whose final, highest, and most serious moment takes place in the most private realm of the human being—in the psychic self. In a vulgarization of this process, the left intellectual indulges himself in cheap angst, but, at its highest moment, the process is intended to reconstruct not simply society but ontology itself.

It is this deepened possibility of liberation that is the true concern of the Frankfurt School. Beyond simply searching for a more sophisticated mode of social analysis, and beyond the desire to create a suitable ontology to put in effective opposition to Heidegger, the real intention of the School is to deepen the possibility of liberation. As in a game of chance, the worse the odds, the higher the possible payoff must be. With the revolution becoming more and more problematic and with the wages of a failed revolution becoming more and more horrible, the payoff, the new existence that stands at the end of the Frankfurt School's gamble, must be that much more alluring. The deepening of historical pessimism over the possibility of an authentic revolution must raise optimism concerning what such a revolution could be. The liberation of the most profound realms of human existence is the only payoff worth the horror of revolutionary terror. Thus the turn to Freud is also a search for the profoundest possibilities of human existence.

8. *Judaism*

Between Marxist optimism and Spenglerian pessimism, there was an enormous pressure on the Frankfurt School to escape into the depths. They turned to Freud because they sought to deepen the meaning of liberation. In part they did this because they had lost the certainty of liberation. The risks involved in revolution had become too great to allow for revolt without the most thoroughgoing of rewards.

A mode of thought was available to them which regards redemption as both problematic and profoundly transformative; that is, Jewish thought. For the Jew, the problematic nature of the Messianic intrusion deepens the possibilities that redemption holds out. Thus it is appropriate that the Frankfurt School (all of whom were born to Jewish families; Adorno's father was Jewish, his mother, whose name he adopted, was Italian) turned to a Jewish motif for the formulation of their thought.

To Marx, the problem of being Jewish was the archetypical social problem of modernity; it was the problem that encapsulated the social dilemma of liberation and of Communism. As Marx puts it in his not-accidental early work, *The Jewish Question:*

> We discern in Judaism therefore, a universal antisocial element of the present time, whose historical development, zealously aided in its harmful aspects by the Jews, has now attained its culmination point, a point at which it must necessarily begin to disintegrate.
>
> In the final analysis, the emancipation of the Jews is the emancipation of mankind from Judaism.[1]

To Marx, as we see, the Jewish Question is not a peripheral problem that would be solved in the course of events. It was a metaphor

---

1. Marx, "The Jewish Question," in *Marx-Engels Reader,* Tucker, ed., p. 47.

Judaism

for the essential problem, involving the very principle of existence in bourgeois society. It would be solved only as the riddle of history was solved. Indeed, it was the Jewish Question that needed to be solved if history was to come to fruition. For Marx, the Jewish principle of huckstering had become the universal principle; the solution was to abolish the principle by abolishing Jewishness.

But interestingly, Marx posed the problem of Judaism in Jewish terms. Marx's metaphor for the solution was the movement of man from the realm of the profane to that of the sacred. To the Jew, life is profane, except during specific times (the sabbath and the holy days) in which the profane is put aside in order to experience the sacred intimations of the Messianic. To Marx, the Jewish indulgence in profane hucksterism had abolished the sabbath: hucksterism had become the universal principle. Hucksterism had made the world radically profane and "dirty Judaical."[2] The practical side of Judaism, the god of commerce, had overwhelmed and obliterated the sacred possibilities of man.

The profanation of the sabbath could not be solved by returning the realms of the sacred and profane to their proper places. The prophecy could no longer be partial. The only solution was to take the profane world and make it totally sacred. It was through the moment of the Messiah that being Jewish could be abolished. Marx, of course, meant the abolition of the profaned sense of being Jewish; but, in the orthodox sense, to be Jewish also has meaning only in the profane realm. With the coming of the Messiah, God's law will be fulfilled and then will need no keepers. To Marx, the problem of history was to take the God whom man had hypostasized in heaven and force his historical coming on earth—to reconcile man and God sensually.[3] Marx's preoccupation with the abolition of the Jews has about it a strange and not quite expressed Jewishness.

It is in this spirit that the Frankfurt School writes. But their work comes after Auschwitz (even Benjamin, who wrote before, sensed the coming of such a crisis). It is difficult to know how they felt about being Jewish, even in the face of the holocaust. Their writings, except for Benjamin's, take on an oddly antiseptic cast when they write on Jewishness and antisemitism. Scholars do not agree

2. Ibid., pp. 48–49.
3. Marx, *Critique of Hegel's "Philosophy of Right,"* pp. 131–32.

on their attitudes. Jay reports that Adorno disapproved of Benjamin's explicit Jewishness; Hildegaard Brenner writes that Adorno endorsed this side of Benjamin.[4] Horkheimer showed an odd dispassion. He concluded an essay on the German Jews: "Men should become sensitive not to the injustice against the Jews, but to injustice as such, not to the persecution of the Jews but to any and all persecution."[5] This is an essay that touches on the most profound experience in his life, the experience of being a German Jew, and he ends it with an empty universalism for which Marx excoriated Bruno Bauer. When considering their Jewishness, they kept an ambivalent distance. At times, they seemed willing to buy objectivity at the price of sterility.

This is an age in which being Jewish and being part of the Enlightenment are bound together socially. At the same time, the Enlightenment was impotent in protecting the Jews of Europe. The Jewish intellectuals on the Left seem either to fall silent or to sound foolish when confronting the failure of the Enlightenment and of the Jewish alliance with it. This seems to be true of Horkheimer, Adorno, and Marcuse. Yet even while the members of the Frankfurt School lapse into the now-empty phrases of the Enlightenment, the problem of Judaism that formed the basis for Marx's work, formed and conditioned their own problematic. Like Marx, they superficially ignored their Jewishness, all the while trying to cope with its meaning.

The first area of Judaic influence on the Frankfurt School is Benjamin's vision of generational unity. To the Jew, it is the Fifth Commandment, which demands honor for parents (and for their covenants), that forms the root and bond of society. The redemption by the son of the promise of the father is what inextricably makes one a Jew. Indeed, it is the task that makes the burden of being a Jew bearable. It is this which is the essence of Benjamin's historical vision. Benjamin writes:

> Social Democracy thought fit to assign to the working class the role of the redeemer of the future generations, in this way cutting the sinews of its greatest strengths. This training made the working class forget both its hatred and its spirit of sacrifice, for both are nourished

---

4. Jay, *Dialectical Imagination,* p. 201; Brenner, "Theodor W. Adorno als Sachwalten des Benjaminischer Werke," in *Neue Linke nach Adorno,* pp. 168–75.

5. Horkheimer, "The German Jews," in *Critique of Instrumental Reason,* p. 118.

by the images of enslaved ancestors rather than of the obliberated grandchildren.[6]

Judaism is rooted in the past; it is nourished by the tears shed for the suffering of the people of Israel. Some tears are shed for this moment. Fewer are shed for the future, for there reside the children and, therefore, the hope: the Messiah may enter at any moment hence. The most bitter tears are for the past, for the sufferings of the past are in the simplest sense unredeemable. Insofar as they can be redeemed, through the reverence of this and future moments, the tears are the bitterest. Redemption rests unremittingly upon this moment; one can move on to the next moment only through the annihilation of the hope that this moment held out: the Messiah did not come. But this bitterness is still bound up with hope. The Messiah may come and if he does, then the burdens of our fathers, to whom we are eternally obligated, can be redeemed. The Jewish hope is for the redemption of the past. Even the profound love of children rests upon this solitary possibility.

Benjamin turns Marxism into a Jewish event. To the Marxist, the hope had always been the future—"Do what we must to get through this moment, for it will all be worthwhile when our grandchildren see the world that we made for them." This was the rationale for horror. Even critics of this stance criticized it as would a hedonist—"Of what use will be the future if there is no pleasure in the present?" Benjamin radicalizes a dispute between deferred and realized pleasures. He transcends those limited boundaries to speak for the past. "Who will speak for the suffering of our fathers?" is the question he raises. He argues that the strength of socialism, as of Judaism, is the undying obligation to avenge the past, however historically or divinely necessary its sufferings may have been. The redemption of the past comes through the realization of what the people of the past had hoped for, through living as they did and through abolishing their own damaged lives. The child's success redeems the father's suffering: the strength of the Jewish son is in the burden that he bears. The strength of the proletarian is in his burden, successfully abolishing the conditions that made him necessary. Benjamin's gentle twist of sensibility toward the past imbues the struggle of the proletariat with a Jewish aura. His sensibility

---

6. Benjamin, "Theses on the Philosophy of History," in *Illuminations*, p. 260.

differentiates itself from Christianity by its undialectical, catastrophic Messianism.

Benjamin was concerned with this Messianism throughout his mature life. As early as 1920–1921, he had written, "Only the Messiah himself consummates all history, in the sense that he alone redeems, completes, creates its relation to the Messianic."[7] He saw in the Messiah the metaphor for the historical problem. History was, by nature, profane. It was the realm of necessity and hence of unfreedom. Man, in entering a realm of freedom, a sacred realm in the sense of being most truly human, had to leave history. History, however, could not set its transcendence as its own task.

The problem of language was such that a linguistic formulation of the sacred was impossible: the sacred cannot have images made of itself because the objectification by language of the inherently indeterminate freedom falsifies that freedom. The injunction against graven images is an injunction against reification—against falsification. Thus the Messiah is the force that transcends history but cannot be historically formulated. As a result, historical language cannot grapple with transcendence. The problem of the revolution can only be understood as the problem of the Messiah, a force that is formally outside of history. This is because the ends of revolution are the abolition of the ground of history: profane need. The means falsify the end. Dialectical language is imprisoned in need. Thus the Messianic force is the result of the need for revolution in the face of the problem of language in history.

To Benjamin, there are two kinds of language: one whose object is the world, the other that is without object.[8] The first sort of language is the prison of necessity: its prosaic surface hides the horrors of reification. This language faces the world from the standpoint of need: its obsession is with the technical manipulation of the world, of which the end is survival. In the second sort of language, which exists at the beginning and at the end of time, is freedom. The essence of this sort of language is the act of naming. In naming things, we address ourselves not to the thing named but to language as such. The name incorporates the thing within the structure of language, freeing it from its prosaicness, uniting it with the transcendence of language. Language's object is itself. This re-

    7. Benjamin, "Theologico-Political Fragment," in *Reflections*, p. 312.
    8. Benjamin, "On Language as Such and on the Language of Man," in *Reflections*, p. 318.

Judaism

flexiveness renders language free from the prosaicness of positivity. So it was at the beginning of Genesis, so it shall be at the end. The Messiah is a name, metaphorical by nature, but as a metaphor, radically free. As Benjamin puts it, "In naming, the mental being of man communicates with God."[9]

This leaves the present with the task of finding the Messiah. The past can be redeemed only through the Messianic. It is because of the burden that Benjamin puts on the present that the search for the revolutionary subject (to burst apart the bonds of history as would the Messiah) takes on the desperate significance that it has for the Frankfurt School. To Benjamin, the revolutionary act is bound up in the Messianic one; the intention of the revolutionary, like the Kabbalist, is to discover the formula that will invoke the sudden and miraculous intrusion into history of an exogenous force, thereby shattering the structure of time and opening the path to redemption.[10] Indeed, Benjamin sees the entire revolutionary act as bound up with the problem of the Messiah:

> A historical materialist approaches a historical subject only when he encounters it as a monad. In this structure, he recognizes the sign of a Messianic cessation of happening, or, put differently, a revolutionary chance in the fight for the oppressed past. He takes cognizance of it in order to blast a specific era out of the homogeneous course of history—blasting a specific life out of the era or a specific work out of lifework.[11]

The revolutionary's approach to history is the attempt to transform time, that is, to remake the very structure of time in such a way as to redeem the past by annihilating the suffering that constituted its essence. In this act and in this moment, "flecks of messianic time" can be seen. The chance (note that it is possibility and never, at *this* moment, certainty) of redemption, of the invocation of the historical and revolutionary subject, is in its form and nature, Messianic.

The Messiah ushers in the redeemed Zion. The structure of the redeemed realm is ineffable, according to Benjamin, as it is to the Jews. It is ineffable because profane language cannot speak without

---

9. Ibid., p. 318.
10. See Benjamin, "Theologico-Political Fragment," in *Reflections,* pp. 312–13; "Theses on the Philosophy of History," in *Illuminations,* p. 263; also see Weber, "Walter Benjamin," in *Unknown Dimensions,* pp. 251–52.
11. Benjamin, "Theses on the Philosophy of History," in *Illuminations,* p. 263.

having something to speak of. In the sense that it originates in need and concludes by speaking of the triumph, the language of history is unfree. The conquest of nature is the preface to redemption, but only the preface, because the second problem is not solved. Language must turn to itself through naming in order to be purged of the profane. Language is fated dialectically to move between the thing it names and its own freedom. When it names the thing, it falls into identity; when it speaks to itself, it seems to fall into ontology.[12]

Thus Benjamin in "On Language as Such and on the Language of Man" subtly turns to the later theme of Adorno's *Negative Dialectics*. Both are seeking a linguistic entity that fulfills the Jewish concept of language: the naming of things without capitulating to them, the purity of language without forgetting men and the divine, as such. Language thus mediates between the sacred and profane, but in such a way that it blocks our entry into the realm of the redeemed. This also allows us to speak of redemption metaphorically. Only the metaphor frees us from identity but roots us in reality. Jews speak of God and redemption metaphorically. Identity and abstraction are catastrophic to them. So, too, Benjamin and Adorno speak metaphorically. But where the Jewish conception of redemption is a metaphor of a thing unimaginable—redemption—the Frankfurt School's is a metaphor for a metaphor. They use the Jewish formulation of language to explain their own epistomological dilemma: language is the ground of freedom but simultaneously of imprisonment. Redemption requires the Messiah who would cut the dialectical knot.

The linguistic problem is drawn by Benjamin directly from Judaism: "After the Fall, which, in making language mediate, laid the foundation for its multiplicity, it could be only a step to linguistic confusion."[13] Men fell into this condition because language could never remain pure—men had to eat of the tree of knowledge. The problem is to escape this fate: "All higher language is a translation of those lower, until in ultimate clarity the word of God unfolds, which is the unity of this movement made up of language."[14] For Benjamin, the word of God is a metaphor. Just as for the Jews,

12. Benjamin, "On Language as Such and on the Language of Man," in *Reflections*, p. 318.
13. Ibid., p. 328.
14. Ibid., p. 332.

Judaism

the word is a metaphor and a shield for God's ineffable name. His name is ineffable because we are compelled to name things and God is beyond the profanity of compulsion. So too, Communism is beyond profanity. Benjamin chooses a Jewish *metaphor* for Communism because his alternative is a Greek *image*. An image is, however, on a continuum with the original and is thus dialectically bound up with it. The point of Communism is that it is a radical break with the past—a Messianic break. As such, we have only metaphors with which to peer into the future, just as the Jews had metaphors but had to ban images as fearfully impotent. The problem is the leap from metaphor to reality.

This problem is necessarily Messianic rather than dialectical. To the Frankfurt School, the dialectic itself had moved to self-exhaustion. This can be seen in Adorno and Horkheimer's *Dialectic of Enlightenment* as well as in Marcuse's *One-Dimensional Man*. History's self-movement had ceased to move us at the penultimate moment of capitalism. The historical materialist's only hope is in the chance, in the possibility, of finding a power outside of this historical moment with which to "blast a specific era out of the homogeneous course of history." In that the event is contingent rather than certain, and in that the agent cannot come from within the confines of the historical dialectic (since that dialectic has become utterly absorptive and affirmative), the search for the revolutionary subject is metaphorically the search for the Jewish Messiah.

Between the granting of the law and the coming of the sacred realm of an utterly redeemed Zion, time is homogeneous. It is differentiated by events, but the events themselves are on a continuum that is itself essentially undifferentiated in the most profound way: in being singularly unredeemed. The movement from this realm of events to the sacred realm of being is promised but is at no moment certain. Each discrete moment of time may be the moment of redemption; no moment need be that time. The Jews' task is to keep the Law, which is the texture of the intervening time; to the Kabbalist, perhaps, the task is to search for the formula that forces the coming. But the Messiah comes from outside of time, for the homogeneous time of the Law in itself possesses no possibility of yielding the Messiah—its very nature is in opposition to the Messianic nature. The Messianic intervention into a seamless time blasts that moment and that time into nonexistence, thereby redeeming its suffering.

To the Frankfurt School, time in the era of administered man had become seamless and homogenous; the dialectic had ceased to differentiate between moments. The possibility now was open that history would form a permanence outside of a realm of redemption—that is, within a still inhuman framework. The absorption of the hitherto revolutionary subject, the proletariat, into the social structure raised the specter that that structure would become permanent—and if this happened, the plastic homogenization of time and life would occur. The Frankfurt School's certainty of revolution was reduced to a contingent event: the search was for a revolutionary subject.

The subject had to come from outside of history; what was historical had been absorbed and what had been absorbed had ceased utterly to be revolutionary. The marginal elements of society from outside the historical process were sought—students, blacks, the third world. The search among these groups was not a search for the negation of the negation. Such a search is unnecessary: the authentically dialectical negation presents itself. Rather, the search was for the Messiah in the social eddies that the Frankfurt School had perceived as being excluded from the realm of historical time. The School's later work echoed the Jewish rumination about the proper method to invoke the Messiah (the proper way to force the groups to take upon themselves the redemptive role) and the problem of identifying him (who was truly revolutionary?). The political task of Critical Theory was to establish a prismatic formula through which the Messianic entity could be invoked and identified. They moved into a Jewish motif through a realization of the Jewish tragedy: the failure of human history, as *human* history, to redeem Zion.

Without a redeemed Zion—that is, without the revolutionary transformation of the world into the sacred realm of the truly human society—history was left in a profane limbo. Always flecked with elements of hell, such as Auschwitz, but never so terrible as to be indistinguishable from hell; touched by a sense of the possibility of the sacred through the conquest of nature, but never heavenly—history stood still in the homogeneous limbo of permanent profanity. Neither damned nor redeemed, history exhausted itself, suspended between hope and horror. The Frankfurt School searched for the Messianic portal that would allow (and necessitate) the entry into the sacred realm of redeemed time.

Judaism

This was the theme of both Marx's Introduction to the *Critique of Hegel's "Philosophy of Right"* and his *Jewish Question*. To Marx, however, the movement into the sacred realm of Communism has a historically dialectical certainty. As such, the tragic sense is alien to it. To the Frankfurt School as to Judaism, even the redemptive is drenched in tragedy because its origin is in a suffering redeemable only in the most tenuous of senses. To Judaism, the tragedy is attenuated by the presence of God; to the Frankfurt School, time presents an unredeemable tragedy.

Still, to the Frankfurt School all serious philosophy must be conditioned by an entry into a sacred time. As Adorno puts it:

> The only philosophy which can be responsibly practiced in face of despair is the attempt to contemplate all things as they would present themselves from the standpoint of redemption. Knowledge has no light but that shed on the world by redemption: all else is reconstruction, mere technique. Perspectives must be fashioned that displace and estrange the world, reveal it to be, with its rifts and crevices, as indigent and distorted as it will appear one day in the messianic light.[15]

If the task of the Messiah and of those who would invoke him is to move the world to the sacred from the profane, then the task of philosophy, of Critical Theory, in a profane age is to view the world through the prisms of the Messianic redemption: to view the world through the scraps of the divine that have been left in the world in the Text. Critical Theory, like the Midrash, becomes the profane hermeneutic of the utterly sacred. Both are the attempt of the unredeemed to glean visions of redemptions from the words that mediate between the sacred and the profane.

But, as to the Jew, the viewing of the sacred is radically impossible in the realm of the profane. The Jews were forbidden to pronounce the ineffable name of God. So Critical Theory (and Marx himself) can view the world from the standpoint of the sacred but can never tell us the nature of the redeemed realm of Communism. As Benjamin puts it:

> We know that the Jews were prohibited from investigating the future. The Torah and the prayers instruct them in remembrance, however.

---

15. Adorno, *Minima Moralia*, p. 247.

This stripped the future of its magic, to which all those succumb who turn to the soothsayers for enlightenment.[16]

The past can be viewed from the perspective of the Messianic, but the nature of the trans-Messianic is ineffable. So Marx falls silent on the precise organization and structure of Communism; so the Frankfurt School lapses into the metaphors of mythology to comprehend its sense, if not its formal structure. The nature of existence in Communist society could not be explicated, for just as the ineffable name of God could not be spoken by the profane because of a profound break in the ontology of the realms and thus the hermeneutics governing each time, so the radical difference between Communism and that which went before it created an unbridgeable gap. The distance between the sacred and profane cannot be fully bridged by language. But the Messianic moment looms as the eternally possible bridge in each monad of time.

The movement of the Frankfurt School into Judaism is rooted thus in Marx's own concerns and in the desperate ambivalences of the enlightened Jew in an age after Auschwitz. Through Marx, they became comfortable with the motif of the sacred and profane. Further, they knew that the experience of Auschwitz must be universalized if philosophy was to have meaning any longer.[17] Thus, both routes led them into Judaism. But it was the tragic recognition of the failure of history that drove them most firmly and subliminally to the Jewish motif. To maintain the Marxist hope in the age of Auschwitz, only the Messiah was sufficient, secularized though he may have become. The tragedy of the age, in the end, was what drove them into a Jewishness even beyond Marx's dialectical faith in the sacred. The tragedy drove them into a prayer for the Messiah, a prayer couched, in the end, in the language of modernity. Dissonant, the aura of the Jew nevertheless permeates their work. Their task, like the Jew's task, was to plumb and bridge the gap between the sacred and profane.

16. Benjamin, "Theses on the Philosophy of History," *Illuminations*, p. 264. Also see Horkheimer, "The German Jews," *Critique of Instrumental Reason*, p. 113; and Adorno, *Minima Moralia*, p. 242.
17. See Adorno, "Erziehung nach Auschwitz," in *Erziehung zur Mündigkeit*, pp. 88–104.

9. Conclusion

We have seen that the Frankfurt School was grounded in the Hegelian-Marxist nexus, in the sense that their concerns were conditioned by the concerns of Marx and Hegel. What distinguishes the Frankfurt School from other forms of Hegelianized Marxism is the way that their historical and social concerns were mediated through a mélange of other, at times antithetical, sources. The impact of Nietzsche, Heidegger, Spengler, Freud, and Judaism created a Marxism that was, in the end, less a Marxism than a complex struggle within the structure of thought.

The intention of the Frankfurt School was to save Marx from institutional Marxism. What Marxism had become upon entering the world of political practice horrified them. On the one hand, it tended toward the philistine ossification of the Western European Social Democrats; on the other hand, it moved toward the brutal millenarianism of Stalin. The Frankfurt School faced the problem of all intellectuals in the twentieth century. To have remained within the intellectual structure of the reformist socialist parties would have meant, from their point of view, an effective capitulation to the more reified elements of bourgeois thought. To have moved toward the most radical position available and endorsed or ignored Stalin's thuggery (as Brecht did early on and Lukács did later) would have been to endorse precisely the brutalization of Enlightenment that had been the prime object of their critique. The alternative was simply to move in opposition to the Left, toward simple conservatism.

They were caught, therefore, on the horns of an almost insoluble dilemma. On the one hand, if they endorsed official Marxism, they would give the illusion of effective opposition to the dehumanization of the century while actually and objectively endorsing it. If, on the other hand, they endorsed the opposition to the Left outright, they would have been endorsing the political manifestation of that movement—fascism. Even a moderate movement to the Right would have meant abandoning the Messianic hope of Marxism. In effect, they would have left the past utterly unredeemed and denied it the hope of redemption. Finally, the problem on each side was compounded by their uncertainty whether there actually were any real historical solutions to the complex of illusory alternatives.

The movement toward Critical Theory was based upon the hopelessness of the situation. No effective and systematic opposition was conceivable. Their solution was to be ineffective, abandoning political practice for the more ethereal reaches of the theoretical and unsystematic. Marxism, in which they had placed their hopes and which was historically and theoretically betraying them, had to be subjected to the withering and unsystematic criticism of the other side. Each of the alternatives—Freud's and Nietzsche's, for example—had to be used to criticize and deepen the understandings possible to Marxism. At the same time, Marx had to be employed to criticize and reduce the autonomous viability of any alternatives. The megalithic systems faced by the Frankfurt School, which occupied the intellectual space they inhabited and made the creation of new, exogenous alternatives impossible, had to be annihilated through their affirmation. The Frankfurt School sought simultaneously to affirm and relate impossible alternatives. They could not live on the Left or on the Right. Rather than abandon the field, they decided to live in both simultaneously, thereby attempting to create a new possibility.

There is a deeper side to this attempt. The problem of the bourgeoisie and of the embourgeoised proletarian is the problem of meaning. The triumph over nature has robbed men of the sensibilities necessary to enjoy that triumph. Empty calculation over things rendered trivial through their attainment left a vacuum in bourgeois culture that it could neither fill nor even reflect on. Pointless, unreflected, and unrefined activity was the narcotic salvation offered by modernity. Affirmation without criticism was its only possible defense.

Marx was no solution. Indeed, in many ways, he was the heart of the problem. To industrialism, he could juxtapose only more industry; to reason, only more rationalization. His silence on Communism's true nature was in part ontological shyness; a gloomier reason for his silence was the realization of the towering emptiness

Conclusion

that accompanied Communism. Marxism turned the world, in Horkheimer's phrase, into a giant workhouse in which labor became its own end. Thus, bourgeois activity became just more activity and the senses were buried under action.

Only on the Right was the opposition to modernity fastidious. Nietzsche opposed the Enlightenment in all its parts; those things that he admired about it, such as its thoroughgoing ruthlessness, were things alien to Enlightenment's spirit. Only the Right supplied the fastidious strength necessary to stand in opposition to modernity's strength. To understand the Frankfurt School, one must understand that their opposition to capitalism was an opposition to the ground of capitalism, an opposition to modernity. It is necessary to understand that they drew their strength from the Right, modernity's most radical opponents.

The problem with the Right is that while its opposition to modernity is far more thoroughgoing than the Left's, its opposition is never fully principled. The Right always has hidden agenda, for in condemning modernity it wishes to resurrect the past rather than to create a future. The Right's antimodernism is a defense of nobility and a defense of transcended ages. Even Nietzsche, who perhaps understood most about the unforgiving texture of time, could consider the future only through metaphors dredged from the past. In the past, there was no room for the equality of man or for universal excellence. The excellence of Tragic Greece was luminous, in part, because of the vices of others.

Thus a universal excellence could not come from the Right. An opposition to modernity that was both fastidious and principled, that praised the past without ultimately making a case for its resurrection, could not come from there. Nor, for that matter, could it come from Marx or Hegel. It required a new diagnosis and a new cure, a cure grounded in the past but free of it. This new diagnosis and cure, rooted as much on the Right as on the Left, was the project of the Frankfurt School.

In order to save Marx, they subjected him to Freud, a theoretical antithesis. Where Marx was a teleologist, Freud saw cycles. Where Marx saw progress, Freud saw permanence. Where Marx saw hope, Freud was filled with hopelessness. However, by imbuing Marx with Freud's sense of the psychic and Freud with Marx's historical sense, the Frankfurt School sought to solve the problem of both. A psychic dimension would save Marxism from the shallowness of a purely political and economic liberation, and a historical dimension would liberate the psychic possibilities embedded in Freud's system. They sought to liberate each thinker from the reified limitations in which they had placed themselves.

Similarly, they attempted to save Hegel from himself. Hegel had held forth the certainty of a historical resolution for the opposition of reason to the world. But in so doing and in proclaiming the abolition of the antimony, he had created a circumstance in which reason, having lost its critical function, also lost its subjectivity and hence its freedom. By subjecting both Hegel's ontology and teleology to the criticism of Nietzsche, Heidegger, and Spengler, the Frankfurt School reopened the possibility of a critical reason. Paradoxically, they employed the critics of reason to resurrect reason's critical possibilities. By subjecting Hegel to their criticism, they reopened the door to the possibility, if never the certainty, of a reason permanent in its negativity. At the same time, they raised the possibility of integrating their critique of Hegel's ontology into Hegelianism itself, thus creating the possibility of a permanent negative dialectic—a negativity built permanently into the dialectical moment.

Finally, almost as if to keep the centrifugality of these relationships from utterly destroying each other, leaving nothing but the void of nihilism, they structured about them the aura of Judaism, almost as an encapsulization. One profound aspect of Judaism is to be found in the Messianic hope and redemptive sensibility of its deepest vision. Inasmuch as the attempted reconciliation of modern radicalism with Judaism left only a little room for hope, they sought the only certainty possible: that in any moment there is hope for the coming of the Messiah.

In the end, they found Marxism, even a Hegelianized Marxism, untenable in the face of both history and the withering criticisms that had been mounted against it. Yet the hope that was there, a hope to be found in Judaism as well, had to be retained.

At the same time, the understanding and possibilities of Marxism had to be deepened. Thus they went far outside Marxism in order to search out in its enemies the potential for preserving it. The question, of course, is whether this movement from outside Marxism and Hegelianism strengthened even the intent of those systems or whether the Frankfurt School represents the theoretical *coup de grâce* to Hegelian-Marxist tradition. The issue is whether the

Conclusion

Frankfurt School represented the salvation of the teleological hopes of Marx and Hegel or the final and utter exposure of the impotence of those hopes in the face of history. The issue is whether the Frankfurt School, objectively, is the redeemer or the executioner of the teleological hopes of the Enlightenment. That is the issue and dilemma that causes us to turn to the structure of the thought of the Frankfurt School.

PART II
POSING THE PROBLEM
OF MODERNITY

10. The Crisis of the Enlightenment

The centerpiece of modernity's faith is its belief in Enlightenment. The Enlightenment held out the possibility and desirability of a demystified world. To the Enlightenment, it seemed that the world had, for the millennia of human self-consciousness, been shrouded in the mists of mythology. Under the veil of myth, the world was a cruelly harsh place, cruel far beyond its intrinsic nature. From the earliest myth to the sophisticated metaphysic of Christianity, the shrouded world was, from the viewpoint of the Enlightenment, cloaked in irrationality and hence in suffering.

The Enlightenment proper launched a campaign to demystify the world, which it saw as a fundamentally beneficent place, or one which could be made so if understood and manipulated correctly. Through demystification, the suffering, ignorance, and injustice that had hitherto been the fate of the world would be abolished. As Peter Gay puts it: "The men of the Enlightenment united on a vastly ambitious program, a program of secularism, humanity, cosmopolitanism, and freedom, above all freedom in its many forms."[1] Gay obviously refers here to the men of the eighteenth century who placed their faith in reason as a way to master the world.

The Enlightenment, however, goes beyond the eighteenth century. It is rooted, albeit without Condorcet's or Hegel's element of teleological certainty, in the thought of Plato, and, according to the Frankfurt School, in the critical myth of the West—the myth of Odysseus.[2] The dominant motif of Western thought is the vision of

---

1. Gay, *The Enlightenment*, vol. I: *The Rise of Modern Paganism*, p. 3.
2. On the Enlightenment and Positivism of Plato's thought, see Adorno, *Zur Metakritik der Erkenntnistheorie*, p. 132; and Horkheimer, *Eclipse of Reason*, pp. 7, 59. On the Odysseus myth, see Adorno and Horkheimer, *Dialectic of Enlightenment*, pp. 46–47.

rational men dispelling the darkness shrouding the world in order to explicate its subterranean orderliness, thereby conjuring a knowledge and possibility of a life that is naturally good. To Plato, this hope was tempered by the thought that it was impossible to translate the *possibility* of knowledge of the naturally good into *actual* knowledge. But here, in both mythic and philosophic Greece, is to be found the conceptual impetus for Enlightenment—the assumption that through reason or cunning, the natural can, somehow, be known to man.

As Hegel placed myth and philosophy on the continuum of the Spirit in history, so too he combined the mythic cunning of Prometheus and Odysseus with the philosophic reason of Plato. The cunning of reason proclaimed to Hegel that the triumph of Enlightenment was a historical certainty. What was developed in Kant, the certainty of reason unfolding in history, culminated in Hegel in the declaration that the distinction between the actual and the rational had been abolished.[3] The problem after Hegel became the epilogical transformation of the thoughtful triumph of Enlightenment into a worldly triumph. What to Plato could have only lived in speech came to Hegel a thing that must live in history. The just city became and had to become the principle of the world.

What Diderot, Kant, Hegel, and Marx shared was a certainty that reason could dispel myth and that to do so was desirable. To each, the root of evil was man's ignorance of the world. The world would yield its theoretical and sensual bounties if only one could finally grasp its principles. Between this end and man stood the intellectual format of man's darkness—myth. It was myth that kept science from probing the nature of the world. But science possessed its own power: by its nature, science progressively dispelled myth. As reason and science triumphed, the historical millennium would be ushered in.

Against the Enlightenment and its process stood arrayed the perceived forces of darkness. The first unexpected opposition came from philosophy itself. Rousseau sounded the warning against Enlightenment: "Peoples, know once and for all that nature wanted to keep you from being harmed by knowledge just as a mother wrests a dangerous weapon from her child's hands; that all the secrets she hides from you are so many evils from which she protects you."[4] If

3. Kant, *Critique of Judgment*, pp. 500–502.
4. Rousseau, *Discourse on the Arts and Sciences*, p. 47.

The Crisis of the Enlightenment

Rousseau suspected that the Enlightenment might be a disaster rather than the solution to the human problem, Nietzsche declared this danger to be the principle of the age.[5] By the twentieth century, what had been almost unambiguously good in the eighteenth had turned itself into the great problematic.

Reason, which had dispelled the myths of the world, had destroyed horizons, leaving man empty and aimless. Science, which had sought to subjugate nature, had succeeded but had subjugated man as well. Freedom, which had been the promise and premise of reason and science, receded either into an empty formalism or into outright barbarism. What had held forth so much hope before still maintained itself and its principles in theory, but it had turned into horror in practice.

The problem of the Enlightenment was the starting point for the political philosophy of the Frankfurt School. As students of Hegel and of Marx, they had learned that the historical struggle between reason and nature was only the preface to a truly human existence. Only with the triumph of reason could man live a truly human life. Yet, in their words, "the Enlightenment has always aimed at liberating men from fear and establishing their sovereignty. Yet the fully enlightened earth radiates disaster triumphant."[6] This age, which should have been the most humane had the promise of the Enlightenment been true currency, was instead the most horrible. Its symbol was not Beethoven's *Ninth Symphony*, but Auschwitz.

To the Frankfurt School as to Hegel, reason, at least abstractly, is capable of positing the historical solution to the human problematic.[7] Reason, when considered as a historical possibility and abstracted from concrete historical practice, is capable by its nature of negativity. That is to say, reason criticizes reality in a way that paves the way for the reconstitution of history. Marcuse praises reason perhaps the most highly of them all:

> Under the name of reason it conceived the idea of an authentic Being in which all significant antithesis (of subject and object, essence and appearance, thought and being) were reconciled. Connected with this idea was the conviction that what exists is not immediately and al-

---

5. Nietzsche, *Use and Abuse of History.*
6. Adorno and Horkheimer, *Dialectic of Enlightenment,* p. 3.
7. Horkheimer, *Hegel und das Problem der Metaphysik,* p. 91; Adorno, "Erfahrungsgehalt," *Drei Studien zu Hegel,* pp. 78–82.

ready rational but must rather be brought to reason. Reason represents the highest potentiality of man and of existence; the two belong together.[8]

So viewed, reason holds forth all the possibilities of a truly human existence.

The Frankfurt School never abandons this point of view; for them, reason perpetually constitutes the hope. This then is the crisis of the Enlightenment: if there is hope, the hope is found in the functioning of reason in history. The Frankfurt School discovered, however, that the function of reason in history is subject to transfiguration; it turns itself into its opposite, just as reason turns the world into the opposite of what it once was.

To Hegel, history resolutely unfolded itself. At various historical points, reason showed a different aspect of itself. At each moment, as the rationality of practice within the particular epoch turned itself into irrationality when viewed from outside (that is from the perspective of the Absolute), reason recoiled into negativity and the outmoded historical practice was transcended. The essence of historical rationality was in its negativity. At the final historical moment, however, as the world and reason lapsed into identity, positivity came to rule. It is this ultimate positivity of reason that the Frankfurt School perceives as a crisis of reason, in and of itself; it is also a crisis of the entire historical process of the West.

A limited critique might charge here that Hegel's problem was allowing the moment of identity to occur before an authentic historical resolution. Thus rationality would rule internally while the external irrationality would become the essence of the historical practice. Such was the format of Marx's critique of Hegel, and the Frankfurt School surely shares it.[9]

The Frankfurt School, however, sees the crisis of reason as having two other successively deeper levels. Concerning the first level, they raise the possibility that the current historical practice is rational (if inhuman); that is to say, society has, in the Weberian sense, rationalized itself successfully.[10] Society may be seen as successful

8. Marcuse, "Philosophy and Critical Theory," in *Negations*, pp. 135–36.
9. Marx, *1844 Manuscripts,* pp. 185–91. For examples of the frequent critiques of the irrationality of bourgeois life in practice, see Adorno, "Veblen's Attack on Culture," in *Prisms,* p. 85, or Marcuse, *One-Dimensional Man,* pp. 4–5.
10. See Adorno, "Spätkapitalismus oder Industriegesellschaft," *Gesellschaftstheorie und Kulturkritik,* pp. 167–69; Marcuse, "Industrialization and Capitalism in Max Weber," in *Negations,* p. 205.

The Crisis of the Enlightenment

in two ways. First, in maintaining itself without the threat of its dissolution through an immanent critique. This then raises the possibility that reason can no longer dialectically develop such a critique. Second, society may be seen as successful in succeeding in doing what reason had initially set out to do—conquer nature. Through the objectification of nature in current historical practice, objectivity and subjectivity may be seen as having been reconciled.[11] The problem with both of these successes, however, is that in achieving them the world has relapsed into inhumanity rather than having realized the humane promise of reason. Thus the Frankfurt School adds to the Marxist critique of Hegelian society the possibility that a historical realization of reason will manifest itself in inhumanity—an inhumanity predicated upon reason.

The second level of the critique of reason goes deeper. It postulates a failure within reason itself, a failure manifested at the moment when reason becomes successful. This critique raises the possibility that the reconciliation of antinomious elements into identity, which is the dialectical goal of reason, is the root of the problem of reason. The crisis of reason derives from its own successful creation of harmony, since the essence of reason is seen to lie in its disharmonious dialectic. As Adorno puts it:

> The force of consciousness extends to the delusion of consciousness. It is rationally knowable where an unleashed, self-escaping rationality goes wrong, where it becomes true mythology. The ratio recoils into irrationality as soon as in its necessary course it fails to grasp that the disappearance of its substrate—however diluted—is its own work, the product of its own abstraction. When thinking follows its law of motion unconsciously, it turns against its own sense, against what has been thought, against that which calls a halt to the flight of subjective intentions. The dictates of its autarky condemn our thinking to emptiness; in the end, subjectively, the emptiness becomes stupidity and primitivity. Regression of consciousness is a product of its lack of self-reflection. We can see through the identity principle, but we cannot think without identifying. Any definition is identification.[12]

This passage of Adorno's denoted the central crisis of reason; this crisis is the real ground of the social crisis of rationality.

Reason, to Hegel, is consciousness. Paradoxically, it works itself

---

11. See, for example, Marcuse, "Neue Quellen zur Grundlegung des historischen Materialismus," *Die Gesellschaft*, IX (August 1932), pp. 145–48.
12. Adorno, *Negative Dialectics*, pp. 148–49.

out unconsciously, in the sense that before the very end it never fully recognizes either its task or even itself. Reason historically destroys the ground of its own practice. Hence, capitalism's rationality, according to Marx, is destroyed by its own success. At the same time, capitalism fails to understand the process. Reason itself, because of its dialectical un-self-consciousness, is fated to lapse into "stupidity and primitivity."

To Adorno, the only solution is to promote a moment of fully self-conscious reason. Reason thus might recognize its own failure, and remake itself. Unlike Hegel and Marx, Adorno considers this transformative moment of reason almost as an act of will, a willingness of reason to recognize its own failure. To be more precise, reason must be unwilling to exist affirmatively; reason must will itself out of its contentment. The social counterpart of this epistemological act of will is seen in Marcuse's and Benjamin's willing the revolutionary act.

Thus the failure of reason is rooted in its own dialectical practice. Because it is necessarily unconscious, because the Owl of Minerva can only fly at dusk, reason perpetually falls into an objective irrationality from which only a willed act of consciousness can save it. Reason seeks the success of identity, but this success is also its failure. Only a willed act of overcoming can save reason from itself.

In this willed act of consciousness, however, there is a further danger. The reconciliation of elements falls into identity. Reason invariably loses its critical faculty at the precise moment of its greatest success. With the triumph of reason, the rational becomes an instrument of the existent social structure, thereby losing the essence of its nature—negativity. Thus, reason inevitably turns itself into a failed act. The only hope for rescue lies in consciously repudiating the event of identity. Only the conscious recognition of the failure of reason, a failure rooted in its success, can rescue rationality.

This recognition is also doomed to identity, in a way. "We can see through the identity principle, but we cannot think without identifying. Any definition is identification." The act of definition depends on reconciling the contentless concept with the unthought object, on the idea becoming identical with the thing. The end of reason, identity, is also its only mode of operation. At the very moment when reason realizes the moment of identity, it is threatened with the mode of escape, negativity, becoming indistin-

The Crisis of the Enlightenment 117

guishable from the problem because of the very functioning of the process. Reason can proceed only through the process of reconciling thought with its opposite. Hence, even as it succeeds, it threatens to lapse into failure. To be sure, Horkheimer holds out hope for a nonidentitarian definition, for otherwise all would be lost.[13] Still, for now, the crisis of reason is rooted in the nature of reason itself.

Thus while reason formally holds out the promise of a negativity that would free itself from the historical irrationality of the world, it has another side. First, the Frankfurt School sees an utterly rationalized world as a crisis precisely because reason has conquered the world. Second, it sees a crisis in the unconsciousness of the rational process, in the tendency of reason not to know itself, which paves the way for reason to collapse dialectically into its opposite. Finally, it sees reason in crisis because reason's very mode of procedure tends to force it into an identity that violates its critical nature.

None of this crisis was manifest before the penultimate historical moment of capitalism. Previously, the unconsciousness of reason was bearable, since the gross opposition between the world and reason forced the rationality of each epoch to move beyond itself. When an age proclaimed itself just the declaration flew in the face of the gross and overwhelming suffering inherent in the world; need forced reason into a negative and revolutionary stance. In the penultimate moment, however, the opposition between the theory of justice and existence becomes subliminal. The abolition of scarcity allows the inhumane to masquerade as the human. Irrationality appears to be reason. It is at this point that reason lapses into identity, unless a gross historical event forces it out of its complacency. It is at this moment that will rather than dialectics is necessary; and it is precisely at this moment that the historical manifestations of reason make such an act problematic. The Frankfurt School believes that Enlightenment begins to go wrong because its agent, in both its being and movement, has a profound flaw. The resurrection of the Enlightenment becomes problematic for the same reason.

The current historical practice of reason is such that it may be seen to be moving away from its abstract purpose. Rather than

---

13. Horkheimer, *Zum Begriff der Vernunft,* p. 15.

serving the search for truth, it serves an instrumental and utilitarian function.[14] As reason lapses into identity with its object and is not shocked out of this stance by overwhelming historical circumstances, reason comes to serve the existing social order. Reason becomes a technical enterprise in which it proves its social usefulness over and over again by becoming an instrument of productivity and social stability.[15]

Positivism becomes the ideological expression of this movement of reason into affirmity. To the Frankfurt School, philosophical and practical Positivism (a term used by the School to denote many movements united primarily by a regard for the facticity of a thing and of the world) constituted the end point of the Enlightenment.[16] The social function of the ideology of Positivism was to deny the critical faculty of reason by allowing it only the ground of utter facticity to operate upon. By so doing, they denied reason a critical moment; reason, under the rule of Positivism, stands in awe of the fact. Its function is simply to categorize the fact.[17] Its task ends when it has affirmed and explicated the fact. Thus, in post-Weberian Social Science, reason's social role is to place an affirming mark upon the social order. Under the rule of Positivism, reason inevitably stops short of a critique.

That Positivism comes to rule the world of social consciousness is not, to the Frankfurt School, an accidental outcome of the process of Enlightenment. They already find the roots of Positivism in Plato. For example, Horkheimer argues that Plato's Philosopher-King is the theoretical counterpart to the modern technocratic social engineer. The essential similarity is that both the Platonic ruler and the bureaucrat intend to subject society to the rule of reason and to reason's perception of the true. Horkheimer obviously acknowledges a radical difference between Platonism and Positivism. Plato intended to transfigure the social order so that it became a replica of the philosophical. The intent of Positivism is to make philosophy subject to the social order, since it cannot allow philos-

---

14. Adorno, *Negative Dialectics*, p. 149.
15. See, for example, Marcuse, "Industrialization and Capitalism in Max Weber," *Negations*, pp. 207–8.
16. Horkheimer, *Zum Begriff der Vernunft*, p. 9; Marcuse, *Reason and Revolution*, p. 323, on Positivism as the outcome of Hegelianism.
17. Adorno, *Negative Dialectics*, p. 166.

The Crisis of the Enlightenment

ophy to escape from brute facticity.[18] Both, however, wish to move toward an ultimately administered society. This is the impetus that, according to the Frankfurt School, Plato gave the Enlightenment.

Positivism clearly perverts the will of Plato. Plato desired the identity of philosophy and society only abstractly; he recognized that historically they could not coincide. Philosophy is affirmative only in an abstracted sense; its concrete practice is always to stand in opposition to the inevitably less-than-just world.

In Hegel, however, the purely abstract possibility of Plato becomes embedded in a historical teleology. Plato's unrealizable hope becomes Hegel's inevitable necessity. Hegel makes the purely abstract concept of the Philosopher-King into the concrete practice of the Prussian civil servant. If Plato gave the impetus for the Enlightenment, then Hegel proclaims its realization. After the proclamation of the reconciliation between reason and reality, the social practice of philosophy must issue in Positivism.

The Hegelian dialectic set out to obliterate the distinction between appearance and reality. The underlying truth of the world somehow had to be made coincidental with the social appearance of the world. The distinction between the thing and its essence, which was the root of Kant, had to be historically reconciled into a single entity. The real and the ideal possibility hidden behind the real had to merge. Positivism was the theory of the social practice that followed this reconciliation.

Positivism, which regards the given fact as inviolate, also denies (without a historical ground, however) the distinction between appearance and reality. To Positivism, appearance constitutes the sole knowable attribute of a thing. Appearance does not shroud a core of authentic being (as in Kant); it is the *sole* ground of being. Thus, to Positivism, apparent facticity, the thing by itself, gains undisputed hegemony over the world. At the same time it achieves hegemony over thought. The fact of things is the single origin of what can be known. Since the fact is the sole gorund of knowing, a simultaneous criticism of the fact is not possible. Hegel thought that, before the end of history, the fact would yield its own rational and historical refutation. At the end of history, the fact, having had its antinomious elements (appearance and reality) reconciled,

---

18. Horkheimer, *Eclipse of Reason*, pp. 59, 60.

stands beyond criticism. Positivism adopts precisely the same stance. In a sense it is Hegelianism of the end. It is the only philosophy possible at the point at which history realizes and exhausts itself.[19]

To the Frankfurt School, Positivism is justified insofar as it attacks false metaphysics and mythologization.[20] Such is also the case with the Enlightenment, of which Positivism is only the final expression. But as is the case with the Enlightenment, the moment of triumph against the false traditions carries with it the burden of a new failure. As Adorno puts it:

> The theoretical levelling of essence and appearance will be paralleled by subjective losses. Along with their faculty of suffering and happiness, the knowers lose the primary capacity to separate essentials and unessentials, without anyone really knowing what is cause and what is effect. The stubborn urge to check the accuracy of irrelevancies rather than to reflect on relevancy at the risk of error is one of the most widespread symptoms of a regressive consciousness. No background world annoys the latest type of backwoodsman; he happily buys what the foreground world will sell him on, in words or in silence. Positivism becomes ideology in eliminating first the objective category of essence and then, consistently, the concern with essentials.[21]

The intent of the Enlightenment was to annihilate the shrouds covering the essence of the world. Positivism, as both a perversion and fulfillment of the Enlightenment, abolishes the shrouds surrounding essences by declaring that essences do not exist. To be more precise, according to Adorno, Positivism declares the essences to coincide with appearance; reality is present only in fact.

The outcome of the triumph of Positivism, and thus the outcome of historical Enlightenment, is the loss of true subjectivity. It is lost, in the first place, by the collapse of the discriminatory faculty. To distinguish between things, one must perceive an essential value embedded within each. The abolition of essences means the lack of fundamental differences between things. All things share the same essence, a basic facticity, and thus all are equal. Man is faced with

---

19. On the relation between positive philosophy and Positivism, see Marcuse, *Reason and Revolution*, p. 327.
20. Horkheimer, *Eclipse of Reason*, p. 86.
21. Adorno, *Negative Dialectics*, p. 170.

The Crisis of the Enlightenment

an incomprehensible world. The multitudinous facts yield nothing beyond themselves. With Positivism, Enlightenment takes the easy way out, abolishing essence without realizing the essential. Yet it was forced into this stance, since the very structure of reason craves an identity on whatever terms are available.

With the abolition of essences, philosophy loses its critical function. The status of philosophy following the completion of Hegel's work becomes problematic; it appears that critical philosophy had abolished itself with the Hegelian act. So too with Positivism, philosophy has lost its critical function. Instead of criticizing and transforming the facticity of the world, philosophy under the auspices of Positivism affirms that world. It can do nothing else, since it recognizes no standard beyond the fact. It possesses no historical sense because it can allow itself to conceive of no essence, no subterranean realm in which the insufficiencies of a fact can work themselves out. Indeed, one can conceive of no insufficient fact. Thus philosophy loses its social function. Philosophic reason, the essence of the Enlightenment, exhausts itself through its very success.[22] As Horkheimer puts it, "At the moment of realization, reason had become irrational and stultified."[23]

The social result of the rise of Positivism to be the dominant expression of reason is that reason has turned into an instrument to be used for the support of the social order.[24] Positivism served two social functions. In the first place, by declaring the rule of the fact, Positivism left no space for a critique of the social order. Moreover, it tended to transform the functioning of society into objective reality. That is, it transformed society into an objective reality that transcended subjective consciousness or will. It turned the social order into natural law.[25] Clearly, Marx had also attempted to do this to society but had mitigated the result by including the historical element. For Positivism, the historical was lacking, since a concept such as history partook of essences. Thus, the social science of Positivism became a social static.[26]

In the second place, reason comes to function simply as an instrument of social production. Rather than having the criticism of

---

22. Horkheimer, *Eclipse of Reason*, pp. 73–81; Marcuse, *Reason and Revolution*, p. 327.
23. Horkheimer, ibid., p. 128.
24. Horkheimer, *Zum Begriff der Vernunft*, pp. 9–13.
25. Marcuse, *Reason and Revolution*, pp. 331–32.
26. Ibid., pp. 375–79.

inhuman social circumstances as its highest purpose, reason becomes a tool for maximizing wealth by increasing technological rationality.[27] By doing this, reason serves to make the social structure more workable, allowing it to produce more and more wealth and more and more efficient (and unsubliminal) modes of social containment.[28] In this way, reason abandons its critical stance entirely. Subjectivity comes to serve utter objectivity, the productive mechanism, and thus buttresses the social system.

Reason comes to support the existing state of affairs in three ways. First, it produces an ideology that forces the rational to focus only on one side of reality and to declare the other side to be pure illusion. It does this by achieving the *formal* historical task that it set itself and by thus abolishing the need to criticize the real—hence, Positivism. Second, reason comes to occupy this space in a way that forces effective opposition over into abstract metaphysics, thus making criticism appear guilty of irrelevance. Worse, it may actually force the opposition into embracing an affirmative ontology.[29] Finally, reason serves the social order concretely by fostering productive and political efficiency and containment.

All of this represents more than simply the rise of a new ideology for the support of a soon-to-be-superseded ruling class. If it were that, its taxonomy would be essentially insignificant. What makes the outcome important is that it is rooted in the very process of reason itself; it creates social conditions and philosophical circumstances that hold open the possibility that this ideology might maintain itself in perpetuity.

As we have seen before, Adorno maintained that reason itself possesses an inherent drive for identity. Thus reason—not simply in its historical form but in its very ontology—creates a format for itself that would deny, in the end, a critical moment to thought. Reason seeks to exhaust its critical faculty and begins to do so in its first successful act: sheer definition. In so doing, it wishes to make the surface of a thing identical with the essence.

More significantly perhaps, the Frankfurt School does not see Positivism as preparing the way for it to dialectically transcend

27. Marcuse, "Industrialization and Capitalism in Max Weber," in *Negations*, p. 204–6. Horkheimer, *Eclipse of Reason*, p. 94.
28. Marcuse, *One-Dimensional Man*, pp. 22–34; Adorno, "Notiz über sozialwissenschaftliche Objektivität," in *Gesellschaftstheorie und Kulturkritik*, pp. 154–55.
29. That is to say, Heidegger.

itself. In seeing its social manifestation as possibly maintaining itself in perpetuity, they see society's theoretical counterpoint maintaining itself as well. In the first place, by creating social circumstances in which wealth is perpetually increased, it does not allow the growth of a gross opposition between its social promise and its realization. Simply put, instrumental reason delivers. It increases the productive capacity while creating social stability. Through the rationalization of the productive mechanism, it creates social (as distinct from psychological) circumstances that could maintain instrumental reason as an ideological principle in perpetuity. It allows no gross dissonance to creep in.

In the second place, Positivism itself lacks internal contradictions. By denying a priori the metaphysical reality of things beyond facts, it develops an internally consistent method of viewing the world. Its ground is in self-sufficient identity. It has reconciled discordant elements either by denying their existence (and socially making a good case for either their non-existence or practical uselessness) or by absorbing them into a category of fact. For example, neo-Freudian Positivism denies certain elements of Freud's later metapsychology (such as an autonomous and thus nonadministrable death wish) while transfiguring other abstract elements into brute and unarguable fact, as it does with the notion of the Oedipal.[30] Under the rule of identity, the concept is self-sufficient; it itself requires nothing else. As with society, for the concept to break out of its self-satisfaction requires an act of self-conscious will rather than dialectical movement.[31]

Finally, Positivism maintains itself by denying alternatives a solid ground to stand on. Any form of rationality that would partake of facts seems fated to partake of them under the scientific orders imposed by Positivism upon fact.[32] The alternative that presents itself, metaphysics, has been subjected to the criticism of Positivism and, moreover, tends to make the practitioner irrelevant to the social practice as determined by Positivism. Positivism, having become enormously powerful in the first place, is in the second place powerful enough to deny a space for the organization of an effective opposition.

The only opposition perceived by the Frankfurt School is that of

---

30. Marcuse, *Eros and Civilization*, pp. 224–66.
31. Adorno, *Negative Dialectics*, pp. 146–47.
32. Horkheimer, *Eclipse of Reason*, p. 75.

Heidegger. And they argued that he offered only the illusion of opposition, since he actually constituted the opposite side of the coin of Positivism. The essential unity of Heidegger and Positivism is to be found on the level of their social functioning. Positivism lacks a critical faculty. Heidegger, while opposing Positivism, recapitulates its objective social function by similarly lacking a critical faculty in relation to society. As Adorno puts it:

> The jargon must defend, so as not to be lost, transitory social forms which are incompatible with the contemporary state of the forces of production. If it wanted to mount the barricades itself, then it would have to engage itself not only for a position much scorned among its believers, but possibly also for that rationality which the exchange society both promises and denies, and through which that society could be transcended. The bourgeois form of rationality has always needed irrational supplements, in order to maintain itself as what it is, continuing injustice through justice. Such irrationality in the midst of the rational is the working atmosphere of authenticity.[33]

Thus Heidegger performs the same social function as Positivism—the affirmation of existing condition.

The roots of this affirmation are to be found in Heidegger's "sleight of hand" concerning the distinction between the ontic and ontological[34] Heidegger's pretense is to seek a ground of Being beyond that of mere facticity, beyond the ontic. Adorno argues, and Heidegger could not dispute him without lapsing into idealism, that "there is not Being without entities."[35] Heidegger attempts at times to avoid entities. When he does so by attempting simultaneously to avoid the conceptualization of Being or its concretization, he lapses into nothingness.[36] Practically, however, unless it is to lapse into silence, ontology must partake of either the concept or the fact. Being must have a root in what exists, either in the world or in thought. To postulate a thing of the world but not in it, which does not partake of theoretical substance, is logically impossible. To be free of both matter and thought is not merely unthinkable but also

---

33. Adorno, *Jargon of Authenticity*, p. 47.
34. Adorno, *Negative Dialectics*, p. 121.
35. Ibid., p. 135.
36. Ibid., p. 115.

The Crisis of the Enlightenment

unlivable. Heidegger, by wishing to do neither, actually vacillates between both. On the one hand:

> Heidegger, his assurance to the contrary notwithstanding, puts the alleged antecedent of the ontological difference on the side of essence: as the difference expressed in the concept of entity is denied, the concept is exhalted by the nonconceptuality said to be beneath it.[37]

On the other hand, socially:

> The eulogized undividedness of existence and essence in Being is thus called by name as what it is: the blind context of nature; the doom of concatenation; the absolute negation of the transcendences whose tremolo notes quiver in the talk of Being. The illusion in the concept of Being is this transcendence; but the reason for it is that Heidegger's definitions—deducted from Dasein, from the miseries of real human history to this day—dispense with the memory of those miseries.[38]

Notice what has happened. In searching for a ground of Being that is immune to entities either of concept or of object, Heidegger, by the very abstractness of the project and his fastidiousness in relation to things, lapses into the concept—into a pure idealism. At the same time, however, the inherent identity within the category of Being requires it to possess simultaneous facticity. Ontology cannot afford to allow anything to escape from its grasp.[39] What creeps in is allowed to do so only brutishly; it is both unsubtle and low. What intrudes is the brute and low reality of the existing social circumstances, a willingness to tolerate intolerable social conditions. By abstracting ontology from facticity on the level of private Being, Heidegger unifies social being and the brute fact. He tends objectively to confirm the fact of social circumstances while attempting to help Being escape from a social context.

From opposite viewpoints, therefore, Heidegger and Positivism attempt to accomplish the same social function. This can be seen, according to Adorno, on the level of language: "The jargon shares with Positivism a crude conception of the archaic in language. . . .

---

37. Ibid., p. 117.
38. Ibid., p. 119.
39. Adorno, *Jargon of Authenticity*, p. 140.

The jargon simply ennobles the antiquity of language, which the positivists just as simply long to eradicate."[40] What each does, one by failing to realize the nonmagicality of language, the other by willfully ignoring its authentic magicality, is leave language untouched. Heidegger plunges so deeply into language that no trace of him can be found. Positivism touches language so superficially that no mark has been made on its surface. Both are objectively unified in their practical impotence.

Positivism intends to be subservient to the fact; it intends to allow facticity to rule. Heideggerianism, on the other hand, pretends to be fundamentally beyond the fact. It attempts to take Being beyond both fact and concept; Adorno holds that it succeeds in neither. At first it plunges into concept. Then, seeking an identical hegemony over everything, it allows the fact to reenter, both because the ontological is practically incomprehensible without reference to the ontical[41] and because the objective social function of Being is to raise the unscathed social fact to the level of an Untouchable—low, but as such, utterly free from the Brahmin Being. "Heidegger transposes the empirical superiority of the way things are into the realm of essence."[42]

Between Positivism and Heideggerianism, the philosophic possibilities are, for this age, exhausted. Heidegger offers the only conceivable solution to Positivism by refusing to answer it on its own ground. Those modes of thought that would adhere to the fact would also, of necessity, be forced to adhere to the laws of facticity as promulgated by that handmaiden of the Enlightenment, science. By becoming scientific, the thought predicated upon the fact would be in perpetual and almost inescapable danger of being drawn to identity. At that moment, thought would end its opposition to Positivism, which has already proclaimed identity to have been achieved. Heidegger's strength is that he eschews the fact. He denies its hold upon him by predicating the ground of Being on something that is neither in the realm of concept nor in the realm of fact. In so doing, he gives the illusion of effective opposition. Heidegger's sleight of hand, his own quest for a universal identity, is to lapse into both metaphysics and facticity at the same time that he seeks to do neither. Thus the only conceivable systematic opposition to

40. Ibid., p. 42.
41. Adorno, *Negative Dialectics*, p. 108.
42. Ibid., p. 100.

The Crisis of the Enlightenment

Positivism, one that is systematically outside the fact, fails by falling into facticity against its will.

No effective opposition to the hegemonic consortium represented by Positivism and Heideggerianism is conceivable as long as it is systematic. Neither the need for facticity nor the imperative to move beyond it can be avoided. Putting a foot in either camp is to take a step on the road to affirmation. Only an unsystematic approach that is able to be inconsistent in order to avoid the affirmative dialectic can survive intact. Critical Theory, as we shall see, is that attempt.

For now, the point is that the movement into facticity is rooted in the very process of the Enlightenment; this movement is inescapable as long as we remain under the aegis of the Enlightenment. At the same time, an escape from the Enlightenment is problematic. Thus the crisis both of Positivism and Heidegger is the crisis of the Enlightenment. As such, it is the crisis of the West itself:

> The prime cause of the retreat from Enlightenment into mythology is not to be sought so much in the nationalistic, pagan and other modern mythologies manufactured precisely in order to contrive such a reversal, but in the Enlightenment itself.[43]

The cause of the retreat from reason and Enlightenment is to be found in reason and Enlightenment themselves.

The initial object of the Enlightenment was the natural world. On the one hand, the Enlightenment intended to demythologize the natural world. On the other hand, it intended to turn that world to man's use, with reason serving as an instrument in subjugating the world.[44] In attempting to do this, Enlightenment's reason inevitably turns itself into modern science.

The intention of the Enlightenment and the intention of science were identical: to demythologize the world.[45] In order to do this, the concept of the world had to be concretized. The first move in this process was the rise of philosophic materialism. In its simplest form it served the task of concretization by denying the reality of the abstractly metaphysical; materialism insisted that the ground of all phenomena was to be found in matter. By reducing the world to

---

43. Adorno and Horkheimer, *Dialectic of Enlightenment*, pp. xiii–xiv.
44. Horkheimer, *Eclipse of Reason*, pp. 92–94.
45. Adorno and Horkheimer, *Dialectic of Enlightenment*, pp. 3–4.

quantities, that is, to discernible things, the Enlightenment laid the basis of modern science. Things are perceivable. Those things that can be sensually perceived are inherently quantifiable. The true test for the authenticity of phenomena is thus to be found in their quantifiability. Whatever cannot be counted, that is, involved in a concretely mathematical event, is unreal. The effort to drive myths and demons from the world gives rise to the test of modern science: can the event be quantified?[46]

The Enlightenment, in order to search for the authentically true and unmythical, impels itself to adopt the stance of science. It must be incredulous toward, potentially abstract events, so it adopts the stance of modern Positivism toward quanta. Indeed, in trying to avoid a metaphysical understanding of events, it abandons even the concept of sensual causality. Since the true cause can never be simply perceived, probability rather than causation must rule the world. Even the concept contains the seed of myth; the concept is expelled in favor of the statistic of probability.[47]

However respectful Enlightenment must initially be toward the metaphysician, it is ultimately forced to adopt the stance of the empiricist and positivist in order to protect its integrity against the encroachment of illusions. To stand with metaphysics is to be on perpetually uncertain ground. The only solution is to adopt the agnostic approach of science. The concept itself must be expelled from the process of thought; the conceptual and empirically unknowable certainty of causality must give way to the agnosticism of statistics. All admissible concepts must pass one criterion of judgment—quantifiability. Enlightenment, which initially promised truth, must wage a war against the concept in order to prevent the intrusion of the mythical.

Science, having reduced the world to a sensually perceivable fact, must now justify itself. Myth promised the secret of the world; metaphysics held open the possibility of salvation; science holds forth the possibility of the conquest of nature.[48] This could be its only justification for the exorcism it had performed upon the human mind. Having reduced the world to the facticity of matter, science can relate only to the material contained in the world. En-

---

46. Ibid., p. 7.
47. Ibid., p. 5.
48. Horkheimer, *Eclipse of Reason*, p. 92.

The Crisis of the Enlightenment

lightenment created science to carry out its task. Science, in its turn, must also create a mode to mediate between itself and the perceived essence of the world. What stands between science and the world is technology.

Science held forth the promise that it would subjugate nature to its will. Otherwise, removing the world's shroud of enchantment would have been pointless by the only standards that science ultimately could allow itself—sensual standards. Science created the structure of technology to carry out its task. Science is methodology that has an abstract relationship with its object (material world). This relationship is predicated on the theoretical side of its practice. If science is to conquer the world, however, theoretical practice is utterly insufficient for that purpose. The relationship between science and the world must be made concrete. Technology, rooted as it is in the abstract method of science and in the ontic reality of the world, is the concretion of the relationship of science and world. Moreover, technology represents the social side of the relationship between science and nature: what science promises theoretically, technology grants sensually and socially. Nature is subjugated and exploited. Finally, technology conforms to the dictates of the scientific method. It works not through abstract concepts or through images of things but through unmediated formulas and method— that is, through formulas and method that stand in direct relation to the essential stratum of the natural and, at the same time, show sensually verifiable results through increased productivity.[49]

The technological process irretrievably completes the development of Enlightenment. Enlightenment, having set out to disenchant the world while seeking to make man utterly at home within it, has no clearer indication of its success than in the working of technology. On the one hand, technology acknowledges no stratum of the real world that is beyond its reach. Having been born from science's transformation of the world into absolute material facticity, it abstractly denies the possibility of any other realm to which man might return, while at the same time it seeks to work and rework the structure of sensual nature. On the other hand, technology seeks to make men utterly at home in the world by conquering and objectifying nature, and it succeeds. By giving man dominion over nature, technology places man in the position of having utterly

---

49. Adorno and Horkheimer, *Dialectic of Enlightenment*, p. 4.

disenchanted the world: he has made himself into something identical to enchantment—God.[50]

It is at this point that the Enlightenment faces its crisis. Having sought to disenchant the world, it returns to mythic forms by casting man in the role of the enchanted. Enlightenment, despite its promise, never actually breaks free of myth. It has its opening motif in mythology and, in its form and structure, is intimately bound up with the task of the same mythologization that it had cast as its mortal enemy. Myth is, in and of itself, a lie. It is an untruthful representation of the nature of the world. At the same time, it is truthful in its lying. The manner in which myth lies reveals ancient and profound truths concerning the needs of men. Moreover, myth is necessary to life: it gives a structure to inchoate existence. Thus myth must be both abolished and maintained.

Enlightenment is bound up with mythology in the simplest sense: it gains both its impetus and its practical motif from a mythological conception of man's relationship to the world. The most obvious example raised by the Frankfurt School is the myth of Prometheus.[51] Prometheus, from Marcuse's point of view the patron saint of labor and of suffering, constitutes the basic motif of the Enlightenment. Science sees itself as an essentially divine enterprise gaining fire for man through the use of cunning reason. As the cunning of men replicates the divine wisdom and charity of a God, nature itself can be conquered and turned to the benefit of man. The selection of this motif is more than simply a rational recognition of human possibilities. Rather, it represents a selection among many possible myths of the relationships of man and nature. In other words, Enlightenment is itself a myth.

Horkheimer and Adorno also see myth at the root of the Enlightenment, the myth of Odysseus the trickster, who constitutes himself as the disenchanter of the world.[52] Odysseus, a human Prometheus, places himself in the role of the enemy and destroyer of myth. Through the abandonment of his home (and the redirection of libido from the erotic to the explorative) and the willingness to endure suffering, empowered by a cunning that substitutes the image of sacrifice for the authentic experience of sacrifice, Odysseus comes to symbolize the Enlightenment of the West. With real and

50. Ibid., p. 9.
51. Marcuse, *Eros and Civilization*, p. 146.
52. Adorno and Horkheimer, *Dialectic of Enlightenment*, pp. 49–52.

The Crisis of the Enlightenment

imagined suffering and with authentic cunning, Odysseus roams the world slaying whatever is enchanted, eluding and deluding those magical things that only can be dealt with so.

The Promethean and Odyssean myths are unified by their unswerving opposition to whatever is outside of or opposed to the human subjugation of the world. Enlightenment both historically and conceptually gains its impetus from the myth. Myth is its form, if not its content, for Enlightenment need not cast itself in the role it adopts. It need not be unswervingly hostile toward the naturally uncontrollable and divinely unknowable. Enlightenment could seek to explicate the mysterious in a way that would reconcile man to the perpetuity of the unknown. It chooses not to, because of its mythology concerning itself. Enlightenment is not so much false as it is untrue; more precisely, it is no more and no less true than are other myths. Enlightenment posits its horizons on the basis of formal and substantial mythology as much as do its avowed enemies.

Moreover, Enlightenment is rooted in myth because it recapitulates the function of the myth:

> Hence, enlightenment returns to mythology, which it never really knew how to elude. For in its figures mythology had the essence of the status quo, cycle, fate and domination of the world reflected as the truth and deprived of hope. In both the pregnancy of the mythical image and the everlastingness of the factual is confirmed and mere existence pure and simple, expressed as the meaning which it forbids.[53]

The formal function of mythology is to affirm the permanence of the human condition. Even the apparent impermanence of specific forms of existence in the myths of Prometheus and Odysseus reappears as permanence when mediated through the prism of the lonely suffering that they demand. Facticity is the affirmation of permanence. Even as it seeks to subjugate nature, the Enlightenment confirms the thing as essentially uncriticizable—it can be used; it cannot be refuted. In the social realm, it sees a permanence (in the Enlightenment's final statement, Positivism) in the human condition, not that the condition is unchangeable but that the proper direction of change is perpetually unknowable. Thus both in the formally unchangeable structure of the scientific method and in

53. Ibid., p. 27.

the unchangeability of the fact as both the critical monad of reality and an unchangeable entity, the Enlightenment never escapes mythology but recapitulates myth in rationalistic form.

Freud, according to Horkheimer and Adorno, attributed magic to the human desire to rule the entire world. It is magic that seeks the domination of the world by the human will. If this is so, then the Frankfurt School sees the Enlightenment as essentially magical in its intentions.[54] Just as myth and Enlightenment share the desire for permanence, so they share the desire for totality.

In the end, this desire shows itself in the Enlightenment's recapitulation of mythic fear. The Enlightenment began by promising to banish the unknown and, with with the unknown, fear. It succeeded in the first task but merely intensified the second:

> Man imagines himself free from fear when there is no longer anything unknown. That determines the course of demythologization, of enlightenment, which compounds the animate with the inanimate just as myth compounds the inanimate with the animate. Enlightenment is mythic fear turned radical. The pure immanence of positivism, its ultimate product, is no more than a so to speak universal taboo. Nothing at all may remain outside, because the mere idea of outsidedness is the very cause of fear.[55]

In other words, Enlightenment made man imagine himself free from the unknown by denying the very existence of things unknown. There was hope in this stance, but behind it lurked fear. Like myth, Enlightenment could not tolerate things that were outside its ken. Like myth in its most radical form, Positivism is rooted in the terrible fear of being refuted by things beyond its paradigmatic comprehension. Positivism tabooed anything that was not fact. It did not refute it but, like myth, swept away that which was outside by dictate—by an act of faith. Positivism, as mythology, shares the desire for totality. It cannot tolerate anything outside of its structure. The desperate fear of Positivism is that there is something that it cannot deal with; something incomprehensible to it. Positivism's mockery of metaphysics shrouds its profound fear of metaphysics' contents, which it can neither own nor refute. It lapses into fear, as would the most primitive myth, at the thought of its enemies.

54. Ibid., p. 11.
55. Ibid., p. 16.

The Crisis of the Enlightenment

Enlightenment thus falls into its archenemy's form:

> Just as myths already realize enlightenment, so enlightenment with every step becomes more deeply engulfed in mythology. It receives all its matter from the myths, in order to destroy them; and even as a judge it comes under the mythic curse. It wishes to extricate itself from the process of fate and retribution, wihile exercising retribution on that process.[56]

In addition to replicating myth in its origins, in its desire for totality, and in its fear of anything outside itself, Enlightenment recapitulates the mythical in its intentions. Each myth wishes to subject all others to a retributive annihilation. This is what Enlightenment wishes to do to myth in general.

Thus, in refuting the myth, the Enlightenment becomes a myth in its own right. In disenchanting the world, it re-enchants it in the image of reified man as God. All of this is not accidental:

> This did not happen merely to his philosophy as the apotheosis of progressive thought, but to the Enlightenment itself, as the sobriety which it thought distinguished it from Hegel and from metaphysics. For enlightenment is as totalitarian as any system. Its untruth does not consist in what its romantic enemies have always reproached it for: analytical method, return to elements, dissolution through reflective thought; but instead in the fact that for enlightenment the process is always decided from the start.[57]

The success of the Enlightenment was known to it from the very beginning. Like all myth, it could not fail, for it had set the terms for its own dialectic. Those elements that did not conform were ruled out of existence. Those elements that did conform were integrated into a precreated structure of thought. Enlightenment as myth was its final reality, because like myth, its fate was decided before its attempt.

The rediscovery that the Enlightenment was rooted in myth was not merely a scholarly enterprise for the Frankfurt School. They began with a quest for the reason that the Enlightenment, instead of fulfilling its promise, had returned to barbarism. It emerged that the return to barbarism was the return of Enlightenment to a more

---

56. Ibid., pp. 11–12.
57. Ibid., p. 24.

naked form of its mythologized brutality. Like myth, the Enlightenment could tolerate nothing outside of its boundaries. Totalitarianism came as easily to Enlightenment's apparent toleration as it did to mythic intolerance. The return to barbarism resulted from the Enlightenment's failure ever effectively to abandon the mythological. It could not do so because it was mythology itself.

Enlightenment's mythology was compounded by the crisis of its agent, reason. Historically, Enlightenment had been seen as reason positing problems and creating solutions. This was at the root of both progress and of a rational ontology. Today, reason posed a problem for which it had no solution: it presented itself as a problem. Its principle of operation was negation. Yet the act of negation was only the intermediate stage in the rational intention. Reason sought identity, and identity was rooted in the very format of its operation. Reason sought to come to rest. Enlightenment and reason simultaneously posited the irreduceable, sensual, and positive fact as the monad of reality. Enlightenment did it by seeking a ground that would apparently ban the mythical. Reason did it by discovering the entity that was utterly identical with itself and presented the opportunity for elegant conceptualization.

Thus, at one and the same time, the uncriticizable fact emerged as the monad of reality, and the Enlightenment most radically fulfilled its mythic mission—the conquest of the world through disenchantment. At the same time, reason denied the possibility of criticizing what it could comprehend, and Enlightenment sought to annihilate all that positivistic and scientific reason could not comprehend. Historically, it became a moment of utterly uncritical totality. Enlightenment had delivered its promise. Nature had been conquered. With that act it fulfilled itself and laid claim to its due—the world itself. Having gained control over the world, it saw fit to lay claim to man himself.[58] The mode of operation of the natural sciences was to be applied to the social sciences. Reason as an instrument of technology was also to become an instrument of social technology—bureaucracy. Enlightenment, critical toward myth, and reason, negative toward recalcitrant facticity, both turned positive simultaneously, because of the conquest of nature and the subjection of the entire world to facticity.

The crises of Enlightenment and reason were these: if the highest

---

58. Ibid., pp. 31–42.

moment of reason was in the act of negation, and that which had to be negated had been negated, and if the purpose of Enlightenment was demythologization, which had in turn turned itself into myth, then all that was left for man was to decline into brute facticity and historical brutality toward the recalcitrant. If reason and Enlightenment had exhausted themselves, what was left beyond exhaustion? On the one hand, there was the nihilism of Heidegger's pseudo-ontology. But it carried with it the corollary brutality of the Enlightenment: that of the Nazis (whom the Frankfurt School saw as no accident, either historically or in their connection with Heidegger). On the other hand, there was the hope of creating a new critical theory. The latter was their intention. But before that was realizable, the crisis of the Enlightenment would have to be worked out aesthetically, psychologically, and, most importantly, historically. Above all, the general crisis of culture arising from the crisis of Enlightenment was essentially the crisis of reason realizing and thereby exhausting itself. Reason had lapsed into an affirmation of whatever was, becoming the servant and instrument of the existent. This affirmative stance was at the root of the crisis of culture itself; and the crisis of culture was the towering crisis of our time.

11. The Crisis of Art and Culture

The Frankfurt School focused its most intense attention on the cultural realm; that is, on the aesthetic dimension. The relationship between culture and history has always been a mysterious element in the Marxist canons. That cultural transformation was central to political and economic liberation was clear to both Marx and Engels and was certainly clear as well to Lenin, Trotsky, and Mao. The ambiguity was in the question of cause and effect. This issue was not actually critical to Marx. On the one hand, he could argue that the economic constituted the essential substratum of history. On the other hand, his dialectical methodology allowed him to move back and forth between the two realms, achieving an implicit balance between the two. By positing the existence of two realms, each affecting the other, he managed to draw a formal balance between the economic and cultural.

Later, politicized Marxism relegated culture to the realm of the epiphenomenal. Engels abandoned the relative dialectical equality of the two realms in Marx for a more purely causal relationship between economic reality and art and culture, with economics clearly constituting the primary realm.[1] Each official variation of Marxism further vulgarized the relationship. These versions tended to wed culture more and more closely to particular class interests in which they thought to find the origins of the particular work of art. Thus, someone like Plekhanov, who actually had a foot in both the Communist and Social Democratic camps, could write, "On the given economic foundations there rises up fatally the ideological

---

1. See Engels, "The Part Played by Labor in the Transition from Man to Ape," in Baxandall and Morawski, eds., *Marx and Engels on Literature and Art*, p. 56.

superstructure appropriate to it."[2] Such a simplistic position could not stand for two reasons. First, the political practice that would arise from such an attitude would be singularly ineffective. Concentrating on the purely material transformation of existence did not, as a matter of practice, yield anything beyond itself. The transformation of consciousness, of which the cultural was the external manifestation, simply did not occur once the economic substratum had been transfigured, as Lenin noted obliquely when he declared that the proletariat, left to its own devices, would only create a trade union consciousness.[3]

Second, as Marx knew full well, such a simplistic notion of the relationship between culture and economics could not be maintained theoretically. There was a dialectical unity between the two realms. Both in the sense that the aesthetic and cultural realms operated by their own unique principles and in the sense that the cultural had a unique ability to affect the material realm, a more sophisticated and subtle relationship between culture and economics had to be developed. Thus, Trotsky could say (while remaining a Marxist), "Yes, art has to be approached as art, literature as literature, that is, as a quite specific field of human endeavor. Of course, we have a class criterion in art too, but this class criterion must be refracted artistically, that is, in conformity with the quite specific peculiarities of that field of creativity to which we are applying our criteria."[4] Marxism, which at one point adopted a vulgar and mechanistic stance toward the relationship between culture and economics, was forced by both its own sophistication and the realities of political practice to abandon economic monism in favor of a more subtle notion of the interplay between the two realms. It recognized the autonomy of the aesthetic.

As reality forced sophistication on the Left, the Frankfurt School also came to its position on the centrality of culture through the influence of the philosophic Right. Clearly, figures such as Nietzsche, Heidegger, and Spengler made the turn to the cultural. For each, in somewhat differing ways, the cultural and the aesthetic came to signify the core of the historical experience. They did not see the cultural as simply the after effect of some hidden reality but

---

2. Plekhanov, *In Defense of Materialism*, André Rothstein, trans. (London, 1947), p. 192.
3. Lenin, *What Is to Be Done?* Connor, ed., pp. 40–41.
4. Trotsky, *Class and Art*, Siegel, ed., p. 76.

rather as the ground on which the essential reality worked itself out. Art and life were intimately bound up together.

It was out of the confluence of Marxism's renewed concern for the function of the aesthetic and with the philosophic Right's vision of the unity of the aesthetic and the human that the Frankfurt School's understanding of culture flowed. On the one hand, as they sought to create an effective historical practice, they had to replicate Lenin and Trotsky's return to culture as a medium of historical activity.[5] On the other hand, they saw the aesthetic not only as an effective arena for political activity but rather as a world intimately bound up with life itself. To them culture and aesthetic sensibility constituted the ultimate existential dimension. The sensual experience of material production—that is, economic life—had an aesthetic impact on the experience of the class man and to that extent it was critical. But this importance extended only to its effect on the experience of sensibility. The existential sensibility constituted and created by art and culture were what was, in and of itself, the core of existence. The Frankfurt School, like Nietzsche, saw history as the unfolding of an aesthetic sensibility; the transformation of that sensibility was the end point of the revolutionary transformation of existence. Life and art were, to them, inextricable.[6]

To the Frankfurt School, the ultimate aspect of the crisis of the Enlightenment is the crisis of aesthetic taste. As Adorno puts it: "Taste is the most accurate seismograph of historical experience. Unlike almost all other faculties, it is even able to register its own behavior. Reacting against itself, it recognizes its own lack of taste."[7] Taste stands as the core of the expression of historical experience. It is, indeed, the formal structure through which the experience is mediated. How we respond to our life is determined by the cultural constructs and expectations through which we filter and evaluate the world. Our tastes determine our experience of the world.

Culture, the realm of taste, is also able to be reflective. Culture's most profound object is itself. Embedded in the aesthetic, as the

---

5. Horkheimer, "Notes on Science and the Crisis," in *Critical Theory*, p. 9.
6. Marcuse, *Essay on Liberation*, pp. 23–48; Horkheimer, "Authority and the Family," in *Critical Theory*, pp. 59–68; Benjamin, "Literaturgeschichte und Literaturwissenschaft," in *Der Stratege im Literaturkampf*, pp. 11–13; Adorno, *Philosophy of Modern Music*, pp. 3–4.
7. Adorno, *Minima Moralia*, p. 145.

counterpoint of taste, is the beautiful.[8] Culture, which may or may not possess taste—that is, may or may not be beautiful—consistently subjects itself to analysis and criticism. This means, in the first place, that culture possesses a dialectical movement of its own, predicated not simply on its relationship to economic things but also derived from its own intrinsic reflexiveness. In the second place, it means that the critic's role is pivotal in relation to culture.

The movement of culture, like the movement of all dialectics, tends toward this resolution of its antinomious tensions. In this case, the intention of culture is to make taste and beauty identical. In the end of the history of culture, beauty should, first, be pervasive in the world, and, second and most important from the perspective of taste as such, be appreciated.

Culture, however, possesses another side: "Culture is only true when implicitly critical.... Criticism is an indispensable element of culture which is itself contradictory: in all its untruth still as true as culture is untrue."[9] The dilemma is this. The implicit movement of culture to criticize itself is a tendency toward good taste—that is, toward an appreciation of the beautiful. Yet, if culture were to come to rest, it would become in some sense untrue. Culture, like reason, falsifies itself as it comes to its end. Thus, the crisis of culture at the end of history is the problem of meaning without ends; it is the problem of beauty when everything is beautiful.

On this level, the contradiction is profound: it is the status of the work of art after the world has become beautiful. But this is not yet the crisis that the Frankfurt School perceives to be crucial. The first crisis that must be faced is the failure of culture even before becoming beautiful. The triumph of bad taste and horror, coupled with the failure of cultural criticism to shatter the self-satisfaction of an insufficient and distorted culture, is the crisis:

> Cultural criticism finds itself faced with the final stage of the dialectic of culture and barbarism. To write poetry after Auschwitz is barbaric. And this corrodes even the knowledge of why it has become impossible to write poetry today. Absolute reification, which presupposed intellectual progress as one of its elements, is now preparing to absorb

---

8. On this, the Frankfurt School seemed to take its bearings from Hegel. See Hegel, *Philosophy of Fine Art*, pp. 194–96.
9. Adorno, "Cultural Criticism and Society," in *Prisms*, p. 22.

the mind entirely. Critical intelligence cannot be equal to this challenge as long as it confines itself to self-satisfied contemplation.[10]

Poetry after Auschwitz—that is, the contemplation of beauty in the face of overwhelming horror—is barbarism. Auschwitz, until fully expiated, has abolished the right to the celebration of poetry. The beautiful has utterly expelled itself from the world. The world, in its penultimate moment, has become utterly ugly. As such, the aesthetic sensibility that can appreciate the world as it is has become absolutely tasteless. This same tasteless cultural criticism has come to occupy the space meant for authentic criticism. Cultural criticism has become affirmative. It affirms culture as it is rather than compelling it to move beyond itself. Adorno calls for the replacement of the current cultural criticism with dialectical criticism, which would have as its task the creation of a new, once again reflective moment of taste.[11] Thus the Frankfurt School launches its criticism of culture from the point of view of the whole, the parts, and the genesis. Critical Theory has its first moment in attempting a revivified and broadened cultural criticism.

The first question that must be addressed is the origin of the crisis of art and culture. Marcuse defines the work of art as follows:

> Like technology, art creates another universe of thought and practice against and within the existing one. But in contrast to the technical universe the artistic universe is one of illusion, semblance, *Schein*. However, this semblance is resemblance to a reality which exists as the threat and promise of the established one. In various forms of mask and silence, the artistic universe is organized by the images of a life without fear.... The more blatantly irrational the society becomes, the greater the rationality of the artistic universe.[12]

The work of art, obviously, is creative. But what is properly created in the work of art is not merely the object as such but a criticism of the existent universe. The work of art, as Trotsky implied, operates through a dialectical movement of its own. But, as he also implied, this movement is not unrelated to the world of practice. Marcuse clarifies this relationship. The task of the work of art is to partake of and constitute a universe in appearance that stands as a threat to

---

10. Ibid., p. 34.
11. Ibid., p. 77.
12. Marcuse, *One-Dimensional Man*, pp. 238–39.

the insufficiency of the "real" world. Replicating Hegel's notion of the status and function of art,[13] the work of art is to stand in a critical relationship to the world as it is in order to create the sensible longing for the beautiful that would overthrow, in political practice, the ugliness that constitutes reality.

The root of the cultural crisis is the failure of the work of art in this age to take a critical stance. Rather than upholding the beautiful as a historical alternative to the ugly irrationality of the world, the work of art either lapses into historical irrelevance or into a positive affirmation of the world as it is. Just as philosophy splits itself into the illusory alternatives of Heidegger's abstractedness and Positivism's concretion, both constituting in practice social affirmation, so the work of art casts itself into two realms, apparently distinct but practically identical.

The first alternative parallels Heidegger's abstractedness and might even be said to have its roots in his aesthetic conception—that is, in the notion of the work of art as utterly abstracted from real, sensual life. Horkheimer writes:

> In the modern period, however, sculpture and painting were dissociated from town and building, and the creation of these arts reduced to a size suitable to any interior; during the same historical process, esthetic feeling acquired independent status, separate from fear, awe, exuberance, prestige and comfort. It became 'pure'. The purely esthetic feeling is the reaction of the private atomic subject, it is the judgment of an individual who abstracts from prevailing social standards. The definition of the beautiful as an object of disinterested pleasure had its roots in this relation.[14]

The root of the idea of "art for art's sake" is to be found in the modern notion of individuation—that is, in a Heideggerian ontology. This prevalent modern notion of the function of art serves the same purpose in the cultural realm as Heidegger's ontology serves in the philosophic. It abstracts the work of art from its sociohistorical context, rendering it impossible for it to posit the beautiful for the world or to juxtapose the beautiful to the world. In this context, the subjectivist paintings of Rousseau or the music of Richard Strauss are to the point, as is Ezra Pound's aestheticism. The appar-

---

13. Hegel, *Philosophy of Fine Art*, pp. 42–43, 263–64.
14. Horkheimer, "Art and Mass Culture," in *Critical Theory*, p. 273.

ent abstractness tends to turn a culture operating under its aegis into an objective affirmation of the ugly as an existential, if not aesthetic, mode.

The second alternative seems to parallel the Frankfurt School's conception of the function of Positivism, where the work of art becomes identical with the world. Examples might be Andy Warhol's ultrarealism or "realistic" movies. As Adorno and Horkheimer put it:

> The earth, now rational, no longer feels the need of an aesthetic reflection. The demonic element is wiped out by directly applying the desired imprint on mankind. The domination no longer needs numinous images' it produces them itself on an industrial scale and uses them as a more reliable means of winning over the masses.[15]

Here, the world having been rationalized in the Hegelian and Weberian senses, the opposition between the work of art and reality is apparently ended. The work of art can drop its critical stance not by levitating into abstractness but rather by affirming what already exists.

Under this conception, the task of the work of art is to reproduce the existent faithfully. Manifesting itself in the ultrarealism of Zhdanov in the socialist camp and of Warhol in the capitalist, the work of art intends to capture the real, not in order to subject it to an immanent criticism but to discover and affirm the beauty proclaimed to be inherent in it. If the essence of the aesthetic is criticism, then the work of art loses the aesthetic in order to establish a harmonious relationship with the world.[16] Art, like Positivistic philosophy, comes to support the established order by faithfully replicating it abstractly, thus rendering impotent the realm whose task is the creation of alternatives.

Utter abstractionism and ultrarealism debate each other perpetually as if they were the only conceivable cultural modes. In the sense of Heidegger and Positivism, they are. It is not that art is transhistorically impossible. Indeed, the Frankfurt School intends to recreate the historical moments in which art can go beyond the sterility of affirmation. At this moment, however, the structure of creativity tends to preclude such a possibility. The reification of consciousness

---

15. Adorno and Horkheimer, *Dialectic of Enlightenment*, p. 251.
16. Adorno, "Perennial Jazz," in *Prisms*, p. 131.

The Crisis of Art and Culture

that takes place under capitalist production and organization denies thought any possibilities outside of being an absolute affirmation of the things that it produces or utterly irrelevant to the entire question of production. Art can be only useless abstraction or pointless concretion.

Just as the philosophic dialectic has been suspended, so has the aesthetic. Georg Lukács first described this phenomenon: "The reified consciousness must also remain hopelessly trapped in the two extremes of crude empiricism and abstract utopianism."[17] To Lukács, the origin of reification—that is, the transformation of subject into an object—is in the very mode of capitalist production. The task of capitalism is to transform the world into an object. This is also the task of Enlightenment. What capitalism does is to go far beyond the Enlightenment's objectification of nature to an objectification of man. Just as the initial stage of capitalism regards a naturally occurring object, a tree, as something subject to itself, its object, so too, at its end, capitalism comes to regard men as equivalent objects. In the end, even man sees himself as an object.[18] He comes to conceive of himself either as a cog in the productive mechanism or, wishing to save itself, as pure subject, utterly free from it. Utter concretion and utter abstraction are the only two alternatives that Lukács acknowledges as real possibilities under the domination of late capitalist reification.[19]

This reification of consciousness is the central crisis within culture: "Once culture itself has been debased to 'cultural goods', with its hideous philosophical rationalization, 'cultural values', it has already defamed its raison d'être."[20] For Adorno and for the rest of the Frankfurt School, Lukács' understanding of the status of consciousness is the basis for their own critique. Culture, like everything else in bourgeois society, has been turned into an object. It serves a concrete, internal social function, and it is produced through the complex of artistic machinery operating under the auspices of the system. Its purpose is, on the one hand, to affirm the existing social condition and, on the other, to provide a safe and meaningless outlet for discontent—through "pure" (socially meaningless) art. Its production becomes like the production of all other

17. Lukács, *History and Class Consciousness*, p. 77.
18. Ibid., pp. 83–103.
19. Ibid., p. 77.
20. Adorno, "Cultural Criticism and Society," in *Prisms*, p. 22.

commodities.²¹ Objectification of culture, however, is not merely another event; in the end it represents the reification of mind itself.

Thus far, the critique of reification is relatively unimaginative. Marx clearly foresaw it, and Lukács had analyzed it. Benjamin, however, radicalizes the analysis by rooting it not simply in bourgeois culture but in all culture created under the technological auspices. Benjamin's analysis in "The Work of Art in an Age of Mechanical Reproduction," is both the basis of the historical pessimism of all of the Frankfurt School and of the sometimes modified fear of technology presented by Marcuse in *One-Dimensional Man* and by Adorno and Horkheimer in the *Dialectic of Enlightenment*.

Benjamin saw the crisis of modern culture as being rooted in the technological mode involved in the creation and the dissemination of the work of art. The technological component, as we saw in the preceding chapter, was by no means accidental. It was at the heart of the Enlightenment's drive to subjugate the world. Thus, the crisis of culture, which Benjamin sees arising from technology, is itself rooted in the dialectical movement of the myth of the West. And just as that crisis might prove to be insoluble, so too might the crisis of culture.

For Benjamin, the work of art in our age takes on a radically new cast: it is the product of mechanical reproduction, which transfigures the very being of the work of art. Benjamin sees the work of art as always having been potentially reproducible. The potential for reproduction, however, was realized only on the smallest scale, leaving the work of art itself essentially untouched. Thus the work of art possessed a singular quality. First, it existed in only one space and only within a finite period. Second, viewing the work of art was tightly bound up with ritual. Art's specific location and uniqueness required and created an aura around the work of art.²² It is the loss of this aura that is crucial to Benjamin.

The mechanical reproduction of the work of art shatters art's structure and radically transforms its existential circumstance. With reproduction through technology, the work of art is suddenly freed from its physical constraints. The entire perception of the work of art is thereby transformed. No longer are the rituals of viewing

---

21. Adorno and Horkheimer, *Dialectic of Enlightenment,* p. 157.
22. Benjamin, "The Work of Art in an Age of Mechanical Reproduction," in *Illuminations,* pp. 218–19. On the rituals of viewing art, see Adorno, "Valéry-Proust Museum," in *Prisms,* pp. 183–85.

necessary for enjoyment. Art is freed from the traditions that surrounded its appreciation as well as from the sheer physical scarcity that conditioned its availability to men before its liberation.

The crucial first step in the transformation of the work of art through mechanical reproduction is that it loses its place in space and time:

> Even the most perfect reproduction of a work of art is lacking in one element: its presence in time and space, its unique existence at the place where it happens to be. This unique existence of the work of art determined the history to which it was subject throughout the time of its existence.[23]

What is lost is the sensual historicity of the object of art. The reproduction may be physically faithful, but the true work of art is more than physical structure. The work of art is a complex of sensual events impinging upon its being; it is the *context* of its representation. The reproduction, as would an artificially created fully mature man, lacks something to make it authentic. What it lacks is its own history. Like an artificial man, it has no past of its own. Further, it has lost its preciousness; it is infinitely reproducible. The careful rituals of the viewing place, the rituals of the museum and the gallery, are unnecessary, superfluous. Like the artificial being that it is, it is a substance that on closer inspection is radically insubstantial.[24]

Art, like man in an age of mechanical reproduction, has lost its authenticity:

> The authenticity of a thing is the essence of all that is transmissible from its beginning, ranging from its substantive duration to its testimony to the history which it has experienced.... And what is really jeopardized when the historical testimony is affected is the authority of the object.[25]

What is lost, Benjamin goes on to say, is the "aura."[26] The work of art before reproduction intervened was surrounded by the aura

23. Benjamin, ibid., p. 220.
24. Ibid., p. 220.
25. Ibid., p. 221.
26. Ibid., p. 221.

of the rituals necessary to experience it. Viewing the work of art was mediated through the historical patina surrounding the object, the sheer knowledge of its profound history and historicity. This scarcity and historicity created the rituals that surrounded our experience of the work of art. With reproduction, this aura is torn away.

The shattering of the aura of the work of art breaks apart the tradition of art. The work of art is separated both from its past and from its place. Each reproduction of the sculpture or the symphony stands now within the context of the viewer's or listener's choosing. The work of art ceases to rule through the power of its aura over all who come into its presence. Now, the work of art becomes an object, subject to the will of the mass of men free to view it.

That the work of art as reproduction is intimately bound up with the rise of the mass (that is, mass culture itself) is obvious. What is more radical is Benjamin's treatment of the political implications of reproducible art:

> For the first time in world history, mechanical reproduction emancipates the work of art from its parasitical dependence on ritual. To an ever greater degree the work of art reproduced becomes the work of art designed for reproducibility. From a photographic negative, for example, one can make any number of prints; to ask for the 'authentic' print makes no sense. But the instant the criterion of authenticity ceases to be applicable to artistic production, the total function of art is reversed. Instead of being based on ritual, it begins to be based on another practice—politics.[27]

The reproduction of art, therefore, takes a strange twist socially. At first glance, reproduction appears liberating; it frees both object and subject from the constraints that previously had been physically imposed on the event. But the illusion is short-lived, for a problem arises. What now is the basis for determining what is a work of art?

Art cannot stand by itself. It requires constraints to determine its structure as well as a structure to determine the format of its experience. With the loss of the constraints imposed by the sheer uniqueness of the object, the work of art is cast free, yet it still needs a ground. The ground is to be found in the social event that it created—the mass. The mass becomes mass instead of mob pre-

27. Ibid., p. 224.

The Crisis of Art and Culture

cisely because of the mass communication that is the substructure behind the reproducible work of art. Without the shared experience of the universalized art that is mass culture, the mass would remain individuated, a mob. It is mass art that creates its own audience, mass man. The work of art as a reproducible object could be experienced by the masses of men. It brings the marginal monads of society, hitherto scattered and ineffective, together through the web of its own manifoldedness. The new ground of the work of art is the mass.

The constraints of reproducibility condition the aesthetic possibilities available to the artist. The physical requirement that the work of art be reproducible determines, in advance, what the limits of creation are. Nowhere is this more apparent than in what Benjamin calls the most perfectly modern aesthetic form: the movie.[28] What is technically possible in movies, in production and presentation, determines what will be shown.

Furthermore, the possibility of reproduction requires the creation of economic circumstances under which reproduction and dissemination are feasible. The reproduced work of art requires customers in order to be practical. Thus, the work of art becomes subject to the demands of the marketplace. A mass market is created to consume mass art.

The conditioning of the work of art by the consumer is by no means new: it is as ancient as the poor artist and the wealthy patron. What is unique is the structure of modern patronage. The individual patron could demand and receive a work of art suitable to his tastes, demands, and interests. This was a private, and at worst, philistine arrangement. The circumstances of the demand for mass culture are by no means so private.[29] The demand is formed in the churning and public masses. As such, the demand for mass culture is by its nature political. The political formulation of the requirements of the masses determines the type and content of the art that the masses will consume. Politics becomes, says Benjamin, the new ground of art.

Having torn the work of art from its previous context and cast it naked into the political maelstrom, modern technology has created not simply a new form of art or a new possibility for the aesthetic.

---

28. Ibid., pp. 221–22, 229–30.
29. Horkheimer, "Art and Mass Culture," in *Critical Theory,* pp. 274–76.

Rather, it has created a new historical problematic from an ancient philosophical problem: the relationship between art and politics. Obviously, two relationships are possible. Politics can determine art, or art can determine politics. According to Benjamin, the issue is between the former, which is Communism, and the latter, which is fascism.[30]

To Benjamin, the aestheticization of politics can only mean war.[31] Only the violence of combat offers the grim beauty sufficient to satisfy art; only violence can come to the fore when politics is faced with the requirement to be beautiful. Moreover, when art has been forced into the context of a mass culture and thus has faced the problems relating to politics, the fascist can avoid subjugation to the aesthetic demands of the masses only by subjecting the masses to the demands of aesthetics. The fascist creates an aesthetic ideal and proceeds to subject the masses to its standards.[32]

The only alternative is to subject art to the demands of politics. To Benjamin, this is the stance of Communism, and as such, is praiseworthy.[33] But it would appear that it is praiseworthy only insofar as it avoids war and fascism. The work of art is still lost; its aura is ripped away and it loses its autonomy. It becomes the subject of the masses. Of course, a new age is gained, but the aesthetic sensibility of the old is lost. Further, the authentic ability to appreciate the work of art is also lost.

Modern art requires only limited attention; it can tolerate, and even requires, the distractedness of the masses. If the archetypal aesthetic and cultural mode of the new age is the film, then the mode of viewing the film relates to all of modern art:

> Reception in a state of distraction, which is increasing noticeably in all fields of art and is symptomatic of profound changes in apperception, finds in the film its true means of exercise. The film with its shock effect meets this mode of reception halfway. The film makes the cult value recede into the background not only by putting the public in the position of the critic, but also by the fact that at the movies this

---

30. Benjamin, "The Work of Art in an Age of Mechanical Reproduction," in *Illuminations*, pp. 241–42.
31. Ibid., p. 242.
32. It is interesting to note that Marcuse, distinctly in opposition to Benjamin, calls for the aestheticization of politics. See *Essay on Liberation*, pp. 40–45.
33. Benjamin, "The Work of Art in an Age of Mechanical Reproduction," in *Illuminations*, p. 242.

position requires no attention. The public is an examiner, but an absent-minded one.[34]

There is in Benjamin both a profound sorrow and an authentic sense of triumph in this. Clearly, the rise of mechanical reproduction was inevitable. The absentmindedness of the masses induced by the soporific structure of the new art tended to make the masses prey to their own aestheticization, that is, to fascism. Yet, there was some hope, in that this might be avoided. Perhaps, through the creation of the mass by the work of art in a reproduced form, the mass might seize control of the work of art, saving themselves from fascism, ushering in the millennium.

It is clear that Benjamin was suffused with a melancholy nostalgia for the lost art, and, more, for the lost sensibility that appreciated art. There was in this nostalgia something that opened him (and, in a way, the rest of the Frankfurt School) to the lure of the aestheticization of politics, to the hope of somehow retrieving the lost aura of the work of art. Benjamin wrenchingly and consciously avoided this danger. As Fredric Jameson puts it:

> But of nostalgia as a political motivation is most frequently associated with Fascism, there is no reason why a nostaliga conscious of itself, a lucid and remorseless dissatisfaction with the present on the grounds of some remembered plentitude, cannot furnish as adequate a revolutionary stimulus an any other: the example of Benjamin is there to prove it.[35]

He avoided the danger of aesthetics only by both abandoning the past and living with the profound reality of reification.

Even if fascism were avoidable, the aesthetic consciousness that would survive would be both free and somehow deformed. In the first place, it could never see the work of art as anything but an instrument. Benjamin knew this use of art to be necessary; it was the basis for his endorsement of Berthold Brecht.[36] But at the same

---

34. Ibid., pp. 240–41.
35. Jameson, *Marxism and Form*, p. 82.
36. Benjamin, *Briefe*, 2:549; Benjamin, *Versuche über Brecht*, pp. 87–91; Scholem, "Walter Benjamin," in *Leo Baeck Yearbook*, 4:130, calls Brecht's influence disastrous. The openness of Benjamin to Brecht would appear theoretically justified as well as rational, however, in light of Benjamin's conscious need to subject art to politics, which was Brecht's position and task.

time it allowed the triumph of a deformed consciousness that, by its nature, was devoid of an authentic aesthetic sensibility. Such a sensibility was no longer possible because the new consciousness had as its object a work of art stripped of its aura. Seeking a renewed sensibility out of the new sort of art would be dangerous. One would either be overwhelmed by nostalgic grief for what had been lost or would go over to the other side and try to recreate a moment of aesthetic triumph. The only realm left for that was politics; the only outcome of such an attempt, war and fascism. Thus, aesthetic sensibility, even in the best of circumstances, was forever lost. As such, the beautiful itself was lost.

There were only two hopes. The first was that the situation could not maintain itself. The second was that a Communist regime would arise that would be authentically Messianic. Benjamin's movement toward Judaism was more than heritage; it was the conscious search for a *deus ex machina* to ensure, through the certain virtue of the Messiah, that Communism would administer the work of art—and hence, consciousness—righteously. This was the reason that Benjamin metaphysicized the proletariat—to ensure its righteousness.

Adorno in particular comes to share Benjamin's analysis of media, applying it particularly to radio and television. Through the utter dissemination of the work of art through radio and television (the extent of which even Benjamin couldn't imagine, let alone appreciate), art becomes nothing more nor less than a backdrop to life. It loses its distinct status as an element opposed to the world by being absorbed in the world.

Nowhere is the loss of the aesthetic clearer than with jazz. Adorno writes:

> To the masses of young people who, year after year, chase the perennial fashion presumably to forget it after a few years, it offers a compromise between aesthetic sublimation and social adjustment. The 'unrealistic', practically useless, imaginative element is permitted to survive at the price of changing its character; it must tirelessly strive to remake itself in the image of reality, to repeat the latter's commands to itself, to submit to them. Thus it reintegrates itself into the sphere from which it sought to escape. Art is deprived of its aesthetic dimension, and emerges as part of the very adjustment which it in

---

37. Adorno, "Perpetual Fashion," in *Prisms,* p. 131.

principle contradicts. Viewed from this standpoint, several unusual features of jazz can be more easily understood.[37]

Jazz, playing in the background, allows itself apparent freedom, but only by perpetually recapitulating, with only technically approved variations, the required and approved theme. Technical virtuosity is raised above authentic freedom. Jazz, both as background music and formal structure, affirms the existent. Moreover, jazz is not merely a peripheral event; it is the essential component of modern culture.[38]

Radio and television serve similar functions. They integrate culture into society by slipping into the background. Television and radio are always there, always heard, but rarely consciously.[39] As do movies with Benjamin's semiconscious movie goer, television and radio slip their message across subliminally.[40]

The essential point is that Adorno and the rest of the Frankfurt School agree in essence with Benjamin's analysis of the status of art under mechanical reproduction and they take their bearing from it. While Adorno was clearly unhappy with a number of aspects of Benjamin's work on art and in particular with his affinity for Brecht (because of what Adorno regarded as Brecht's vulgar Marxism),[41] what remains indisputable is that there existed no conflict between their formal analysis of the status of modern culture.

It is necessary to pause here to consider the much-reported discord between Adorno and Horkheimer on the question of Bertolt Brecht. Susan Buck-Morss, for example, claimed that Benjamin's arguments on art "managed to tread on all ten of Adorno's intellectual toes."[42] It is certainly true that there was a debate between Adorno and Benjamin, in which much turned around the figure of Brecht, with whom Benjamin stood much to the chagrin of Adorno. But it is not at all clear that the apparent tension had a fundamental theoretical base.

We can see that Adorno's criticism was neither thorough-going nor consistent. In *Negative Dialectics,* he writes, "Benjamin's defeatism about his own thought was conditioned by the undialectical

38. Ibid., pp. 128–35.
39. Adorno, "Prolog zum Fernsehen," in *Eingriffe,* pp. 70–74.
40. Adorno, "Fernsehen als Ideologie," in *Eingriffe,* pp. 90–92.
41. See Tiedemann, *Studien zur Philosophie Walter Benjamins,* pp. 89–90.
42. Buck-Morss, *The Origins of Negative Dialectics,* p. 148.

positivity of which he carried a formally unchanged remnant from his theological phase into his materialistic phase."[43] This sums up quite elegantly Adorno's criticism of Benjamin and also shows us its limits. Adorno is trying to determine here the origins of Benjamin's philosophic pessimism—the reason for his doubts about reason. Adorno finds its roots in a kind of theological Positivism—a commitment to objective revolution.

There is something very strange in this criticism. First, Benjamin (in the "Theses on the Philosophy of History") had himself accused materialism of hyper-Positivism. Thus Benjamin was aware of the dangers of Positivism and sought refuge in a theological sensibility to *avoid* Adorno's charge. Second, *Negative Dialectics* also bases hyper-Positivism on materialism's self-assured identity—its certainty of unity with the concept. Third, both Benjamin and Adorno see Positivism as giving rise to puerile optimism rather than to philosophic despair. Finally, his despair about reason can be found in almost all of Adorno's work (*Minima Moralia*, the essays published in *Prisms*, and even in *Negative Dialectics*).

To untangle this strange web of accusations, let us consider what prompted them. In *Negative Dialectics*, Adorno sets himself two tasks: first, to rescue Hegel from Positivism and, second, to break the false authenticity of Heideggerian ontology. In both these tasks, he had an almost identical intent: to allow a moment of human comprehension without allowing the concept to become identical with its object. In other words, he sought an unending dialectic that met the requirements of attained truthfulness and ceaseless search. Now these are clearly difficult goals to achieve and in the *Dialectic of Enlightenment* and much of the later work, he despaired of attaining them. It was only in *Negative Dialectics* that he thought he could find this moment.

Benjamin had early on sought this ineffable moment in which all things could both be and not be. His criticism of the Positivism of Social Democracy was that it felt at ease with itself, that it thought that the dialectic had come to rest in itself, that subject and object had been reconciled. Benjamin knew, however, that the relationship between a thought and a thing was far more ambiguous. He writes that a thought, however true it may be in one's heart, becomes false at the moment it is uttered. The very act of speaking renders the

---

43. Adorno, *Negative Dialectics*, p. 19.

thought fixed, and it is that fixedness, that mere existence, which renders it false. Benjamin's search is for a language that partakes of historicity, that is at ease with the fact, and that possesses in its purity the dialectical ability to criticize itself: in other words, he seeks a true negative dialectic in which opposites are united without having the essence of negativity abolished. Thus Benjamin turns to the text, to the history of language's highest moment, searching for what is still alive in the concept, for what is true without falling into Positivity. Benjamin had a theological sensitivity and not Positivity. It was not despair but a hope.

Adorno knew this well, as he writes in his "Portrait of Walter Benjamin":

> He [Benjamin] transposed the idea of the sacred text into the sphere of enlightenment, into which, according to Scholem, Jewish mysticism itself tends to culminate dialectically. His 'essayism' consists in treating profane texts as though they were sacred. This does not mean that he clung to theological relics or, as the religious socialists, endowed the profane with transcendent significance.[44]

What Benjamin saw in the text was live language—language that both had captured the true and had not succumbed to complacent Positivity. In the text of the world-historical work are the chips of truth embedded within the falsehood of the text's historicity. The struggle between historicity and transcendental truth keeps that truth both alive and preserved—objective without reification. Thus Benjamin's theological Positivism is known by Adorno himself to be something quite different from quietistic despair. Adorno acknowledges this even more clearly in *Negative Dialectics:*

> Philosophy rests on the texts it criticizes. They are brought to it by the tradition they embody, and it is in dealing with them that the conduct of philosophy becomes commensurable with tradition. This justifies the move from philosophy to exegesis, which exalts neither the interpretation nor the symbol into an absolute, but seeks the truth where thinking secularizes the irretrievable archetype of sacred texts.[45]

---

44. Adorno, *Prisms*, p. 234.
45. Adorno, *Negative Dialectics*, p. 55.

Textual exegesis, the practical activity of Critical Theory, was born of the same need as Benjamin's worldly Talmudism: to capture truth without reification, to conjure the radical possibilities embedded in the tradition without falling into reaction. In the exegetical moment, where translation takes place over the gulf of culture and history, the dead are brought back to life in order to slay living monsters. Thus Adorno's criticism of Benjamin is gratuitous and he knows it to be such. The procedure that Adorno adopts is Benjamin's. It is precisely the methodology they have in common.

Theodor Adorno and Walter Benjamin shared a concern for the relationship between language and truth and both sought to solve the problem of language and negativity by focusing on language congealed into a text: in other words, they were intent on language bound up with history. Truth was to be found in language rather than floating free in the world, as Positivism would have it. Manipulating the matrix of language in order to conjure the opposition that is truth is problematic, however. It was problematic both in its possibility and in its consequences.

This is the great problem of both Benjamin's "Theses on the Philosophy of History" and Adorno and Horkheimer's *Dialectic of Enlightenment.* For both, history has become the great question mark. Just as the epistemological optimism of Marxism was held in doubt, so the historical optimism resulting from the philosophic variety was open to doubt. Benjamin spoke of the growing philistinism and barbarism of the worker movement at the hands of the Social Democrats; so, too, Adorno addresses himself to the growing historical barbarism of those countries operating under the formal aegis of Enlightenment—mass society.

There is a real parallel in Benjamin's and Adorno's political outlook. Both raise doubts about the revolutionary subjectivity of the proletariat and its ability to carry out its historic task, and both doubt that the attained outcome, the Positivity of an achieved order, holds the answer. Why, then, do Benjamin and Adorno appear to differ on political matters? This brings us back to the problem of Bertolt Brecht.

As we have seen, Adorno viewed Brecht as a vulgarian and regarded his influence on Benjamin as catastrophic. In particular, Adorno laid Benjamin's continued support for the Soviet Union at Brecht's door.[46] What is not clear is whether Adorno fully under-

---

46. Buck-Morss, *Origins of Negative Dialectics,* pp. 151–53.

stood why Benjamin was attracted to Brecht. Indeed, there was a profound tension between the two. Benjamin reported his essay on Kafka had been criticized by Brecht as contributing to Jewish fascism.[47] Brecht charged that Benjamin had obscured the problem of Kafka by focusing on Kafka as such rather than on Kafka the exemplar of certain general conditions. In this, Brecht was not mistaken, but the charge shows the chasm between Benjamin and him. What Brecht drew from Kafka's *Trial* were certain social propositions: the complexity of mediations and entanglements in the city. What Benjamin drew was that "the true measure of life is remembrance."[48] A chasm separated their sensibilities. To Brecht, life was lived in large things; history was sweeping. To Benjamin, life was in the small; history was a collection of nuances. For Brecht, politics was in the mass; for Benjamin it was buried in a small miniature of the individual. Thus Brecht was far removed from Benjamin.

Why then did it appear to Adorno that Benjamin and Brecht were allied? Remember that in "The Work of Art in an Age of Mechanical Reproduction," Benjamin wrote that either art could rule politics or politics could rule art; for art to rule politics was fascism, for politics to rule art was Communism. These choices were not altogether pleasant for Benjamin, for they represented the collapse of art as an autonomous realm, but they were the historical choices. It was not Brecht's political understanding that was attractive to Benjamin but his desire to subjugate art, and so avoid fascism.[49] Thus Benjamin's attraction to Brecht was a response to fascism more than any attraction to vulgar Marxism. Benjamin, along with Adorno, understood that the available political possibilities were severely limited; the choice was between decadence and barbarism. Benjamin understood the need to live within those boundaries while searching for formulas to resurrect the humane tradition. Thus, Adorno's criticisms of Brecht never cut to the heart of the matter and do not signify an absolute break between the two. What was involved was relatively superficial: the need to temporize with history. Brecht violated Benjamin's sensibilities as he did Adorno's; but Benjamin saw Brecht as a bulwark against fascism.

This matter was a relatively minor tactical disagreement, because Benjamin and Adorno were engaged in the same project. Both sought the formula which would break the bonds of the historical

47. Benjamin, "Conversations with Brecht," in *Reflections*, p. 208.
48. A hint of this reasoning is in ibid., p. 211.
49. Ibid., p. 210.

dilemma. To avoid fascism without losing the aesthetic sensibility was the crisis of the age.

The advent of technology had brought about the crisis. Technology had made a radical break in the format of art. It shattered the traditional structure of presentation through utter reproducibility and absolute dissemination while creating a situation in which art's prime relationship is with politics. Under those circumstances art, rather than exercising its authentic function of criticizing reality moves to become either the ruler of the real (fascism) or, more frequently, an instrument of affirmation through either catering to the manipulated taste of the mass and reaffirming the manipulation, or serving the objective interests of the masses.

The only outcome for the work of art as an instrument of affirmation is to be made trivial and mediocre.[50] A work of art that fails to fulfill its social function is, by its nature, mediocre. What is meant by 'social function' is not the contemporary usage of the phrase, meaning affirmation, but the historical purpose of art, meaning criticism. The work of art, having necessarily become subject to politics in order to save itself from the worse fate of fascism, becomes propaganda. At best, as with jazz, it becomes the subliminal affirmation of the existent through turning consciousness into a pattern of acceptable rhythms. Under such circumstances, the work of art irretrievably loses the greatness that was once its reason for being. What art remains great (Joyce, Picasso) is destroyed through the consciousness that experiences it.

Both the best and the worst are catastrophic to the work of art. Under the worst circumstances, art triumphs over the world. But this triumph involves a terrible price. First, the art is transfigured into historical horror: the work of art knows of no way to make itself manifest other than by portraying horror. Second, even if by some sleight-of-hand war and fascism are averted, art must give itself up by abandoning its distance from the world and thereby abandoning its authenticity. If art comes to rule the workd, then art's mediation through the object would be lost, and it would lose itself in the world. The price would be the same that reason under the reign of its identitarian principle had to pay: the loss of its functional essence, negativity.

50. Marcuse, *One-Dimensional Man*, pp. 239–40; Horkheimer, "Art and Mass Culture," in *Critical Theory*, pp. 277–79; Adorno and Horkheimer, *Dialectic of Enlightenment*, pp. 125–31.

The Crisis of Art and Culture

Even under the best of circumstances the work of art would have to pay the terrible price of reification.[51] By becoming an object of politics, the work of art loses itself to propaganda even while it maintains a formally critical stance toward existent mundane circumstances. It becomes pure object, not merely in its mediation but also in its very being. Brecht and Zhdanov, however historically necessary they may be, deliver the coup de grâce to the work of art. Art, as such, is lost even under the best of circumstances. Whichever way history moves, reification appears to be art's ultimate fate.

This analysis tends to posit that the formal problem of culture in an age of mechanical reproduction is insoluble. On the one hand, the success of art means fascism; on the other hand, the subjugation of art means the loss of the aesthetic through reification. Even maintaining the status quo means that the work of art will be lost without the social benefits of Communism making up for that loss.

The ultimate problem, however, is deeper. The historical task of the work of art, like that of philosophy, is to posit the subliminal path to liberation through radical criticism.[52] The crisis of reification in culture thus leads directly to question the very possibility of a critical theory of culture. If the work of art is lost forever, then the question arises whether or not any sort of authentic cultural liberation is possible. Adorno sees this as the problem of all socialist criticism; he thereby rejects Zhdanov and Brecht, obviously, but also in the process he takes issue with and hopes for a solution to Benjamin's insight:

> This explains the inadequacy of most socialist contributions to cultural criticism: they lack the experience of that with which they deal. In wishing to wipe away the whole as if with a sponge, they develop an affinity to barbarism.... The blanket rejection of culture becomes a pretext for promoting what is crudest, 'healthiest', even repressive; above all, the perennial conflict between individual and society, both drawn in like manner, which is obstinately resolved in favor of society according to the criteria of the administrators who have appropriated it.[53]

---

51. Adorno himself sees this dilemma in Benjamin; see "A Portrait of Walter Benjamin," in *Prisms*, p. 233.
52. See Marcuse, *Eros and Civilization*, pp. 130–31; Adorno, "Cultural Criticism and Society," in *Prisms*, pp. 29–34.
53. Adorno, ibid., p. 32.

The subjugation of art to the "administrators"—that is, to politics—is Benjamin's only solution. Obviously, by moving into the metaphysics of politics, by positing a Messianic possibility as the basis for the administrator, Benjamin shows that he both understands the problem and wishes to avoid it. He avoids it, however, only as an *auto-da-fé*. The rest of the Frankfurt School, using Benjamin's analysis of the structure of the work of art, cannot stand the solution, which is reification.

Thus both Adorno and Marcuse posited solutions that would have been unacceptable to Benjamin. Adorno is the more moderate, seeking to minimize the reification of art and culture by distancing it from the identitarian and rationalistic imperatives of philosophy.[54] He does this simply by positing different realms for them, however, distancing art from reification primarily through a formal consideration of its structure and its distance from reason. His intention is clear: somehow to free the work of art from the dialectic of Enlightenment. But he posits the solution only metaphysically. The concrete relation between life and art is left untouched.

It is Marcuse who returns to the most radical formulation of the relation of art and life. To Marcuse, the function of art was to recapitulate phantasy, conjuring in abstract but objectified form, the longings of the utterly repressed.[55] In this he returns to the Hegelian notion of function of art. Marcuse's solution is to allow the work of art to fulfill its function—to criticize life and, ultimately, to reshape its structure.[56] Praising both expressionism and surrealism for their fantastic qualities (which make them radically critical),[57] Marcuse argues that the work of art should come to rest in the world, making itself into the world and the world into a work of art.[58]

What he thus praises is clearly what to Benjamin was anathema. Adorno also looked askance on such an identitarian role for the work of art.[59] We see therefore that the Frankfurt School arrived at three opposed ends from the same analysis. Benjamin, in the first place, was willing to surrender, with melancholy, to the reification of the work of art. His only hope for avoiding the loss of art was the

54. Adorno, *Negative Dialectics*, p. 15.
55. Marcuse, *Eros and Civilization*, pp. 168–69.
56. Marcuse, *Essay on Liberation*, p. 45.
57. Ibid., pp. 31–34.
58. Ibid., pp. 43–48.
59. Adorno, *Negative Dialectics*, p. 8.

miraculous intrusion of the Messianic, creating both a new time and a new texture of being. The melancholia of his analysis led him to metaphysics. In the second place, Adorno apparently took Benjamin's warnings concerning fascism to heart but was unwilling to accept Benjamin's Brechtian resignation. Thus rather unsatisfactorily, he sought to cordon art off from Enlightenment formally (although he was forced to reunite them in the *Dialectic of Enlightenment*) in order to preserve the negativity of the work of art. In the third place, Marcuse took Adorno to his logical conclusion, accepting the crisis of reification that Benjamin saw but rejecting his fears. Marcuse allowed art to return to its critical function and, considering the state of history in its penultimate format, hoped that art would condition the world. Marcuse, therefore, by Benjamin's lights, flirted with fascism. But, just as Benjamin was willing to accept reification as the price of avoiding fascism and gambled on a transfigured history to salvage the beautiful, Marcuse was willing to gamble with fascism. Reification was too high a price; he was willing to gamble with war and chaos in order to find a solution.

The split within the Frankfurt School did not, it should be noted, center on the analytic structure of "The Work of Art in an Age of Mechanical Reproduction." The outlines of that analysis were accepted. The School went even further, seemingly accepting that the primary relationship to consider was not between art and its own standards but art and politics. The rise of mass culture had necessitated such an outcome, since it brought about mass society. What the disagreement concerned was the historical alternative to be accepted. Benjamin alone was willing at times to accept the price of Socialist Realism and its political substructure. Marcuse led the way to gambling with fascism. But the roots of both analyses were in the same problematic.

Why Benjamin chose the former path and Marcuse the latter is a subject for speculation. The answer could be as simple as Brecht's influence on Benjamin. More deeply, it might have been that each intimately understood the tragedy of one side of the historical equation. Benjamin understood and feared fascism; Marcuse, through his work on Soviet Communism, tried to understand Stalin. Each rejected the thing he knew best. It thus might be said that each was the antipode of an insoluble dialectic. Each accepted the unaceptable because he thought the other possibility to be worse. Perhaps the split in the Frankfurt School points not to a solution but to the profound insolubility of the problem of culture and art in an age of mechanical reproduction. Perhaps both Benjamin and Marcuse had to lose their gambles; there may be no solution. This view is supported by the Frankfurt School's analysis of the part of the culture industry in the crisis of art.

There is a dialectical correlation between the reification of culture and of the work of art and the structure of the industry that produces cultural goods. Technology cannot stand by itself. On the one hand, it requires a social organization to administer and serve it. On the other hand, and dialectically connected, it must itself become the principle that controls the social organization. Technology rationalizes society, thereby making itself the principle of social organization. This is concretely manifested in the aesthetic sphere by the rise of the culture industry. Only a bureaucratic, utterly rational social form can satisfy the requirements of technologized art. In the first place, only bureaucracy can effectively control the technology of culture, coping both with the physical machinery behind it (financial and administrative) and with its myriad internal social consequences (the mass control of personnel required by the industry). In the second place, only a rationalized social structure can effectively contain the creation of mass culture: mass society. The social outcome of technological aesthetics are the masses of men integrated into a single structure of consciousness. Only a rationalized bureaucracy can cope with this creation. Thus, from the standpoints of both the work of art and the consumers of art, the mammoth rationalized culture industry is the necessary and logical outcome.[60]

The same tendency to monopoly that Marx sees as determining the development of capitalism as a whole is particularly at work in the culture industry. This tendency is reinforced by the peculiar position of culture itself. Under capitalism, culture becomes merely another industry. But unlike the functions other industries, the function of the culture industry is pivotal to the maintenance of the system. It is through the structure and content of culture that consciousness is formed; and it is through the creation of a repressed consciousness that the system maintains itself. The political system

60. On this see Chap. 13.

The Crisis of Art and Culture

requires an undifferentiated presentation of the content of culture, and this presentation requires an undifferentiated technical and economic structure. Both these requirements reinforce the natural tendency of the culture industry to monopoly.

The monopolistic tendency of the industry as a whole is reinforced by the technology that it administers (note that the following was written in 1944):

> Television aims at a synthesis of radio and film, and is held up only because the interested parties have not yet reached agreement, but its consequences will be quite enormous and promise to intensify the impoverishment of the aesthetic matter so drastically, that by tomorrow the thinly veiled identity of all industrial cultural products can come triumphantly out into the open, derisively fulfilling the Wagnerian dream of the *Gesamtkunstwerk*—the fusion of all the arts in one work.[61]

The drive of modernity is for identity. It intends to come to rest, and toward this end it bends all hitherto critical and negative structures to the task of affirmation. In television, the ultimate mechanical means for reproducing works of art joins with a unitary industrial administrative structure to achieve the task of making art affirmative.

By its nature, however, art is negative. Only by destroying its authenticity can art be turned to affirmation. Benjamin saw this as the inevitable outcome of technology; the authenticity of temporarlity and mediation had been eliminated by the reconstruction of the work of art itself. Television takes this event to radical extremes. It does not, however, stand alone in turning art to affirmation. The culture industry reproduces in the content of the work of art the structural inauthenticity of the mass-produced work of art.[62] Authentic style—that is, beauty—cannot be presented through the unmediatedness of the current presentational forms; the beautiful must maintain a distance from the subject lest it lose its fastidiousness and become sullied with the ugliness of the existent. The overwhelming directness of modern art makes impossible the presentation of beauty, which is by its nature shy. The structure of presentation for modern art is too brutal.

61. Adorno and Horkheimer, *Dialectic of Enlightenment*, p. 124.
62. Ibid., pp. 127–31.

The structural impossibility of presenting beauty directly, however, is merely one side of the process. The other side is the systematic destruction of any substantial or seductive content. Were such content permitted, the monistic control of the system would be threatened. Hence a systematic campaign against art itself (even though art is structurally impossible) is conducted by the culture industry. The mediocrity of mass culture is the result.

The Frankfurt School's quasi-Romantic critique of mass culture is not based on any kind of inegalitarianism. The mass itself, taken as monads, are not responsible. The creation of the mass, and the circumstances leading up to and currently maintaining it, are at fault. The origin of the mass was in the technology that created the conditions of a mass culture. Once the technology existed, the mass possessed its predicate and created itself. It was the technology, both mechanical and social, that made for the mediocritization of the culture of the mass that it created.

The outcome was a mass society and culture in thrall to the culture industry:

> The stronger the positions of the culture industry become, the more summarily it can deal with consumers' needs, producing them, controlling them, disciplining them and even withdrawing amusement: No limits are set to cultural progress of this kind. But the tendency is immanent in the principle of amusement itself, which is enlightened in the bourgeois sense.[63]

Amusement replaces art as the principle of mass culture. Where art serves a negative, critical function, amusement serves an affirmative function: it soothes the recipient and viewer, calming him into an affirmation of that which is. The culture industry creates a content of amusement in order to maintain itself. With its monopolistic control of the means of entertainment, the culture industry has the power to control the very structure of the consciousness of the mass of men set before it.

The power of the rulers of the media have three roots: first, the already discussed transfiguration of the work of art itself; and second, the sheer economic power of the managers of the culture industry who control both the access to the masses and the means of livelihood.[64] The third aspect is the most profound socially: it

---

63. Ibid., p. 144.
64. Horkheimer, "Art and Mass Culture," in *Critical Theory*, p. 290.

The Crisis of Art and Culture 163

concerns the abolition of the private realm: "The private realm, however, to which art is related, has been steadily menaced. Society tends to liquidate it."⁶⁵

To Horkheimer, the private realm has been under assault since Calvin. The bourgeois work ethic, with its disapproval of play, also necessarily denigrated the realm in which play was the essence: the private. What took place in the private realm was insignificant compared to what occurred in the public workplace. Under industrialization, the public realm grew malignantly while the private realm sharnk. Under the final assault of reproduced art, now in its ultimate form in television, the private realm disappeared almost entirely. The outside world of huckstering assaulted one's innermost privacy. The penetration of the private was the final declaration of the abolition of autonomous art. Art, erotic by nature, can be experienced only privately; experiencing it publicly obscenely transfigures it. The penetration of privacy grants the penetrator unparalleled power. The penetration of the home symbolizes the more profound penetration, that of the psyche itself.

The first task of the penetrators is to advertise:

> Advertising and the culture industry merge technically as well as economically. In both cases the same thing can be seen in innumerable places, and the mechanical repetition of the same culture product has come to be the same as that of the propaganda slogan. In both cases the insistent demand for effectiveness makes technology into psychotechnology, and a procedure for manipulating men ... the object is to overpower the customer.⁶⁶

Economically, the culture industry must push the products that the consumer must consume in order to maintain the productive and, hence, the bureaucratic systems. Thus the culture industry becomes an advertising industry by its nature, because maintaining the economic system depends on maintaining economic demand. Economic demand can be maintained only by a transfiguration and control of the psyches of the masses of men. Art becomes degraded to propaganda, without Benjamin's redemptive possibilities.⁶⁷

The second task of the culture industry is the basis for the first. The industry must maintain itself and thereby maintain the system

65. Ibid., p. 275.
66. Adorno and Horkheimer, *Dialectic of Enlightenment*, p. 163.
67. In this process, the cultural needs of the consumer are themselves conditioned by the producer. Adorno, *Introduction to the Sociology of Music*, p. 199.

it is a part of. It does this by abolishing the distinction between the cultural product and life. Life becomes like a movie, and movies tend to recapitulate life.[68] In this way, no room is allowed for the critical impulse. Through the complex of presentations of what already exists in the form of movies and commercials, the culture industry promulgates a vast imitativeness. All wish to buy the products; all wish to live as the movies and television shows portray life.

The desire for imitativeness is not new; it derives from the mimetic urges that lurk at the core of the structure of myth itself. What is new—and to the Frankfurt School pernicious—is the affirmation of the social structure that lurks behind the current imitativeness.[69] The man who wished to imitate the Greek myths conceived of himself as divine and thereby set himself against the existent social structure. However, the desire to imitate the life of a movie star, both as a lifestyle and as the consumer of particular products, is not negative but the utter affirmation of what is. The current imitativeness creates cravings that are the essence of the social structure. The culture industry has taken the aesthetic and castrated it; the remainder stands as an affirmation of that which denatured it.

Politically, this means that the culture industry precludes the development of any consciousness that might threaten its continued functioning. Formally everyone is free, but the informal structure violates cultural and political freedom:

> Everybody is guaranteed formal freedom. No one is officially responsible for what he thinks. Instead, everyone is enclosed at an early age in a system of churches, clubs, professional associations and other such concerns, which constitute the most sensitive instrument of social control.[70]

In a way, this analysis is quite similar to Tocqueville's understanding of America. What differentiates it from Tocqueville, among other things, is that behind the social institutions of affirmation lurk the technological means for assuring that a revolt against society is not merely painful but effectively and literally unthinkable.

68. Adorno and Horkheimer, *Dialectic of Enlightenment*, p. 126.
69. Ibid., p. 131.
70. Ibid., p. 149.

The Crisis of Art and Culture

Just as there is no room between Positivism and ontology for an alternative, or between the utterly abstracted and utterly realistic work of art, so there is no room for an alternative in the cultural realm created by the culture industry. Marcuse writes:

> The unification of opposites which characterizes the commercial and political style is one of the many ways in which discourse and communication make themselves immune against the expression of protest and refusal. How can such protest and refusal find the right word when the organs of the established order admit and advertise that peace is really the brink of war? ... In exhibiting its contradictions as the token of its truth, this universe of discourse closes itself against any other discourse which is not on its own terms.[71]

The structure of cultural dissemination is so supple in its ability to control discourse that it leaves no space for things outside its grasp to intrude.

It can deny entry into discourse by the simplest means: denying access to the medium of communication. Such crude tactics as outright censorship are not necessary. It can be completely tolerant and allow the most blatant opposition to speak its piece. The culture industry, having worked the ground well, has already created a mass consciousness that will reject the extraordinary as the obvious sign of madness.[72] Neither must the culture industry fear what the critic hurls against it; all that is in the critic was put there by the culture industry. The area of discourse has already been so manipulated by the culture industry that anything authentically negative has been precluded. Indeed, the very structure of art, and the structure of modern rationality as well, tend to rule out the possibility of a statement that would be authentically and radically negative in either structure or content.

If such an event did take place, by definition it would fail. The system is elastic enough to co-opt any criticism. Because of what it is and what it controls, the culture industry can adopt the stance of any opposition, disseminate it, make it its own, and thereby render it harmless.[73] This co-optation of opposition is the ultimate defense

---

71. Marcuse, *One-Dimensional Man*, p. 90.
72. Marcuse, "Repressive Tolerance," in *A Critique of Pure Tolerance*, p. 95.
73. Marcuse, *One-Dimensional Man*, pp. 22–48, 90.

of the culture industry. It is a defense, however, rooted in the nature of modern culture. Culture, predicated on technology, has lost its very negativity because of the nature of that technology. All opposition would seem doomed to failure.

In a way, the culture industry is actually not in control of itself. Its task is to disseminate the work of art in an age of mechanical reproduction; as such it is a response to the technological imperatives inherent in such reproducibility. As Adorno and Horkheimer put it, "The industry submits to the vote which it has itself inspired."[74] It is a prisoner of the technology that created it. Even if it wished to create a negative culture and annihilate itself, it is not clear that it could; technology demands an industry, and an industry has imperatives beyond its intentions. Similarly, having created a demand or, rather, having given content to a demand created by technology, industry is not clearly able to cease catering to what it created.

The inability of the culture industry to do anything beyond what it is already doing is symptomatic of the underlying crisis of culture: like reason, the dialectic failed to move beyond affirmation. Adorno notes that "attempts to break the monopolies by spontaneity and a refusal to make artistic concessions have never broken anyone but the performing artist."[75] This is not accidental. It appears to the Frankfurt School that the crisis is precisely in that no one can break the stranglehold of affirmative culture.

The dialectical cul-de-sac has three aspects in relation to culture. The first, and most profound, is the crisis of the work of art itself. Art has been placed in an untenable position. Technology has destroyed its essential authenticity and autonomy. It can no longer stand by itself as the mediation of beauty but is dependent on things outside itself. The mass, the social circumstance created by art, makes art dependent upon politics or politics upon it. In either case, art loses its essence; it must deny its beauty by promulgating fascist horror, or it must deny its negativity by affirming the existent social structure. The work of art has dialectically lost its previous stance, but it does not dialectically create a new moment that would allow it to remain art.

The second crisis arises from the first, the crisis of culture in

---

74. Adorno and Horkheimer, *Dialectic of Enlightenment*, p. 134.
75. Adorno, *Introduction to the Sociology of Music*, p. 200.

The Crisis of Art and Culture

general. Culture itself becomes affirmative. Worse, through the loss of its aesthetic components and institutional and political imperatives, it becomes mediocre. Culture, rather than constituting consciousness, stands as the denial of consciousness. It stands as the empty recitation of the slogan, since recitation is the only task left for it after the failure of art. The status of modern culture represents a deadend for human consciousness. And precisely its emptiness gives it an utter resiliency, making it essentially immune to opposition through a combination of strength and absorptive ability.

Finally, there is the crisis of institutions. The culture industry stands as an institutional superstructure over the technological transformation of art and culture. Responding to the rationalized imperatives of any bureaucratic structure, as well as to the rationality of support for the economic and political system as a whole, the culture industry is impregnable against either a cultural or political assault.

Each of these crises grows out of the crisis of the Enlightenment, which inevitably created the circumstances that enervated the aesthetic. Its child, technology, transfigured art beyond existence. And its crisis—its own desire for affirmative identity and its own positing of a problematic to which it could internally conjure no solution—served as the format and substructure for the crisis of the cultural dialectic.

With culture as it had with reason, the Frankfurt School faced the possibility that history itself had failed. A circumstance had been created that was insoluble and yet inhuman and unbearable. The emptiness of modern culture dehumanized the social circumstances of existence. Yet the perpetual maintenance of the situation seemed not merely conceivable but probable, inasmuch as reason itself could posit no effective solution. The crisis of culture threatened the infinite perpetuation of the utterly inhuman. The Frankfurt School, however, perceived an even more profound, though dialectically connected, crisis: the crisis of the human psyche itself. The problem of art was the objective side of the problem of the subject.

12. The Crisis of the Human Psyche

Lukács' concern with the problem of reified consciousness points to a critical ambivalence within Marxism. Officially Marxist orthodoxy relagates psychic problems to a secondary status. Yet, both Marx and his later followers were concerned with the problem of the historical function and the ontic structure of the psyche. The problem of psychic alienation (the alienation of man from himself) was the critical ground of Marx's later work; the loss of species-being turned Marx toward his later, more extensive, political and economic work. Even as late as *Das Kapital*, there remained a psychic problem for Marx. Commodity fetishism, which Marx saw as the private motor behind capital accumulation, was a central and utterly psychic dimension in the development of his economic theory.[1] Nevertheless, the psychic side of the historical remained for Marx a secondary if important realm in relation to economics; it never blocked the way either to revolution or to Communism. Marx believed that when objective economic conditions had developed to a sufficient point, the concomitant development of psychic (as well as physical) suffering would force a revolutionary consciousness upon the proletariat. And as man conquered nature, alienation and thus psychopathology would also be abolished.

Two things changed the psychic dimension from an important but soluble concern to the critical problem of the age. Lenin noted the first crisis of the psychic: the failure of the consciousness of the proletariat to keep pace with the development of objective contradictions in the socioeconomic and political spheres. As capitalism and alienation (although this was not a side that Lenin

1. Marx, *Capital*, 1:71–73.

The Crisis of the Human Psyche

himself considered) worked themselves to their heights, the proletariat failed to develop a consciousness suitable to the revolutionary task before them. While history continued to develop in the material spheres, consciousness failed to keep pace autonomously.

Second, and perhaps more significant, neither the conquest of nature in the advanced industrial countries nor the conquest of power by socialist parties succeeded in transforming the psychic structures of those who lived under their auspices. In the West, the conquest of nature and the abolition of the conditions that created scarcity did not lead to the abolition of alienation. On the contrary, as the objective economic conditions developed, the subjective appreciation and experience of the psychic possibilities inherent in the circumstance seemed to diminish. In the socialist bloc, the conquest of political power lead neither to political freedom nor to a reordering of the psychic constructs of the inhabitants.

In both camps, reification of consciousness was the overriding reality. In the West, the development of the consumption economy, with its corollary fetishization of commodities so developed (albeit contrary to Marx's predictions) that the range of psychic possibilities available to men was actually narrowed. In the East, narrow philistinism, coupled with a commodity fetishism at least as virulent as the West's, became the order of the day.

Clearly, something had gone wrong with the development of the consciousness of the masses. Neither the seizure of political power, nor the conquest of nature, nor even the development of objective economic contradictions, propelled the development of human consciousness forward. The task of the revolution was not simply to seize power nor even to equalize the distribution of property; the revolution had to create a new existential condition that would touch not merely the physical conditions of existence but also the very core of being, the psychic.

The failure of history to replace the alienation of the past with a new mode of psychic existence was the primary concern of the Frankfurt School. In the end, the psychic was their crucial concern for the same reason that Marx saw psychic transformation as the end of history. It was on the psychic level that men as men experienced even their most external physical experience. It was by the mediation of such experience through consciousness that history worked itself out. Most important, it was in the innermost psychic realm that historical liberation would be realized. The success of human endeavors in the social, political, and even economic realms constituted, therefore, merely the penultimate moment of the millennium. The ultimate moment came with the transformation not of the external circumstances but of the very ontology of man. The failure of psychic liberation, as the psychic clung to outmoded and unnecessary modes of repressed existence in the face of awesome historical possibilities, formed the core of the historical dilemma for the Frankfurt School.

In order to explain the failure of psychic liberation—that is, in order to understand how a dehumanized culture industry could maintain itself and its consciousness—it was necessary to go beyond Marx. Marx, with his fundamental faith in history's ability to resolve itself, found it unnecessary to delve too deeply into the formal structure of consiousness. He dealt explicitly with the psychic dimension only where it impinged directly on the working out of economic and political problems (as with commodity fetishism) or where the general outlines of the problem would suffice (as with alienation). Similarly, he failed to give an effective definition of a nonpathological psyche. The failure of history to work itself out—the perpetuation of psychopathology as the normal mode of psychic existence—forced the Frankfurt School to turn to Freud, whose speciality was the pathology rather than the teleology of history.

The Frankfurt School (with Marcuse doing the most extensive work in the area) turned to Freud for three reasons. First, the turn to Freud gave them a formal psychological structure to work with (and to criticize). Through this formal structure, they were able to schematize their own, as well as Marx's, analysis of alieniation. Second, through Freud's structure and through his analysis of psychopathology (of both civilizations and individuals), they gained an understanding of the problem of both mass society and the failure of the dialectical development of consciousness. Finally, through Freud's formal structure, they deepened the possibilities of psychic liberation. Embedded in Freud's metapsychology, in opposition to his explicit historical pessimism, was the possibility of a profound transformation in the structure of the psyche, if certain historical possibilities, such as the abolition of scarcity, were attained. To Freud, such an achievement was inconceivable; to the Frankfurt School, it was the essence of the historical reality. Thus, from Freud, they paradoxically achieved a deeper belief in the potential depths of psychic liberation.

Of the explicit teachings of Freud, the point that the Frankfurt School accepted most completely was the notion of the pleasure principle as the governing element of human existence.[2] To Freud, the basic intention of any organism was the attainment of pleasure and the avoidance of pain: "As we see, what decides the purpose of life is simply the programme of the pleasure principle. This principle dominates the operation of the mental apparatus from the start."[3] To Freud, the initial dimension of pleasure was sensual. Later and more refined modes of pleasuring merely represented the sublimation of the earlier, more direct experience. As with Hobbes, however, the desire for pleasure encountered a hostile world. Freud continues:

> There can be no doubts about its efficacy, and yet its programme is at loggerheads with the whole world, with the macrocosm as much as with the microcosm. There is no possibility at all of its being carried through; all the refutations of the universe run counter to it. One feels inclined to say that the intention that man should be "happy" is not included in the plan of "Creation."[4]

Against the intrinsic pleasure principle, the hostile world forces the creation of an exogenous reality principle.[5] For Freud, the irreconcilable antimony between these two principles—the first bent upon pleasure and the second content with mere survival in a cruel world—was the essence of the human condition.

Marcuse acknowledges the centrality of this antimony:

> The replacement of the pleasure principle by the reality principle is the great traumatic event in the development of man—in the development of the genus (phylogenesis) as well as of the individual (ontogenesis).[6]

But, while accepting Freud's view here, they take issue with him on a number of other crucial points.

In the first place, they reject the affirmative character of Freud's

2. Horkheimer, *Geschichte und Psychologie*, p. 129.
3. Freud, *Civilization and Its Discontents*, p. 23.
4. Ibid., p. 23.
5. Ibid., p. 14.
6. Marcuse, *Eros and Civilization*, p. 14.

psychotherapeutic method. To the Frankfurt School, the thread running though this method was the reconciliation of the individual with society's expectations, however corrupt those expectations might be. Adorno writes; "The 'good Freudian' uninhibited by repressions would, in the existing acquisitive society, be almost indistinguishable from the hungry beast of prey."[7] Further, "Psychoanalytic practice, which claims on paper to heal even neurosis, collaborates with the universal and long-standing practice of depriving men of love and happiness in favour of hard work and a healthy sex life."[8] Repeating the standard Marxist argument against Freud, Adorno complains that the Freudian method looks for the roots of psychosis and neurosis only in the individual's maladjustment to society and never in inequities within the social order.

The positions of Freud and the Frankfurt School reflect their different historical conceptions. Freud sees the competition for scarce resources exerting a harsh discipline on the human race. Society originates in this perpetual hostility. Men band together, following the slaying of the primal father, to struggle against the scarcity inherent in nature. For survival, society demands that its members systematically repress the asocial tendencies of the pleasure principle. The pleasure principle (Eros in general), is inherently subversive. Men gripped by the pleasure principle wish gratification regardless of the real deprivation found in their social or natural circumstances. Since Eros is rooted in nature and not history, the demand by society that the individual repress the pleasure principle is not, to Freud, unreasonable. Indeed it is the essence of rationality. Freud argues that it is this conflict that gives rise to neurosis and psychosis; they are the price men pay for survival. Thus psychotherapy's effort to reconcile man to the expectations of society is not unreasonable, but simply man's fate.

To the Frankfurt School, however, scarcity is historical and not natural.[9] The scarcity of the world is precisely the evil that reason, technology, and Enlightenment have set themselves to wipe out. To Freud, perpetual scarcity in nature is the basis of the perpetual instinctual structure of man. Eliminating the assumption of perma-

---

7. Adorno, *Sociology and Psychology*, 2:84.
8. Adorno, *Sociology and Psychology*, 1:80.
9. Marcuse, *Eros and Civilization*, pp. 120–21; Horkheimer, *Geschichte und Psychologie*, pp. 133–34.

nence opens up Freud's system to the possibility of the complete and revolutionary transformation of the psychic structure itself.

Because of this, the Frankfurt School rejects Freud's underlying assumption concerning labor. To Freud, labor is painful even when it is dialectically therapeutic: "As a path to happiness, work is not highly prized by men. They do not strive after it as they do after other possibilities of satisfaction. The great majority of people only work under the stress of necessity, and this natural human aversion to work raises most difficult social problems."[10] In order to labor, man must have energy, something that he has only in finite quantities. Libidinous energy, if the instincts were to remain utterly unimpeded by external reality, would naturally move to satisfy the demands of the id; that is, the pleasure principle would rule. It is the reality principle that diverts libido away from immediate gratification to postponed gratification, or mere survival. The catastrophic truth for the organism is that the world will never allow perpetual gratification. Gratification is available in miniscule amounts only by mediation through inherently painful labor. To Freud, play (that is, gratificatory activity) is a perpetually unfulfilled promise of this world. To the Frankfurt School, play will become the highest principle, which must be fulfilled if the suffering of the past is to have any meaning.[11]

The early Freud considered that where the organism was confronted with the perpetual block to the realization of its erotic potential, it turned to the thantotic—to the death wish.[12] The organism, having failed to achieve pleasure and facing its absolute opposite in labor, chooses surcease. The instincts, facing a perpetuation of suffering, prefer self-annihilation through a seemingly precise hedonistic calculus. In this early formulation of Freud's, the death instinct is not autonomous but rather derives from the failure of the erotic instincts. Later Freud hypostasized that the death instinct is an autonomous element in order to explain the perpetuation of war.[13]

The Frankfurt School rejects the later formulation of Freud as being utterly undialectical.[14] There is a further, simpler, reason for

10. Freud, *Civilization and Its Discontents*, p. 27.
11. Marcuse, *Eros and Civilization*, pp. 170–72.
12. Freud, *Three Contributions to the Theory of Sex*, pp. 21–24.
13. Freud, *Beyond the Pleasure Principle*, p. 51.
14. Adorno, *Sociology and Psychology*, 2:80–81.

this rejection: if the autonomy of the thanatotic is accepted, then there is no hope of creating a utopia. The perpetuity of the death wish, manifested socially in war, would block any transfiguration of the psychic structure of man. Only by regarding the death wish as dialectically derivative could the possibility of transforming the psyche be considered real. Thus the Frankfurt School siezes on the earlier formulations of the death wish in order to use Freud to reveal psychic possibilities. The early Freud held that the abolition of scarcity would mean the abolition of labor, which in turn would mean the end of suffering and the abolition of the desire of the human organism for death. Under those conditions the possibilities for psychic transformation are profound.

Marcuse begins his analysis of labor with a Freudian analysis of man and of man's instinctual structure. Like Freud, he sees man as having one primary drive, the pleasure principle, and a number of derivative drives that result from the interaction of man with external reality. Thus the primary instinct of man is erotic, inasmuch as his primary motive is the search for pleasure and gratification. Similarly, labor has its roots in the erotic, as a manifestation of the pleasure principle: "Man begins working because he finds pleasure in work, not only after work, pleasure in the play of his faculties and the fulfillment of his life needs, not as the means of life, but as life itself. Man begins the cultivation of nature and of himself, cooperation, in order to secure and perpetuate the gaining of pleasure."[15] Thus, although Marcuse's analysis begins with a Freudian conception of man as a being seeking pleasure, he goes far beyond Freud. Starting with Freud's dichotomy between instinct and reality, Marcuse moves beyond him by rooting labor in the erotic instincts, rather than making it simply the necessary and painful mediation between man and a hostile world.

The very beginning of Marcuse's analysis indicates the systematic transformation of Freudianism from a fundamentally pessimistic view of the human condition into a fundamentally optimistic view of the possibility of liberation. This will be accomplished, first, by making Thanatos derivative of Eros and, then, by making labor potentially gratifying although historically painful. By questioning the painfulness of all forms of labor—that is, by subjecting Freud to

15. Marcuse, *Five Lectures*, pp. 11–12.

The Crisis of the Human Psyche

an historical analysis—Marcuse goes beyond Freud to a new level of thought and to new possibilities of psychic and existential liberation.

In analyzing the role of labor in all forms of existence hitherto experienced (importantly excluding the primal form before to the beginning of human history), Marcuse does accept the outline of Freud's system. The starting point of Freud's metapsychology, and therefore of Marcuse's vision of previous forms of existence, is the contradiction between the pleasure and reality principles. Where the id previously demanded immediate gratification, the ego, the level upon which the reality principle operates, repressed the id's demands and channeled libidinous energy away from sexual gratification toward the performance of the labor that was necessary merely to survive. Thus, the demands of life required that the life instincts be restructured in a way that would desexualize man: "Originally the organism in its totality and in all its activities and relationships is a potential field for sexuality, dominated by the pleasure principle. And precisely for this reason it must be desexualized in order to carry out unpleasurable work, in order, in fact, to live in a context of unpleasurable work."[16] The demands of life require that the most profound of human pleasures, the sexual, be transformed and the energies devoted to it be rechanneled in order to make life in a hostile universe at least possible. Any good life remains beyond the reach of men; only mere life is available. To allow the sexual to flourish would be to raise the possibility of the organism's death.

This diversion of energy from pleasure and into labor, although made necessary by the historical circumstances of man's existence, is nonetheless profoundly repressive. Instead of the pleasure that life seemed to promise the id, nature has dictated that labor should form the essence of the human condition, labor, which is repressing gratification sustains life only through pain. Thus labor, in becoming the essential moment of existence, turns life into an essentially painful process.[17]

Domination by the reality principle, however, is never quite secure; the human psyche is defined by the perpetual struggle between

---

15. Marcuse, *Five Lectures*, pp. 11–12.
16. Ibid., pp. 8–9.
17. Marcuse, *Eros and Civilization*, pp. 11–14.

the need for gratification and the need for labor, between id and ego:

> The unconscious retains the objectives of the defeated pleasure principle. Turned back by the external reality or even unable to reach it, the full force of the pleasure principle not only survives in the unconscious but also affects in manifold ways the very reality which has superseded the pleasure principle. The *return of the repressed* makes up the tabooed and subterranean history of civilization.[18]

It is this revenge of the repressed upon existence that Benjamin sees as the historical role of the proletariat: its task is to redeem the suffering of the past, which had to taboo the pleasures it craved.[19] Similarly, Adorno and Horkheimer see the reemergence of myth and of the tabooed despite the best efforts of the Enlightenment—indeed, as the result of the Enlightenment, as the Enlightenment itself—as resulting from the craving of the repressed for reaffirmation, even in the face of reification.[20] Indeed, for Adorno and Horkheimer, modern morality, epitomized by the Marquis de Sade, originates in this revenge of the repressed mediated through the structure of alienation: "Juliette embodies (in psychological terms) neither unsublimated nor regressive libido, but intellectual pleasure in regression—*amor intellectualis diaboli*, the pleasure of attacking civilization with its own weapons."[21] The dialectical movement between repression and revenge is the essence of the Frankfurt School's historic-psychological conception. It is also the basis of bourgeois morality. Unlike Jane Austen, de Sade is fully bourgeois, inasmuch as he captures the revanchist dimension of that which has been repressed under the surface of manners. De Sade represents the bourgeois reality of this return of the repressed. That which had to be put aside lurks to revenge itself upon what had to be. The crisis is not in the return of the repressed, for the return is liberating; rather, the crisis is in the inability of the repressed to manifest itself. The problem is in the eternal selfmaintainance of repression.

To Marcuse and the Frankfurt School, human existence is a cycle within a progression; implicit in the perpetual overcoming of nature, which necessitated the repression of the id and the redirection

---

18. Ibid., p. 15.
19. Benjamin, "Theses on the Philosophy of History," in *Illuminations*, pp. 253–55, 258.
20. Adorno and Horkheimer, *Dialectic of Enlightenment*, pp. 92–98.
21. Ibid., p. 94.

The Crisis of the Human Psyche

of libidinous activity from sexuality to labor, is the cyclical recurrence of the demands of the pleasure principle. The conflict within man is the conflict between human progress and the resultant human cycle. This cycle could never come to rest, could never realize its goal of pleasure, as long as the progress of man's struggle against nature remains the dominant theme of human existence. The painfulness of labor can never be reconciled to the possibilities of pleasure, as long as labor remains rooted in struggle against the world and as long as the world continues to require man to struggle against it. This opposition remained merely tragic as long as nature remained unsubdued; it was simply the unchanging nature of the human condition. The tragedy became inhuman when the struggle became unnecessary.

Marcuse traces the thanatotic drive to the painful relationship between man and nature, as does early Freud. The id, unable to achieve positive gratification (pleasure) seeks instead the negative gratification of nirvana; it seeks the peaceful nothingness of the womb in order to avoid the pain entailed by life. But regression—either biological or historical, either to the womb or to the period preceding the emergence of the species (to an *Ur*-existence)—is physically impossible. Thus, since the id cannot seek the quiescence of the womb and society cannot repeat the mythical peacefulness of prehistory, the organism searches for peace in the certainty of death. If the erotic tendencies in man cannot be fulfilled, then the thanatotic solution is all that is left for man, both as an individual and as civilization. War, suffering, and death must all find their source in the repression necessitated by nature.[22]

The problem of civilization is to harness the death instinct in a way that will bring it into the service of civilization. Thus the definitive problem of human existence is to reconcile the life and the death instincts. The tension is resolved in civilization by harnessing thanatos in the service of Eros and by transforming the expression of eros into a form of thanatos. That is, the death instinct, instead of giving vent to its destructive urges by destroying life, is redirected toward the subjugation of nature. Death serves Eros through forcing nature to gratify the organism's needs. The satisfaction of the erotic is gained not through gratification but subjugation.[23] Thus

---

22. This is the position of the early Freud.
23. Horkheimer sees this in man's conquest of nature and nature's consequent revolt; *Eclipse of Reason,* pp. 92–127.

labor was not a means to satiety, but a redirection of man's self-aggression outward against nature. The purpose of labor was to serve Thanatos, and Thanatos was in the service of Eros. As Marcuse puts it, "In limiting Eros to the partial function of sexuality and making the destructive instinct useful, the individual becomes, in his very nature, the subject—object of socially useful labor, of the domination of men and nature."[24] Thus the presence of the death instinct distorts the purpose of labor, moving it from gratification (both in and of itself and as a means to procure the external, gratificatory objects) toward domination.

Domination of nature is one form of this general movement toward domination. Manifesting itself through technology, which in turn grows out of the Enlightenment in general, the domination of nature by technology is designed to procure gratification from nature for man. However, free and unfettered gratification would result in the weakening of the death instinct; the attainment of gratification reduces the organism's craving for nirvana. The concord between Eros and Thanatos was based upon the respect of each for the autonomy of the other. Only in this concord could the organism preserve itself without self-destruction. The pent-up, self-destructive urges could be redirected toward nature but could never simply be abolished. The technology that had been created through the concord of Eros and Thanatos was allowed to serve only the most minor of erotic impulses: that of survival. The bulk of its energy was turned to domination.

Technology thus becomes an end in itself. However, it supplies not erotic gratification but thanatotic. Thanatos' grantification is rooted in the domination that technology makes possible over nature. The pleasure in technology arises not so much from its immediate benefits as from the sheer act of domination. Under those circumstances the work of technology, apart from the minimum effort required for human survival, is to perpetuate itself as a form of domination: the highest end of technology is technology itself. The needs of technology take precedence over the needs of man. The outward projection of Thanatos is mediated through technology and then redirected inward, toward man. Thanatos cannot completely dominate man because of the strength of the erotic, but its power is manifested in sublimated form in the domination of

24. Marcuse, *Five Lectures*, pp. 11–12.

The Crisis of the Human Psyche

men by the technology that is the concretization of the historical compromise of the two psychic principles.

Human society, in service to Thanatos, becomes organized about the requirements of technology. Not the efficient use of the machine to serve human needs but the efficient use of the machine in itself becomes the organizing principle of society. Man comes to be defined not by his service to himself but by his service to the machine and its abstraction, the economic system. Just as life required sexuality to be sublimated so that the organism might survive, the death instinct requires labor to become its subsidiary in service to domination so that the power of death might be aggrandized. Eros was reluctantly forced to see unfettered gratification as destructive to the organism. The inevitable by-product of repression was the domination by death of society. Thanatos avidly embraced labor as and end in itself. Gratification is the mortal enemy of the death instinct. Thus the presence of the death instinct results in man's enslavement to his own labor and to the institutions and machines that he created to facilitate his labor.[25]

Freud would have found the use of this analysis as an indictment of a particular historical epoch meaningless. To him scarcity was a transhistorical truth, the perpetual reality of the human condition. If scarcity is not inevitable, however—if abundance is a human possibility—then the transhistorical truth of his entire instinctual system is shattered. The instincts would then define man only relative to the level of production in any particular historical epoch. Thus coupling Marx's view of the possibility of abundance for all at the end of history with Freud's theory of instincts opens the way for fundamental changes to be made in the human condition. Freud's pessimism, mediated through Marx, becomes optimism.

Coupling Freud and Marx is precisely what Marcuse in particular, and the Frankfurt School in general, does. The modern view of labor as an end in itself is not the theoretically inevitable form of existence; the present reality does not represent the sole potential form of the reality principle for man. Rather, the present represents a particular form of existence—a form peculiar to this historical epoch. The principle of this epoch is the performance principle, and not merely the reality principle.

There is a dialectic at work in history and within the individual

---

25. Marcuse, "On Hedonism," in *Negations,* pp. 185–87.

himself that tends to go beyond mere reality and its demands to the underlying principles. Marcuse writes:

> We have seen that Freud's theory is focused on the recurrent cycle 'domination-rebellion-domination'. But the second domination is not simply a repetition of the first one; the cyclical movement is progress in domination. From the primal father via the brother clan to the system of institutional authority characteristic of mature civilization, domination becomes increasingly impersonal, objective, universal, and also increasingly rational, effective, productive. At the end, under the rule of the fully developed performance principle, subordination appears as implemented through the social division of labor itself.... Society emerges as a lasting and expanding system of useful performances; the hierarchy of functions and relationships assumes the form of objective reason.[26]

A certain amount of repression is necessary in order to maintain life. Both the repression of the id by the ego and the repression of anarchic elements by social institutions are required if a society and its individuals are to survive.

As the reality principle turns itself into the performance principle, however, necessary repression turns itself into surplus repression. The repression, which was necessary, created a desire in the individual for nirvana; this nirvana principle manifested itself socially in the self-destructive impulses of the social organism. Survival demanded that the self-directed aggressions of society be re-directed against nature. The result was nature's subjugation and the end of scarcity.[27] Under these circumstances, repression ceases to be a necessary component of the reality principle. Neither the repressive division of labor nor the overwhelming repression of the id are required. Still, they continue.

As in the Enlightenment and in culture, the psyche of the organism paid a price for its success against nature. Man's existence was conditioned by the manner in which he was forced to achieve his goal of freedom from want. Until the conquest of nature, the demand for performance was rationally identical with reality: the human organism had to perform in order to survive. Performance acted out as aggression against nature was reasonable under the circumstance. Thanatos, however, became equal to Eros, and

---

26. Marcuse, *Eros and Civilization*, p. 81.
27. Ibid., p. 3.

The Crisis of the Human Psyche

thanatotic social institutions do not give up simply because they have completed their task. Having achieved autonomy, they seek to maintain themselves. The performance principle ceases to be identical with reality. It becomes irrational; that is, it goes beyond the requirements of the human condition. Repression ceases to be identical with the necessary and becomes surplus-repression.[28] As Marcuse puts it, "Objectively, the need for instinctual inhibition and restraint depends on the need for toil and delayed satisfaction. The same and even a reduced scope of instinctual regimentation would constitute a higher degree of repression at a mature stage of civilization, when the need for renunciation and toil is greatly reduced by material and intellectual progress."[29] Nonetheless, the hierarchy of instincts and the division of labor do not let go. Repression, once created, tends to maintain itself.

The transformed nature of reality nevertheless gives man the possibility of going beyond the performance principle. At the same time, the possibility of going beyond the performance principle results in the need to do so. Marcuse here is essentially Hegelian in maintaining that the highest good is freedom—not freedom in the sense of the mere absence of coercion, but in the sense of fully realized potential. The performance principle is outmoded precisely because new forms of existence are now possible. In Freudian terms, the performance principle must be rejected because it is based on the social organization's attempts to deny gratification by means of a repressive organization of the instinctual structure.

Thus an affinity between Freud and Hegel is apparent. To Hegel, the fulfillment of human potential is the highest good: this, objectively if not subjectively, is the source of human happiness. For Hegel, happiness is not psychological in nature. It is the realization of potential. Freud, approaching happiness from the opposite direction, claims that gratification, psychological happiness, is the organism's end. Marcuse, taking Freud beyond his historical pessimism, claims that the highest level of gratification possible is bound up with human freedom. Thus a unity is forged between freedom, the realization of potential, and subjective happiness.

> The concrete form of human freedom determines the form of human happiness. Comprehension of the connection between happiness and

---

28. Ibid., pp. 78–86.
29. Ibid., pp. 80–81.

freedom was already expressed in the ancient critique of hedonism. Happiness, as the fulfillment of all potentialities of the individual, presupposes freedom: at root, it is freedom.[30]

The objectification of happiness, which links it with the notion of the full realization of human potential, the attainment of gratification, creates a significant tension within Marcuse's system: assuming a person to be subjectively happy, why ought he be forced beyond psychological satisfaction?

Marcuse concedes that man, even under the performance principle, experiences subjective happiness.[31] But he asserts that a fundamental objectivity is applicable to happiness. The problem remains essentially as the radical hedonists posed it: happiness, being by its very nature subjective, is incapable of being judged objectively. Only by invoking the Hegelian distinction between appearance and reality can the real subjective experience be declared unreal or trivial. Only through asserting the superficiality of the subjective can one speak of it as being unreal.

Yet, subjective happiness is quite real in the only sense in which happiness as happiness *in and of itself* can be judged: the subject declares it to be pleasant. It is only by linking happiness to other phenomena, freedom and fulfillment, that happiness can be objectively judged. However, linking happiness to other criteria robs it of its essence, its profound and singular relationship to the subject. By objectifying happiness, happiness is eviscerated; it becomes secondary and subject to other criteria. Thus the unity is not one of equals but the subjugation of happiness to other values. Marcuse hurls precisely this charge at the idealistic concept of happiness.[32] Yet by repeating the linkage between the three concepts (happiness, freedom, fulfillment) he repeats the crime. The assertion that happiness is real based upon the full realization of potential is vitiated by its manner of becoming; the process of revolution is imposed and not dialectically developed out of the subject's self-realized inadequacy. Indeed, the revolution can even come in the guise of repression.[33]

This movement from autonomous gratification to gratification linked to exogenous criteria is by no means accidental. It cuts to the

30. Marcuse, "On Hedonism," in *Negations*, p. 180.
31. Marcuse, *Eros and Civilization*, pp. 90–91.
32. Marcuse, "On Hedonism," pp. 159–62; Adorno, *Minima Moralia*, p. 97.
33. Marcuse, *Repressive Tolerance*, pp. 81–82.

The Crisis of the Human Psyche

heart of the psychic dilema. On the one hand: "The high standard of living in the domain of the great corporations is restrictive in a concrete sociological sense: the goods and services that the individuals buy control their needs and petrify their faculties."[34] On the other hand, men don't know it, and they remain subjectively gratified.

The psychic dialectic has encountered two dilemmas. First, the development of Thanatos, necessary as it was, created conditions under which it cannot be abolished. The power of the death instinct as the ruling principle of society is such that it cannot be readily abolished. Indeed, to attempt to abolish it would be to risk abolishing its redirection, allowing it to act directly and brutally upon men; the eternal return of the repressed is not applicable only to the erotic. The second problem derives from the first. The effectiveness of the repression is so powerful that men fail to realize their oppression subjectively: they do not feel oppressed. They are not moved to change their situation. Thus the dialectic cannot proceed. Just as Benjamin turns to the exogenous, to the Messiah, so Marcuse must turn to the exogenous—in this case, to the exogenous concept of objective happiness.

The root of the crisis is in the rational subjugation of the passions, which was the goal of the Enlightenment itself, and in the complex of physical and social technological mechanisms, which was the joint product of the Enlightenment and thanatos. It might be said that the direct by-product of the Enlightenment was man's death wish, to the extent that the Enlightenment intended a transfiguration not merely of nature but also of the human psyche itself.

The system intends to maintain itself both socially and personally. In order to maintain itself, society must create a situation in which the personal repressions are maintained. Thus it must create institutions that maintain the surplus repression characteristic of the performance principle. Maintaining this surplus repression demands an economic system that continues to call for labor even as labor becomes progressively unnecessary for survival. Having conquered nature, Thanatos wishes to maintain its domination of man. In order to do this, it manufactures a complex of false demands for consumption.[35] Thanatos creates the conditions for the perpetuation of labor. The system maintains itself by creating conditions for

---

34. Marcuse, *Eros and Civilization*, pp. 90–91.
35. Ibid., pp. 91–92.

maintaining the psychic structure in individuals on which the entire system is predicated. It does this through planned obsolescence and systematic advertising to create needs. A combination of artificial scarcity and false needs maintains a greater instinctual repression than was demanded of men before the conquest of nature. Even the apparent desublimation of the sexual mores of late capitalism is merely a facade behind which the products of sexuality can be sold and thus produced.[36]

The psychic crisis has a darker side as well:

> Assuming that the Destruction Instinct (in the last analysis: the Death Instinct) is a large component of the energy which feeds the technical conquest of man and nature it seems that society's growing capacity to manipulate technical progress also increases its capacity to manipulate and control this instinct, i.e., to satisfy it 'productively'. Then social cohesion would be strengthened at the deepest instinctual roots .... The supreme risk, and even the fact of war would meet, not only with helpless acceptance, but also with instinctual approval on the part of the victims.[37]

Modern society must come to terms more directly with the death instinct. Having completed the conquest of nature, society needs space upon which to work its aggression. The structure of the economy supplies one outlet, the false labor required to maintain the system, but even this is insufficient. Indeed, as technology progresses and as its sphere of power grows, greater repression than ever is required. Thus the death instinct wants blood: the literal blood of war. Marcuse sees the growing warfare of the West as no accident; it is simply the attempt of the socio-instinctual system to maintain itself through the systematic release of libido-thanatotic energy. In a sense, Nazis and anti-Nazis were equally entrapped in the same dialectic.

This psychic system maintains itself by employing all the means at its disposal. Economically, it is supported by the structure of late capitalism. The affluent society is the product of the repression of instincts mediated through the economic structure. In this structure, art either was expelled from the world by taking utterly abstract forms of it became a recapitulation of the world by simply depict-

36. Marcuse, *One-Dimensional Man*, pp. 74–77.
37. Ibid., p. 79.

ing its surfaces uncritically. Culturally, this de-eroticization of art turned the minds of men from criticism to affirmation—from the pleasures lost to those made economically available to them. Politically, the system of formal tolerance coupled with the systematic exclusion of criticism from the political order serves to prevent a catastrophic break in the structure of consciousness.

Most significantly, the system of surplus repression is self-maintained. It cannot free itself without releasing the complex of thanatotic energies that it has pent up since childhood of both the individual and the race. Just as, according to Benjamin, the world's becoming subject to art would have meant war, so the psyche becoming subject to id would mean war. The Enlightenment has created a profound psychic imbalance in its quest for domination. It is impossible simultaneously to enjoy the fruits of its victories (affluence) and to abolish its price (repression).

Thus man in late capitalism (and in industrialized socialism) faces a crisis. Securing what was essential for human survival resulted in a distortion of what was the psychic structure of men. The greater the subjugation of nature (and therefore the greater the possibilities for freedom from material want), the greater must be the technological and hierarchical structures that support the overcoming of nature. Thus the greater the potential for liberation from material want, the less possible is freedom from psychic distortion. The greater the possibility for liberation of a desublimated psyche in which unnecessary repression is utterly excluded, the less likely is its realization.

The root of the crisis is in the Enlightenment itself; the end point is in the human mind. And with this crisis, the general crisis of history—its failure to move beyond itself—becomes all the more urgent. If there is a solution, it can be found only through the rediscovery of the subversive possibilities of the erotic: in the return of the repressed.

13. The Crisis of History

Each of the preceding three chapters in Part II detailed various aspects of what the Frankfurt School considers the overarching crisis: the crisis of history. The crisis of the Enlightenment, of art and culture, and of the psyche, each critical in its own right, constituted alternative and complementary perspectives of the general crisis. This crisis was the failure of history to transcend itself—the freezing of history at an inhuman moment. As Marcuse puts it: "Nothing indicates that it [history] will be a good end. The economic and technical capabilities of the established societies are sufficiently vast to allow for adjustments and concessions to the underdog, and their armed forces sufficiently trained and equipped to take care of emergency situations."[1] History had reached a point of utter dehumanization. To the Frankfurt School, the most terrifying aspect of the situation was that it showed every sign of being able to maintain itself in perpetuity.

The awfulness can be seen in the collapse of freedom, as the universe of choice is closed off. Chapter 10 details the collapse of philosophical alternatives, as Positivism and Heideggerianism collaborated to close off the universe of authentic (that is, subversive and progressive) choices. Chapter 11 is concerned with the collapse of aesthetic alternatives under the joint assault of a technologized aesthetic and a monopolistic and bureaucratized culture industry. Art, the transcendentally subjective criticism of reality, was turned either into the recapitulation and affirmation of the existent or into

---

1. Marcuse, *One-Dimensional Man*, p. 257; also see Adorno, "Wird Spengler rechtbehalten," in *Kritik,* pp. 94–95, on the failure of the West's hold over itself to weaken even in decline; and Horkheimer, *Critical Theory*, p. vi.

The Crisis of History

a fraudulent abstraction from the concrete. Finally, Chapter 12 considered the collapse of the psychic alternatives, as the rise of the thanatotic principle demanded the systematic suppression of the authentic eroticism possible in human existence.

These three crisis were different aspects of the general crisis of human existence—in a deeper sense, a crisis of everyday life.[2] It is difficult to define the meaning of the crisis of everyday life; its essence, in a way, is in its aura. Just as the aura of the work of art is profoundly indescribable, except for its formal outline (which misses the point), so the aura of everyday life is undefinable. A sense of its meaning can be gleaned from the following passage from *Monuments of Humanity* by Adorno and Horkheimer on what is praiseworthy in everyday life:

> Humanity has always been more at home in France than elsewhere. But the French themselves were not aware of this. Their books simply contained the ideology which everyone already recognized. The better things in life still led a separate existence; the special tone of voice, the feats of gastronomy, the brothels and the cast-iron urinals. But the Blum government already opened an offensive against this respect for the individual, and even the conservatives did little to protect its monuments.[3]

There was something humane in everyday French existence. The humaneness rested in a sensibility toward the functions of existence. A urinal was permeated by the aura of beauty; even the inherently ugly possessed the sensibility of refinement. The sense of humanity was to be found in the regard of French things for the individuals involved. The sensibility of the individual, indeed, the sensibility that is the essence of the authentically self-conscious human being, finds its complement and reinforcement in the things that surround him. But the socialist government of Blum cleared the way for an attack on those sensibilities. What was lost was a sense of uniqueness; what was gained was a mass-produced hygiene. And even the conservatives (perhaps especially the conservatives) did nothing to save the monuments.

This individual sensibility was at the core of the Frankfurt

---

2. The phrase is taken from the title of an essay by Karl Klare, "The Critique of Everyday Life," in *Unknown Dimension*, pp. 3–33.
3. Adorno and Horkheimer, *Dialectic of Enlightenment*, p. 225.

School's concerns: they cared for the private spheres that stood in opposition to the world. Marcuse writes:

> The crime is that of a society in which the growing population aggravates the struggle for existence in the face of its possible alleviation. The drive for more 'living space' operates not only in international aggressiveness, but also within the nation. Here, expansion has, in all forms of teamwork, community life and fun, invaded the inner space of privacy and practically eliminated the possibility of that isolation in which the individual, thrown back on himself alone, can think and question and find.[4]

For the Frankfurt School, the essence of humanity is in its negativity, in its standing against the affirmations of everyday life, in the rejection of the demand to be a member of the group. The attack on this private sphere is the essence of the historical crisis. It is here that the other three crises have their final impact and deepest significance.

The crisis of everyday life is the crisis of the loss of the individual as a realm of sensibility and negativity. There is something profoundly conservative in the Frankfurt School's vision of this crisis. Indeed, Horkheimer writes:

> For the left to help the advance of a totalitarian bureaucracy is a pseudorevolutionary act, and for the right to support the tendency to terrorism is a pseudoconservative act. As recent history proves, both tendencies are really more closely related to each other than to the ideas to which they appeal for support. On the other hand, a true conservatism which takes man's spiritual heritage seriously is more closely related to the revolutionary mentality.[5]

Horkheimer uses the term 'spirituality'; it is an odd word for a Marxist to employ, unless one considers what Marxism's official opposition to spirituality has meant. Adorno and Horkheimer are wistful about the past; they sorrow not only for the failure of socialism to redeem its pledge but also for the failure of conservatism to maintain its heritage.

The immediate culprit in the assault on everyday life is technology, both in its mechanical and social aspect. As Horkheimer puts

4. Marcuse, *One-Dimensional Man*, p. 244.
5. Horkheimer, *Critical Theory*, pp. viii–ix.

The Crisis of History

it, "the dwindling away of individual thinking and resistance, as it is brought about by the economic and cultural mechanisms of modern industrialism, will render evolution toward the humane increasingly difficult."[6] The rise of technology is itself the problem. This has two sides to it. The first is the reification of consciousness and the objectification of life itself. The other is the potential for sheer terror inherent in the system.

Even in the best of circumstances, the significance of technology is its ability to inflict brute terror on the world. This, after all, was the relation of technology toward nature.[7] As an outgrowth of the thanatotic, technology could realize itself only through the logic of domination. But domination quickly turns to terror as the recalcitrant sensibility seeks to resist the incursion of reification.[8] Technology has not only the will, but also the ability to avenge itself upon man in the most brutal ways conceivable. The power of Nazi Germany rested not merely on the Nazi's will to hurt, but on the potential within technology (and within technology's own dynamic will) to inflict suffering through the rational organization of the social and physical mechanisms of terror.

The brutality of the technology of Nazi Germany was merely the most visible moment of totalitarian terror. It was the most blatant assault upon the private sphere, and for that reason, perhaps the most inefficient. Even when the blatancy of terror is cloaked, and its most primitive moment of brutality nonexistent, technology serves as a totalitarian assault upon the individual. Marcuse writes:

> Today this private space has been invaded and whittled down by technological reality. Mass production and mass distribution claim the entire individual, and industrial psychology has long since ceased to be confirmed to the factory. The manifold processes of introjection seem to be ossified in almost mechanical reactions. The result is not adjustment but mimesis: an immediate identification of the individual with his society.[9]

Although lacking the immediacy of violence, the technological intrudes upon man in such a was as to deny him his individuality and

---

6. Horkheimer, *Eclipse of Reason*, p. 156.
7. Ibid., p. 93.
8. Benjamin, *Zur Kritik der Gewalt*, pp. 47–50.
9. Marcuse, *One-Dimensional Man*, p. 10; Also see Horkheimer, *Eclipse of Reason*, p. 141.

privacy. From the first, the logic of mass production and mass consumption absorbed those who were the cogs of the machine. Production and consumption become tools for affirmation. From the logic of the assembly line to the logic of the advertising industry, the private sphere was systematically invaded by forces seeking to deny the individual his last particle of negativity. The ossification of consciousness was the outcome. Under these circumstances the terror was, if more subtle, all the more complete.

In a certain sense, absurd as it appears, the Frankfurt School is arguing that the United States is worse than Nazi Germany. Outright brutality can be resisted: the logic of the industrial machine cannot be resisted, because it seduces. It promises men not merely the things that they authentically need but also those things that they need only subjectively. To be more precise, their subjectivity is turned into objectivity by the mechanism of industrial psychology and by the logic of the system as a whole. Even more important, technology given men the hope of being whole. The real alienation of the individual is treated by the false integration of man into society through the production line and trade union. The psychic wholeness promised turns out to be merely the wholeness of an affirmation of a society that cannot allow the individual as authentic subjectivity.[10]

Technology, as the very embodiment of reason, comes to rule not only as a mechanical principle but also as a social principle. Having rationalized the mode of production (that is, the struggle against nature), technology turns to rationalize the form of production, and productive control itself. Bureaucracy (in the Weberian sense) is adopted as a social principle; who can argue against the rationality of merit? However, the systematic bureaucratization of society further denies space to the individual. It reduces individuals to ciphers within a statistical universe. Men become significant solely as aggregates; when treated as individuals, they are significant only for their social possibilities. They are taken seriously only as they can help, or threaten, the social order. This bureaucratic conception quickly turns into a self-image. The bureaucrat himself, putatively the rationalized ruler, loses his privacy and subjectivity. Officially praiseworthy, this adherence to exogenously derived rules serves to

---

10. Marcuse, "On Hedonism," in *Negations,* pp. 171-74.

The Crisis of History

imprison all subjectivity in the constraints of objectivity. From both sides, bureaucracy turns man into an instrument.[11]

The assault of technology upon the individual reduced the negativity of even Marx's revolutionary subject,[12] the proletariat:

> Because modern society is a totality, the decline of individuality affects the lower as well as the higher social groups, the workers no less than the businessmen. One of the most important attributes of individuality, that of spontaneous action, which begins to decline in capitalism as a result of the partial elimination of competition, played an integral part in socialist theory. But today, the spontaneity of the working class has been impaired by the general dissolution of individuality.[13]

The sociological manifestation of the collapse of the individual and of the individual's autonomy is found in the failure of the proletariat to fulfill its historical role; the revolutionary transformation of society.

With the loss of subjectivity, the proletariat ceases to be revolutionary, and instead affirms the existent social structure. To be authentically revolutionary, the proletariat must have autonomy in the sense of both consciousness and action. Marx believed, through both a calculus of interest and an understanding of their historical function (the task of theory), the proletariat would freely act to carry out its historic function.[14] This function, however, could be carried out only through a stance of fastidious intransigence on their part. It could be carried out, that is, if the proletariat, although participating in the system as necessary, never allowed the system to intrude into the private core of its being. The bourgeoisie, according to Marx, could grind the proletariat down physically but were incapable of penetrating their realm of consciousness and calculation. Only with this realm intact could the proletariat carry out its historical function.

But the proletariat, according to the Frankfurt School, had ceased

---

11. Marcuse, *One-Dimensional Man*, pp. 32–35.
12. Which to Marx is the absolute negation.
13. Horkheimer, *Eclipse of Reason*, p. 143.
14. The complex of subjectivity and objectivity on the part of the proletariat can be seen in Marx's *18th Brumaire:* "Men make their own history, but not any way they wish"; and in the third *Theses on Feuerbach*.

to constitute the revolutionary subject.[15] Even where there remained the hope of resurrecting the proletariat as a revolutionary force, the subjectivity that made history determinate for Marx, had been lost. The loss of the revolutionary subject was the cutting edge behind the historical crisis as such: history, having been failed by its agent, no longer appeared prepared to move beyond itself.

The causes of the desubjectification of the proletariat are threefold. Each has been alluded to in other contexts, but each has its real historical significance in its effect on the proletariat. First, there is the effect upon the proletariat of technology itself. Marx himself had noted that the mode of production transfigured the self-consciousness of a class and, therefore, its subjectivity. So the Frankfurt School sees technology as having a profound impact on the self-consciousness of the proletariat. But it is an impact that, contrary to Marx, robs the worker of autonomous negativity. Technology intruded upon the very structure of the consciousness of the individual worker. Further, technological production under capitalism regards the proletariat as an object; a commodity to be used. The cult of productivity and objectification, almost a religion with the bourgeoisie, comes to intrude on the proletariat as well. The proletarian comes to believe that which is said falsely about him.[16]

Second, the objective function of the proletarian in the economic system is such as to compel him to see himself not simply as an exchange-value but also as a machine. The proletarian has certain tasks to perform. These tasks, however, are always partial ones. They never take place alone or autonomously. They are always caused by directives outside of himself and they are always performed in conjunction with other men and with other machines.[17] The outcome does not realize Marx's vision of a growing class consciousness and an awareness of the functioning of the mechanisms of production and of the worker's own significance to them. On the contrary, the outcome is the reification of the worker's self-consciousness. Having been regarded as an object, the worker comes to see himself as an object. Rather than self-awareness of

15. See Horkheimer, *Critical Theory*, p. vi; Marcuse, *One-Dimensional Man*, pp. 31–32; Adorno, "Reflexionen zur Klassentheorie," in *Gesellschaftstheorie und Kulturkritik*, pp. 17–18.
16. Horkheimer, *Eclipse of Reason*, pp. 153–57.
17. Ibid., pp. 147–48.

The Crisis of History

power, the worker comes to an awareness of impotence so far as autonomous action is concerned.[18] Reinforced by both overt propaganda and the culture industry's covert intrusion into the consciousness of the proletariat, the working class comes to lose its subjectivity to the objectivity of the system.[19]

The revolutionary's source of energy is his hatred, the knowledge of the suffering that surrounds him. This, coupled with his own sense of righteousness as the just redeemer of the damaged, fuels the revolutionary in moments of danger. His hatred requires two things: an object of loathing and an object of pity. The Frankfurt School believed that the proletariat has been denied both these things. The object of pity was denied by the official doctrine of the Social Democrats—the party of the workers themselves. Benjamin writes:

> Social Democracy thought fit to assign to the working class the role of the redeemer of future generations, in this way cutting the sinews of its greatest strength. This training made the working class forget both its hatred and its spirit of sacrifice, for both are nourished by the image of enslaved ancestors rather than that of liberated grandchildren.[20]

The positive position, which was inherent in Marxism itself, broke the strength of the proletariat. Love and pity for the past was replaced by an inspidly positive vision of the future.

This tendency of Marxist ideology was reinforced by the objective development of the social structure in late capitalism. The apparent contradiction between bourgeois and proletarian, which was the core of Marxism, has been replaced by the illusion of a shared fate between ruler and ruled. Domination has been changed into rational administration, and the rapacious capitalist replaced by the efficient bureaucrat. As Marcuse writes:

> The capitalist bosses and owners are losing their identity as responsible agents; they are assuming the function of bureaucrats in a corporate machine. Within the vast hierarchy of executive and managerial boards extending far beyond the individual establishment into the

---

18. Marcuse, *One-Dimensional Man*, p. 33.
19. Adorno and Horkheimer, *Dialectic of Enlightenment*, p. 167.
20. Benjamin, "Theses on the Philosophy of History," in *Illuminations*, p. 260.

scientific laboratory and research institute, the national government and national purpose, the tangible source of exploitation disappears behind the facade of objective rationality. Hatred and frustration are deprived of their specific target.[21]

The apparent replacement of capitalism by technocracy (in which the Frankfurt School sees a certain truth) robs the revolutionary of his object of hatred. Hatred of an abstraction is as insipid as love for the unborn future. Thus, because of ideology and historical movement, the revolutionary proletariat loses its ability to hate and so loses the source of its energy. The proletariat slips into affirmation because the negative has lost its attraction.

All of this would mean little if the brute reality of the proletarian's existence had forced him daily to consider his own suffering. To Marx, the pauperization of the proletariat was critical, not because the more subtle aspects were insignificant but because, in the end, revolution requires the brute reality of hunger to give it weight. Against starvation, the subtleties of reification would have little strenght. This is why the final explanation of the failure of the proletariat's revolutionary thrust is most significant of all. This reason is the abolition of poverty: the conquest of nature by men.[22]

The conquest of nature freed men from the brutality of want. More specifically, the ability of the capitalist system both to conquer nature and to distribute the fruits of its victory to the mass (the former was known to Marx but the latter unthinkable) freed capitalism from its crisis. The crisis of overproduction and underconsumption that, for Marx, would be the proximate cause for the rebellion of the proletariat simply did not take place. Marx had argued that capital could not expand quickly enough to absorb the growing mass of the proletariat, which would be drawn from the collapsing petit-bourgeoisie and migrating peasantry. He thought that there would be a growing army of unemployed, forcing wages downward toward mere subsistence for the employed and below it for the lumpen mass, causing unrest and finally revolution.

What Marx had failed to calculate was that capitalism not only had conquered nature but was able to expand its conquest and its exploitation of nature rapidly enough to employ the masses. Capitalism was predicated upon overconsumption. It was success-

21. Marcuse, *One-Dimensional Man*, p. 32.

ful because it was able to create new markets not, as Lenin argued, in overseas colonies but domestically in a vast internal consuming empire. The proletariat hoisted itself by its own bootstraps. They did not consume because they had jobs, but, as a class, they had jobs because they consumed. The more the proletarian mass consumed, the more capital expanded, and the more jobs were available, allowing the proletariat to consume more, continuing the process potentially ad infinitum.[23]

In maintaining this system, the culture industry became critical, because it was necessary to create systematically the consciousness of consumption. Late capitalism makes for philistinism and distorted values. It does not create objective sensual suffering. Subjectively, at least, the proletariat is content; objectively, it is relatively free from want. Under these circumstances, history lacks the brute force necessary to convey to the proletariat its objective unhappiness. The satisfaction and oversatisfaction of wants may be inhuman in their particular forms but do not offer a moment of outrage for the masses.[24]

Thus the absorption of subjectivity by the system, the loss of the proletariat's object of loathing, and the overwhelming reality of the affluent society worked together to rob history of its revolutionary subject. Rather than being the cutting-edge of the revolution, the proletariat came to constitute a complacent, conservative class. Having the most to gain from the consumption economy (relative to their previous position) and the most to lose if the economy failed (since they would be the ones hurled into the ranks of the unemployed) the proletariat consumed with abandon, thus maintaining the system and themselves.

Having the most to lose and to gain, the proletariat came to be the most ardent supporter of the existing social structure. Technology had created the conditions for their cooptation. Just as its general category, reason, had created a problem that it could not dialectically solve, so technology had created a circumstance that was beyond its power to solve: an inhuman society, one-dimensional in consciousness and practice, which showed no sign

---

22. Adorno, "Reflexionen zur Klassentheorie," in *Gesellschaftstheorie und Kulturkritik,* pp. 22-23.
23. Marcuse acknowledges the importance of affluence, *One-Dimensional Man,* pp. 48-49, but does not give a detailed analysis of its economic dialectic.
24. Ibid., p. 49.

of negating itself dialectically. Indeed, it was a circumstance in which the historical negative came to constitute the epochal positive, the source of strength and affirmation. The crisis of the proletariat formally paralleled the crisis of reason.

Had the system maintained itself as peaceably as this analysis would indicate, then the Frankfurt School would have been reduced to a critique of the aesthetics of capitalism, much as had Thomas Carlyle and Matthew Arnold. In a way, the aesthetic is the basic level on which the Frankfurt School is operating, hence its serious concern for the problem of culture. But there is another side to the Frankfurt School's perception of the cowlike placidness of late capitalism: war.

Apart from the power of Thanatos over the system (see Chapter 12) or of the aestheticization of politics (see Chapter 11), the system itself objectively requires war in order to maintain itself. Marcuse writes:

> The reality of pluralism becomes ideological, deceptive. It seems to extend rather than reduce manipulation and coordination, to promote rather than counteract the fateful integration. Free insititutions compete with authoritarian ones in making the Enemy a deadly force within the system. And this deadly force stimulates growth and initiative, not by virtue of the magnitude and economic impact of the defense 'sector', but by virtue of the fact that the society as a whole becomes a defense society. For the Enemy is permanent . . . he is thus being built into the system as a growing power.[25]

Surely, the defense industries stimulate production and help maintain the system. But the presence of the enemy is, to the Frankfurt School, the critical element in creating cohesion for the system. It is the final element of stability reinforcing the already reified consciousness of the proletariat. The economic and political tasks coincide and reinforce each other.

To the recalcitrant, the society holds open nothing but the terror of being unheard and the more immediate terror of being physically crushed. The enemy without must also become the enemy within. The systematic search for traitors (manifest in both the West and in the socialist countries) originates both in the subjective need for

25. Ibid., p. 51.

enemies and the objective fear of those who could have the strength to be unreconciled.[26]

Society, having lost the mythic source of the terror it requires to maintain itself, must replace it with an actual one. The core of social stability might be seen as the fear of offending the Power. To the Jew, the fear of offending the Lord drove him to honor mother and father, thus keeping the covenant of the Father Abraham and ultimately maintaining His social structure. The mythic fear of His power, manifested in the Torah, did not have to be repeated continually. God's terror was a perpetual possibility, and only at times did it become a historical reality. At all times, however, this myth of terror bound the people of Israel together. Enlightenment dispelled the mythic but did not dispel the structural need for the mythic terror. Instead, it dispelled the protective envelope of myth, leaving its actual, sensual residue. Mythic terror, having been expelled from heaven, left its mythic form behind and came to constitute the binding power on earth. Being on earth it became actual, utterly brutal, and socially necessary.[27]

Thus what might have been only an aesthetic critique of philistinism becomes, in view of the underside of affluence, a critique of the terror engendered and required by affirmation. The inhumanity of the system consists not only of bad taste but also of utter terror, a terror that, because of both its social and transhistorical necessity, threatens to become permanent. It is a terror that does not threaten to annihilate itself as its last object.

The situation is no better in the socialist camp. Neither the Soviet's nor the Social Democrats, in the view of the Frankfurt School, constituted the historical negation of the negation, since each tended to replicate the Western attitude toward labor, technology, and instrumental rationality. Thus the Soviets lapsed into overt brutality and the Social Democrats moved into a replication of bourgeois philistinism and dehumanization.

In his study *Soviet Marxism*, Marcuse writes:

> The ethics of productivity expresses the fusion of technological and political rationality which is characteristic of Soviet society at its present stage. At this stage the fusion is clearly repressive of its own

26. Ibid., p. 3.
27. Benjamin, *Kritik der Gewalt*, pp. 57–64.

potentialities with respect to individual liberty and happiness. Freed from politics which must prevent the collective individual control of technics and its use for individual gratification, technological rationality may be a powerful vehicle of liberation. But then the question arises whether the ethics of productivity does not contain tendencies pushing beyond the political framework.[28]

But, he goes on, "Needless to say, the present reality is so far removed from this possibility that the latter [hope] appears as idle speculation."[29] The Soviet Union grew out of the confluence of Marxism and Positivism.[30] The Marxist emphasis on industrialism coupled with the Positivist conception of reason produced in the Soviet Union bourgeois notions of reason while reducing reason to a mere instrumentality in practice.

The result was political and psychic repression. Art, philosophy, and culture were all reduced to instruments of affirmation. They served (consider 'Socialist Realism') to buttress the internal structure of the Soviet Union. Theoretically justified by the claim that the historical dialectic had come to a close, the affirmation of the existent served to replicate the repression of consciousness prevalent in the West. The outcome can be most clearly seen in the puritanism of Soviet ethics; its sexual repression, the surplus repression of redirected libido, is as cruel as the West's and is more intensely enforced.[31]

Thus Marx's anticipated political solution failed, not, as the Social Democrats and Mensheviks argued, because the Soviets were forced to skip over historically necessary epochs but because socialism in the Soviet Union, and in the world as a whole (at least in the industrialized portion), had to be mediated through the experience of technology. The problem of the Soviet Union was that it sprang from the same ground of Enlightenment as the West, so that labor and the repression of the instincts of gratification came to be fetishized similarly. Horkheimer came to see in this fetishization of labor the same ideology as ruled in the capitalist world.[32] And

28. Marcuse, *Soviet Marxism*, pp. 239–40.
29. Ibid., p. 242.
30. Marcuse sees this as being rooted in Engels (ibid., pp. 126–29).
31. Repressive desublimation is more advanced in the West; Marcuse, *One-Dimensional Man*, pp. 123–43; Marcuse, *Soviet Marxism*, pp. 216–17.
32. Horkheimer, *Dämmerung*, p. 181; also see Benjamin, "Theses on the Philosophy of History," in *Illuminations*, p. 259, although Marx is spared the onus.

Adorno went as far as to root the problem not merely in the work of Lenin and Stalin but in the ideology of Marx as well; he accused Marx of wishing to turn the world into a gigantic workhouse.[33]

The fetishization of labor is the historical capstone of the failure of the Soviet experiment. It represents the triumph of the logic of aesceticism over the logic of gratification. What was built into bourgeois culture by its ideological and experiential heritage became part of the ideology of the Soviet Union, although it never experienced the bourgeois epoch directly. Indeed, perhaps because of this and because their desire was to replicate the technological triumph of the bourgeoisie, the Soviets were forced to out-do the bourgeois fetishization of labor. In any case, the outcome was the creation of a cult of labor powerful enough to eliminate the possibility of liberation. Thanatos, merely viable in the West, became the dominant existential order in the Soviet orbit. The result was that the same frozen dialectic that existed in the bourgeois countries was extant in the Soviet Union, with the added elements of a powerfully centralized bureaucracy and an institutionalized hierarchy to maintain it.

The situation among the official Marxists in the West was no better. Where the Soviets fetishized labor, the Social Democrats fetishized its historical counterpart, progress. Benjamin writes of them:

> The conformism which has been part and parcel of Social Democracy from the beginning attaches not only to its political tactics but to its economic views as well. It is one reason for its later breakdown. Nothing has corrupted the German working class so much as the notion that it was moving with the current. It regarded technological developments as the fall of the stream with which it thought it was moving. From there it was but a step to the illusion that the factory work which was supposed to tend toward technological progress constituted a political achievement.[34]

The embrace of technology was as much part of the ideology of the Second Internationale as it was of the Third.

In a sense, it is not surprising that official Marxism would come

---

33. Jay recounts this from a conversation with Adorno; *Dialectical Imagination*, p. 57.
34. Benjamin, "Theses on the Philosophy of History," in *Illuminations*, p. 258.

to embrace technology. Technology was the essence of Marx's notion of man's developing relationship with nature and the cutting edge of the notion of historical progress and theoretical Enlightenment out of which Marx sprang. The roots of Marxism in the tradition of Enlightenment naturally turned it toward technology and labor. True, in the end, technology was intended to liberate man from labor. But this had to be mediated through its own dialectical counterpart: the fetishization of labor by the bourgeoisie and by all who wished to replicate their experience of capital accumulation. Under those circumstances, their practice of Enlightenment was as much imprisoned by the logic of Enlightenment as was capitalism. There was no more hope in the Communist world than there was in the capitalist.[35] If there was hope, as we shall later see, it was to be found historically only outside the dialectic of Enlightenment—that is, in the Third World, among the students; or elsewhere outside the system.

Thus, history presented the world with an insoluble problem. In a sense, the promise of the Enlightenment had been fulfilled. Objectively, nature had been conquered. In what had already been achieved by technology, and in view of the potential of technology, it could be said that the grinding and impoverished existence of men had been abolished in the part of the world under the sway of technology. Maldistribution of goods notwithstanding, the fundamental reality of the world was the affluence promised but unimagined by the Enlightenment.

The conquest of nature opened the way to possible political and psychological liberation. Politically, it was now possible to abolish the class antagonisms and oppression that had been made necessary by the niggardliness of nature and the need of men to organize in order to struggle against it. Indeed, the physical conditions that made politics the primary activity among men were no longer the dominant circumstances; politics itself, therefore, stood liable to abolition.

Even more, the possibility of psychic liberation revealed itself. The psychic structure that had developed out of the need to main-

---

35. Marcuse, *One-Dimensional Man*, pp. 48–49, raises the most distant possibility of hope in the Soviet Union, predicated on the clash of official ideology with the repressive and centralized (thus vulnerable) reality. In the end, he regards this as very doubtful.

tain the mere existence of the human organism was no longer necessary. The abolition of repression, except for the minimum needed to maintain enough painful labor to continue the conquest of nature, became possible. Unrepressed and undamaged men were now conceivable. Indeed, their realization seemed implicitly necessary as the logical outcome of history. Utopia appeared at hand.

On a deeper level, the hopefulness of the Marxist vision became profoundly problematic to the Frankfurt School. The same forces that had been necessary to conquer nature created the dynamic of self-maintainance; history showed little possibility of transcending itself. The psychological, aesthetic, philosophic, and political forms of the struggle against nature—that is, of Enlightenment—seemed able to maintain themselves in perpetuity. Psychologically, the repression that labor had required had created a quasi-autonomous principle, Thanatos, that competed on equal terms with the erotic for the loyalty of the organism. Surplus repression, repression beyond the minimum necessary for the self-maintainance of the organism, was the result, and its very dynamic precluded its abolition without a cataclysmic break in the psyche.

Art, which could be universally disseminated through technology, was also faced with the loss of its authenticity. The work of art, robbed by technology of its aura even as it became universally available tended to merge into the background of everyday existence, affirming the world as it denied itself its authentic negativity. Buttressed by the institutional format and power of the culture industry that produced and marketed mass art and art for the masses, art served to support the social order, however, repressive it might be. The original purpose of art, to represent the beautiful and protest the ugly and damaged world, was lost as art came to fulfill its historical mission of universalization. In failing to make the world beautiful, it failed in its real mission. Premature affirmation was its fate; yet even timely affirmation would have destroyed it. Art is intrinsically negative.

Similarly, reason fell into affirmation. Philosophy, instead of continuing its dialectical mission of criticism, became not the cutting edge of Enlightenment's negativity but the instrument of its official maintenance at the moment of its triumph. Reason, having triumphed over the world, regressed into being the world's handmaiden, maintaining itself as the principle of the world but losing its own principle, negativity, in the process. Having triumphed, reason was lost to the affirmation of Positivism and of the Positivistic social sciences. Itself brought to premature affirmation, reason also seemed doomed to inauthenticity even if affirmation had come at the right time. Reason, by its very nature, seemed doomed to castrate itself, to fall into identity instead of maintaining its criticism of the world.

Thus the political outcome of all these forces was a historical immobilism. History, having lost the critical vanguard of art and reason, was left impotent against the forces of affirmation. Without the catastrophe of starvation to force society to reflect on itself, history seemed to have exhausted itself. The proletariat, having been brought off by a society capable of fulfilling its fondest sensual dreams, ceased its revolutionary activity: history had therefore lost its agent. The price demanded by the social system was the loss of an authentic psychic liberation. The personal rule of neurosis and the historical domination of society by war represented the maintenance of repression beyond the demands of history and nature. The crisis was that the forces that had created the conditions for the abolition of psychic suffering were the same that had either denied history the possibility of negating itself or had created autonomous principles for the maintenance of repression.[36]

Enlightenment—progressive as long as it was conquering nature, as long as it was negative—became repressive at the moment of realization. The crisis of history is that the force of liberation became the source of repression and, worse still, created the conditions for its own perpetuation. Man had apparently posed a problem for himself for which there was no readily available solution; indeed, it perhaps might be utterly insoluble. The damaged life might become the perpetual form of existence.

The crisis of history impelled the Frankfurt School to search for a historical, or even antihistorical, solution. Dialectics demanded an interplay between theory and practice. Currently, however, the dialectic created a circumstance in which the theoretical denied to the practical the possibility of transcendence, and the practical denied to the theoretical any sensual necessity for transcendence—all while the distortion of the human condition was left intact. Society's development precluded the development of either a theory or practice of transcendence; transcendence seemed to be confined impotently to the margins of society. Theoretical and practical

36. Ibid., pp. 241–42.

The Crisis of History

power were either repressed or coopted by the overwhelming strength of the dominant culture and society.

The crisis of history presented the Frankfurt School with its own personal crisis: it had to become both relevant and unsubverted. To do this the School had to discover a way to exist on the margins of society, apparently impotent yet practically subversive. They had to create a theory of practice that combined within its format apparently and actually irreconcilable elements. On the one hand, they turned to the marginalia of pure, esoteric theory. Living outside the official ideologies yet taking their bearings from them, they had to discover a means of effective criticism that would not be absorbed by culture's absorptive process. They had to create the idea of negation within the crevices of a seemingly omnipotent affirmative social order.[37] At the same time, since any practical reflection within the social order was liable to absorption, they had to create moments of pure activity, of commitment for its own sake. The student movement of the 1960s, rooted in activism for its own sake, was intended, particularly by the later Marcuse, as a discovery of a mode of practice, a pure practice, that was unsubverted by the practical reflectiveness of the dominant culture. The combination of irreconcilable elements—of pure theory and pure practice—within a single structure of thought pointed to the deepest realization of the Frankfurt School: system was the preserve and prerogative of the Enlightenment. In turning against the Enlightenment itself, while formally adhering to its deepest principle, negativity, the Frankfurt School had to reinstitutionalize opposition.

The unification of pure thought and pure action as opposed poles of a single structure of thought represented the quest of the Frankfurt School for an unsystematic theory. The lack of system of the Frankfurt School's Critical Theory represented their search for a break in a seamless society. A systematic search, by its nature, would fall under the forces of a society that turned system into repression. Critical Theory represented theoretical guerilla warfare, the warfare of irregulars against regularity itself. As such, Critical Theory was the search for the solution to an insoluble problem; the problematic itself was unsystematic. Through antisystematics it might be solved and, in Benjamin's words, "blast open the continuum of history." Thus did the Frankfurt School turn to the problem of a historical solution of history's insolubility.

---

37. Adorno, *Negative Dialectic*, p. 150.

PART III

THE SEARCH FOR THE SOLUTION

14. *The Exegetical Solution*

The impetus for the creation of Critical Theory is found in the opening passage of Adorno's *Negative Dialectics:*

> Philosophy, which once seemed obsolete, lives on because the moment to realize it was missed. The summary judgment that it had merely interpreted the the world, that resignation in the face of reality had crippled it in itself, becomes a defeatism of reason after the attempt to change the world miscarried. Philosophy offers no place from which theory as such might be concretely convicted of the anachronism it is suspect of, now as before. Perhaps it was an inadequate interpretation which promised that it would be put into practice. Theory cannot prolong the moment its critique depended on. . . .
>
> Having broken its pledge to be as one with reality or at the point of realization, philosophy is obliged ruthlessly to criticize itself.[1]

At one point, philosophy had neld open the possibility of its own abolition. The "Eleventh" of Marx's *Theses on Feuerbach* represented the highest historical possibility of philosophy. There, philosophy and reality seemed capable of merging with each other. The distinction between the real and the ideal, in theory and in practice, became trivial and each held the possibility of abolishing the other.

Only then did the attack upon philosophy, represented by the "Eleventh" in *Theses*, seem plausible. The charge that philosophy was contemplative and, as such, was irrelevant to historical practice, was reasonable just at that moment—the moment in which philosophy presented its practical and prosaically consequential side to the world. After that moment had passed and the brutality of the world had barred the potential self-abolition of philosophy as a distinct aspect of life, then the time of the Eleventh Thesis had also

---

1. Adorno, *Negative Dialectics*, p. 3.

passed. To accuse philosophy of being mere contemplation without consequence can have meaning only when it is possible for thought to be consequential. When the moment of consequentiality is past, so is the possibility of valid criticism of philosophy. Enlightenment, having played itself out—indeed, having turned itself into its opposite—must be criticized not for its contemplativeness but for its concrete practice in the world. The failure of philosophy to remake the world had, paradoxically, recreated the space in which philosophy in practice has recreated its existence in theory.

Marxism, and all theories that fail to recognize that the moment for the reconciliation of philosophy and reality has passed, do not see that a theoretical moment cannot be maintained past its historical one. What was true in the nineteenth century, the optimism and the hope, became utter falsehood in the twentieth. Stalin, Blum, and Hitler had given lie to the promise of philosophy. Marx's attack on philosophy, true at the moment of hope, becomes a lie at the moment of despair. Perhaps Marxism was wrong in its initial hope; perhaps only the contents of its hope were misplaced. In any event, the moment of contempt for philosophy is gone.

Now philosophy must leave the alien ground of the world, and return to itself, becoming once more, as it was for Plato, both subject and its own highest object. The concreteness that Marx wished to give Hegel was meaningful only when that concreteness seemed imprisoned in its own dialectic. Only when concrete history seemed about to become identical with truth could philosophy bind itself to it. Now that history has turned into a lie, the moment of intimacy between philosophy and the content of history is past. Now philosophy must once more become contemplative: it must once more become its own highest object.

Marx had expelled metaphysics from heaven so that it might take its rightful place on earth. Now, for the moment at least, metaphysics has hired out as a whore in the brothels of an impure world. The contemplation of the true and the beautiful sold itself to the highest bidder in order to service the false and the ugly. At this moment—and this holds only for the this moment—metaphysics must be driven out of earth and into heaven. Only there can it be purified, and only then can it prepare for its righteous counterattack against the world.

The task of Critical Theory is to preside over the expulsion of philosophy from the world, so that it can be cleansed and purified

The Exegetical Solution

for its earthly resurrection and transcendence. Philosophy, for the Frankfurt School, is historical; at the same time it is bound to ancient truths.[2] It is this dialectical tension between philosophy's ties to the most profound and transhistorical truth concerning man and the world and its rootedness in the historical practice of the moment that causes oscillations in its status. At one moment it is bound to the world; at the next, it must flee in order to save itself. Critical Theory represents the historical moment of flight by philosophy, a return to the ancient truths and to the tradition to which it is bound. The task of philosophy had once been to change the world; the world, however, had changed philosophy. With Critical Theory, philosophy seeks to leave the world once again, for this moment.

Critical Theory's ultimate object is the world. Horkheimer can write that "It is the taks of the critical theoretician to reduce the tension between his own insight and oppressed humanity in whose service he thinks."[3] And both Marcuse and Horkheimer, in their seminal essay introducing Critical Theory, can write as if the initial object of Critical Theory were the concrete social problems besetting the world.[4] But, in the end, the path to the world of Critical Theory is mediated through philosophy. As Horkheimer puts it:

> This theory is not concerned only with goals already imposed by existent ways of life, but with men and all their potentialities.
> To that extent the critical theory is the heir not only of German idealism but of philosophy as such. It is not just a research ... ; it is an essential element in the historical effort to create a world which satisfies the needs and powers of men.... In this it resembles Greek philosophy, not so much in the Hellenistic age of resignation as in the golden age of Plato and Aristotle.[5]

The ancient truths to which Critical Theory is bound are not only mythic truths but also philosophical ones. The opposition between appearance and reality, which was an essential element of ancient philosophy, constitutes the core of Critical Theory. Not abolition of

---

2. Marcuse, "Philosophy and Critical Theory," in *Negations*, p. 153.
3. Horkheimer, "Traditional and Critical Theory," in *Critical Theory*, p. 221.
4. See, for example, ibid., pp. 218–19. In Marcuse, "Philosophy and Critical Theory," in *Negations*, pp. 144–47, it is linked to social practice.
5. Horkheimer, "Postscript," in *Critical Theory*, pp. 245–46.

the distinction between subject and object but the explication and nurture of that opposition is the Frankfurt School's project. Its ultimate end is the world, but it is a practice mediated through philosophy as philosophy fastidiously recoils into itself.

More than simply a return to philosophy, Critical Theory is a return to what is both the most concrete and the most metaphysical element of the philosophic: the text. It is a return to the essence and the residue of philosophy found in the traditions of the West. The same traditions that so exhausted themselves in the Enlightenment must now be resurrected, criticized, and transcended, but always cherished.

Critical Theory has its first moment of practice in a historicized and socialized Talmudism, which it learned from the spirit of Benjamin's work. Benjamin himself never fully embraced Critical Theory. He was too closely tied to Brecht.[6] There was also a serious disjunction in Benjamin's work.[7] On the one hand, he formally placed himself in the camp of materialism. Indeed, Benjamin's positions tended toward the vulgarity that he had learned from Brecht.[8] On the other hand, having embraced the notion of materialism with a vulgarity far beyond what the rest of the Frankfurt School was willing to tolerate, he was capable of demonstrating the most profound metaphysical subtlety time and time again.[9]

I would argue that Benjamin's metaphysical sensibility motivated the formation of the critical practice of the Frankfurt School's Critical Theory. In a letter to Max Rychner, Benjamin wrote that despite his materialism (or rather, complementary to it), he had come to regard the world as he did the Talmud: with forty-nine levels of interpretation embedded within it.[10] For Benjamin, it was in the text (which was the metaphor for the thing) and not in the thing itself that philosophical truth lay. Despite his Brechtianism, Benjamin's notion of truth was Talmudic: what was true in the universe came to man not directly but rather mediated through the word.

6. Jay, *Dialectical Imagination,* pp. 200–202.
7. Gershom Scholem noted this disjunction between Benjamin's "real mode of thought and the materialist one he has ostensibly adopted" ("Walter Benjamin," *Leo Baeck Yearbook,* p. 128).
8. See Benjamin, *Briefe,* 2:594, for an example of his devotion to Brecht. As for Benjamin's praise of crudeness in Brecht, see Benjamin, *Versuche über Brecht,* p. 90.
9. Leading Scholem to call him a philosopher ("Walter Benjamin," *Leo Baeck Yearbook,* pp. 120–22).
10. Benjamin, *Briefe,* 2:524.

The Exegetical Solution

This was why he was concerned for the purity of language. His concern was not with language as such but with the truth that was embedded in the text.

The search for this truth can be seen in his treatment of the translation of a text:

> If there is such a thing as a language of truth, the tensionless and even silent depository of the ultimate truth which all thought strives for, then this language of truth is—the true language. And this very language whose divination and description is the only perfection a philosopher can hope for, is concealed in concentrated fashion in translation.[11]

The task of philosophy is to conquer the true: only in language is such a conquest conceivable. To Benjamin, philosophic truth does not float free in the world (as, paradoxically, it seems to in the methodologies of vulgar Marxism). Philosophy, caught in the vise of language, can express itself only by first entwining *itself* in language and its concretion, the text. The truth of the materialist, to Benjamin, is complex: being dialectical, it presents first one side and then another. A monad of the world, like a passage of Torah, possesses forty-nine levels of truth.[12] Even more like the Torah, the truth of the world, as far as philosophy can conjure it, is embedded in the monads of language congealed in the text. The historical materialist who wishes philosophical truth must turn to exegesis if he is to liberate the worldly truths available to philosophy. Thus all philosophy is the exegesis of the texts that sought truth. To Benjamin, nowhere is this truer than in the task of the materialist. The materialist, most fully wedded to the world, is also most entangled in the speech of the worldly, in language and its textuality.

Adorno saw and appreciated this side of Benjamin:[13]

> He transposed the idea of the sacred text into the sphere of enlightenment, into which, according to Scholem, Jewish mysticism itself tends to culminate dialectically. His essayism consists in treating profane texts as though they were sacred. This does not mean that he clung to

---

11. Benjamin, "The Task of the Translator," in *Illuminations*, p. 77.
12. This was the view of the Talmud toward the structure of Torah.
13. This is so, despite the minor differences reported by Jay in *Dialectic Imagination*, p. 176.

theological relics or, as the religious socialists, endowed the profane with trancendent significance. Rather he looked to radical defenceless profanation as the only chance for the theological heritage which squandered itself in profanity. The key to the picture puzzles is lost. They must, as a baroque poem about melancholy says, 'speak themselves'.[14]

The notion of a sacred text had been the core of the Jewish teaching: the sacred word opposed to the profane world. What Benjamin did was to treat the profane texts of the world as if they were akin to the Holy Book. In this, he was neither a ritual Jew nor a preacher of the social gospel. Rather, he understood that the format of the world's truth recapitulated the format of Jewish truth. Between the subject and the object of both, there was the mediation of the text. Only through the text could the truth of nature and God be conjured. Both philosophical and religious truth were, in essence, wordless. They stood as pure being, prior to all that was profane. The profane could conjure the sacred truths only through the words of those who had captured the truth in the web of language, whether Moses or Plato. The Judaic notion of the sacred text thus entered the philosophic and materialistic world of Benjamin.

Through Benjamin, it touched Adorno and thence the entire Frankfurt School. In *Negative Dialectics* Adorno formally repeats Benjamin's thesis without acknowledgement:

> Philosophy rests on the texts it criticizes. They are brought to it by the tradition they embody, and it is in dealing with them that the conduct of philosophy becomes commensurable with tradition. This justifies the move from philosophy to exegesis, which exalts neither the interpretation nor the symbol into an absolute but seeks the truth where thinking secularizes the irretrievable archetype of sacred texts.[15]

The task of philosophy is textual exegesis and criticism. In a sense, all the world is subject to such exegesis. In practice, only the highest, 'world-historical' texts lend themselves to it, philosophical texts most directly. Philosophy is not an immaculate conception. Its genesis is in the tradition of philosophizing that went before it. As in Benjamin, the text stands between the man and the world. And

---

14. Adorno, "A Portrait of Walter Benjamin," in *Prisms,* pp. 234–45.
15. Adorno, *Negative Dialectics,* p. 55.

The Exegetical Solution

also as in Benjamin, the text stands both in the sacred and in the profane. The task of philosophical criticism is not the hypostatization of the text as the sacred in and of itself. Rather, its task is to accept the text as if it were the secularized manifestation of the general case of textuality. In the treatment of each particular secular and profane text are to be found kernels of the general, and in this instance sacred, task of exegesis.

Thus, Critical Theory as a method is grounded in the exegesis of those texts that stand in the tradition of philosophic development. The act of philosophizing is inextricably bound up with criticizing previous philosophy; the nature of dialectical thought always roots the current attempt in the successes and failures of the past. One turns to the text in order to gain freedom from the prison that its thought and words represented. One does not simply stand in awe of the text as the embodiment of the sacred but negates it as if it were also polluted with the profane; this is the task that Critical Theory sets itself.[16]

Critical Theory is negative in one sense because authentic philosophy is negative. Critical Theory denies that all the content of philosophy originates in class. Authentic philosophy has two sides. The first is certainly its class function and position. But the underlying core of philosophy, the thing that distinguishes the philosophic from mere ideology, is philosophy's transhistoricity.[17] It is this transhistoricity that renders philosophy negative. Philosophy manifests its negation in two ways. Authentic philosophy points the way beyond the current historical circumstances. It criticizes the present and, in order to do so must draw its power from a vision of the human beyond the moment. But this is philosophy's *petit* moment; philosophy here negates what is only temporal by pointing to the next monad of time. Within this action, philosophy touches upon another, more profound transhistorical negativity. The highest philosophy neither affirms the existent nor merely criticizes it on the basis of the possibilities of the moment (or epoch). Philosophy conjures up images of authentic being that are rooted not in time but in the unrealized possibilities inherent in men. In nature, this grand moment is the highest point of philosophy; at this point philosophy

---

16. Ibid., p. 17.
17. To the extent that the Frankfurt School distinguished between philosophy and ideology, they had already radically broken with Marx.

summons its full critical strength. True, to be made historically relevant, it must turn into the petit moment of criticism, but the authentic power of philosophy is in its grand moment.[18]

Thus the negativity of Critical Theory can be seen in its object. Philosophy, which is the initial object of Critical Theory, is itself negative. Its intention is to negate the existent untruth, at least in theory. In proposing that the object of Critical Theory be the texts of a negative philosophical tradition, Critical Theory wraps itself in the mantle of negativity, claiming itself to be negativity's heir. In a sense, Horkheimer's claim that Critical Theory is the true heir of the philosophic tradition makes sense in light of the task that the Frankfurt School, facing the crisis of philosophy after Heidegger and Positivism, has set itself: no less than to resurrect the authentic core of philosophy, its abstract negativity.

Critical Theory is negative in a second sense as well. In addition to adhering to the negative tradition of philosophy, Critical Theory compounds its negativity by being negative in relation to the texts that are its object. If the core of the authentically philosophic is the ancient and transhistorical truths it conjures up for consideration, then its outer husk, the thing that officially presents itself to the world, is nonetheless historical.

Critical Theory sets out to criticize philosophic texts in such a way as to free and absorb the transhistorical insights embedded in their language. In facing the thought that had gained hegemony over an epoch, the Frankfurt School could only plunge down into its depths to conjure what was human and abolish what had become inhuman. In this way, they could possibly free philosophy of its affirmation.

There are many examples of the theoretical practice of the Frankfurt School, but perhaps the most elegant is Adorno's treatment of Spengler. The exegetical method of Critical Theory may be schematized somewhat as follows. First, there is the demonstration of the intellectual and historical significance of the thinker. Second, there is an analysis of the particular insights possessed by the object, the text. Third, there is a demonstration of the partiality of those insights; that is, there is an analysis of the reasons that the texts, despite their virtues, possess a theoretical structure that would tend to render them historically false on the whole. Finally, there is the

---

18. Marcuse, "Philosophy and Critical Theory," in *Negations*, pp. 148–49, 153.

The Exegetical Solution

demonstration of what, in general, was worth learning from the thinker, the manner in which those things could be integrated into a general theoretical critique of the existent.

Adorno begins the first task, the demonstration of Spengler's significance, with the following passage:

> There is good reason to raise the question of the truth and untruth of Spengler's work again. It would be conceding him too much to look to world history, which passed him by on its way to the new order, for the last judgment on the value of his ideas. And there is all the less reason to do so, considering that the course of world history vindicated his immediate prognoses to an extent that would astonish if they were still remembered. Forgotten, Spengler takes his revenge by threatening to be right.[19]

The demonstration of intrinsic worth is made independent of Spengler's class position, historical or intellectual influence, or political and ideological proclivities. It is based on Spengler's sociohistorical insight. At the start, Spengler is stripped of the historical and sociological status that traditional Marxism accords an object it wishes to study. Similarly, Spengler is stripped of any simplistic evaluation of historical consequentiality. Who Spengler was and what in practice he accomplished are, in this initial stage of operation, made trivial in order to focus on the pristine clarity of his vision of the world. Spengler's significance, to Adorno, was in what he knew and not in who he was or what he accomplished. Thus the first step in Critical Theory is to dehistoricize its object. The object is cleansed of both its historical roots and failures.

Only after accomplishing this can Adorno begin to focus on Spengler's particular virtues, that is, his particular insights. These are divided into two categories: general sociohistorical insights and particular historical prognoses. Adorno lists five of the former and four of the latter. Spengler's five general insights are, first, insight into the rise of Caesarism as the new political principle of the age; second, the rise of the new nomadic city-dweller as the manifestation of the fragmentation of the new age; third, the rise of sport as a general and permeating category of activity in the new age; fourth, the rise of education as a new form of propaganda; and, fifth, the rise of propaganda as the dominant form of political discourse in

---

19. Adorno, "Spengler after the Decline," *Prisms,* pp. 53–54.

the modern age. The four historical prognoses for which Adorno praises Spengler are first, the coming of the professional fanatical military corps of the embattled states later in the century; second, the rise of war as the universal experience of the coming time, encompassing continents and beyond the will of men to control; third, the coming collapse of the historical spontaneity of men in the new age; and fourth, the transformation of the political party from a party of participants to a group of followers.[20]

The particular elements are interesting primarily as they influenced the stance of the Frankfurt School toward coming and already existent sociohistorical events.[21] In a number of areas, the influence of Spengler was critical. What I want to point out here, however, is the method by which the Frankfurt School absorbed these elements of Spengler. Their method resembles the dissection of the text. They read Spengler's *Decline of the West,* after they had determined its worth, in order to extricate the fragmentary insights embedded within it. With excruciating care, things of value were plucked whole from the texture of the object and submitted to exegetical scrutiny. The text as a whole is not treated as sacred; rather, elements of the text, little chips of the sacred (or more precisely, the prophetic) embedded in a complex of the profane, are conjured from the circumstances that defile them.

Having extricated the gems, the Frankfurt School now turned to Critical Theory to demonstrate the corruption of the whole. Having distilled from Spengler his unintended negativity, the School applied the principle of negativity to the philosophic system in which Spengler's insights were embedded. Spengler, Adorno notes, has six particular failings. First, since his sympathies are with the rulers, his negativity is subverted into social positivity. Second, Spengler's attempt to be universal, that is, systematic, makes him superior to the particularism of the positivistic social sciences, but in other areas he is inferior because his obsession within an a priori system denies him the space for dialectical action. He gains insights but, rather than propelling him to new levels of historical consciousness, they become the prisoners of the system, caught within the web of its a priori knowledge. In leaving no real room for negativity, Spengler is undialectical. This leads to the third point: he

20. Ibid., pp. 54–59.
21. On this, see above, Chapter 6.

The Exegetical Solution

makes the mass responsible for its ignominy rather than putting the blame where it belongs: on the Caesars. Fourth, Spengler is right to declare the demise of culture, but he errs in also hoping for it. Thus Spengler, in desiring the collapse of culture, is actually guilty of participating in its execution. Moreover, his authentic loathing for culture denies him, once again, the space for a dialectical critique of the social order needed to destroy the cultural: Spengler is once more guilty of positivity. Fifth and perhaps most important of all, Spengler, by no means accidentally, knows nothing about economics. He fails to see the source of the events that he describes as being in the economic sphere. Thus, whatever insights he may have, and whatever virtues those insights may offer in particular cases, the general value of his work is minimal. Indeed, in diverting his followers' attention from the authentic dimension of the problem, he is actually counterproductive. Finally, Spengler is subservient to the general category of power in that the consideration of the achievement and texture of power is the most significant aspect of his work. His work is itself ultimately subservient to the power of the existing social institutions.[22]

The purpose of Adorno's particularistic critique (the second stage of Critical Theory) would appear to be threefold. In the first place, Adorno intends to demonstrate Spengler's simple, ideological biases. The commitment to Caesarism testifies to Spengler's implicit fascism. In a critique of Spengler or of any other thinker, the first stage of Critical Theory calls for the surface layer of bias to be stripped away. The commitment to a particular regime or social order is the first and most blatant obstacle to genuine negativity. The second step of Critical Theory is to demonstrate the structural limitations of the work. By showing that Spengler knows nothing of economics and that his ignorance is willful, one can demonstrate the dialectical limitations of Spengler's chosen structure. The structural limitation differs from mere bias in that it is far more subtle; it masquerades as methodology rather than as opinion. By laying bare the structure of methodology of the texts examined, Critical Theory is able to demonstrate their underlying proclivities. Third, and culminating the first two steps, a total critique of Spengler as a whole is established. Having in the first phase plucked the kernels of insight from the text, Critical Theory now approaches from the other end:

22. Adorno, "Spengler after the Decline," in *Prisms*, pp. 61–63, 68.

the whole is distilled in order to boil off the impurities—the internal biases and structural proclivities that would turn the text toward an affirmation of the existent inhuman social structure. Boiling off the textual pollutants again lays bare the kernels of truth but now they are freed from the clinging inadequacies that might have remained if the first step had been regarded as sufficient.

Finally, Adorno summarizes what has been learned. He considers what is worthy of praise in Spengler, what we must learn from him in order to absorb the particles of negativity embedded in his text. At the same time, the absolute falsehoods of the general level must be laid bare. Adorno believes it necessary to answer Spengler in his own terms: "To answer Spengler on his own terms would be to overcome historically the 'standpoint of actual history' which is not history but nature in a bad sense, and to transform what is historically possible into reality, something Spengler deems impossible because it has not yet been done." Thus Adorno finds it necessary to agree with Spengler that all culture bears the mark of death—that is, that all culture tends toward decay, for: "To deny this would be to remain impotent before Spengler, who betrayed as many of the secrets of culture as did Hitler those of propaganda."[23] It is necessary to deny Spengler's idea of culture as a whole, for to accept the primacy of culture impels one to accept the truth of his insight: culture as pure culture is doomed to annihilate itself.[24]

This summary of Spengler takes Adorno beyond him. Spengler supplies the ground on which his thought will be transcended. Spengler's validity, on the level of particular insights, is praised, but his insights are dialectically coupled with his failures. His profound insight into the structure of culture is linked to the general failure of his system to comprehend the human condition so that one is impelled to use the truth of the insight in order to deny the truth of the system. Thus, Spengler's vision of the collapse of culture leading to brutal inhumanity is used to explode the structure of his historicism. The truth that he knows about culture must deny the validity of his notion of the historical function of culture. Since culture is entropic, and entropic history is a priori inhuman and unbearable, then the entropy of culture must demonstrate the disentropy of

23. Ibid., p. 71.
24. Ibid., p. 72.

The Exegetical Solution

history. History, in the view of the Frankfurt School, cannot simply be entropic.

Note that Adorno doesn't proceed in this particular study to demonstrate his own historical vision. He and other members of the Frankfurt School work that out against other texts. In dealing with Spengler, it is enough to demonstrate his internal contradictions as they are revealed by the application of Adorno's historical assumptions. The insights of Spengler are carefully (and from both ends) dissected from the text. The text as a whole is placed in opposition to its particular parts. The opposition between the system and the monad—the inherent negativity that is the authentic component of all true texts—is used to transcend the text.

Thus Benjamin's notion that all texts (of the highest order) possess forty-nine levels of truth is expanded on by Critical Theory. Truly, all texts have forty-nine levels, but the layers of truth are sandwiched between layers of falsehood. The next is a compound of the sacred and profane. It is not in the text as text that the sacredness resides in its pure form. Rather, sacredness is possible on the level of transcendence. Mediating between the transcendent and the textual is the exegetical. It is in the exegetical act that the opposition between the sacred and the profane in the text is explicated and allowed to explode. Out of the debris (exegetically akin to the historical blast of revolution that Benjamin mentions in the "Theses on the Philosophy of History") are freed the chips of the sacred, of the true, that were embedded in the false. If all the layers were sacred, then dialectics within (as opposed to against) the text would be impossible.

Thus through exegesis truth becomes free but homeless. A transcendent moment, a moment of affirmation, is necessary, as the particles of truth are now to be embedded in a structure of truth. But this structure does not fall into positivity, which the Frankfurt School fears above all. The truth of the new structure of thought is in its general negativity. The exegesis of that opposition is to be revolution itself. The sacred is attainable only through the texts of history, but it is realized only when it breaks free of the profane language in which it is rooted. It achieves a partial sacredness in the renewed vision, but its authentic moment is found only in the historically redeemed Zion that comes after the revolution, after the Messianic mediation has made the sacred sensually real.

Critical Theory is consistent in its methodology of exegesis, but it refused to allow itself to coalesce into systematic theory. In this, Nietzsche's influence is clear.[25] The Frankfurt School believed, in a manner redolent of Nietzsche, that system as such was inherently bourgeois. To the Frankfurt School, systematics marked the presence of traditional theories and worked with those theories to deny consciousness and spontaneity to individuals by subsuming them into the reified categories that the system presented to them a priori.[26] The system was a manifestation of reification; indeed, it was reification. It represented the objectification of subjectivity into formalized and mechanistic categories, which superimposed themselves on the spontaneous subjectivity of being. The system constituted the reification of *Geist* itself.

The opposition to system, however, went even deeper than this. It was rooted in the historical moment. The world had become a realm of total administration. In each of the discrete spheres of human activity, the hegemony of nonalternatives had become established. Historically, the realm of systems had become absorbed by the overarching systematics of the ruling principles. Aesthetically, politically, psychologically, and, above all perhaps, philosophically, the system as system and as particular entity came to represent the enemy. To engage in systematics under those circumstances was to risk either becoming indistinguishable from the ruling entities formally or being crushed by the overwhelming antidialectical strength of the system (overwhelming because it rested on the failure of autonomous dialectics itself).

The historical ground of the antisystematics of Critical Theory is described by Marcuse:

> For the philosophical construction of reason is replaced by the creation of a rational society....
> What, however, if the development outlined by the theory does not occur? What if the forces that were to bring about the transformation are suppressed and appear to be defeated? Little as the theory's truth

---

25. See an acknowledgement of this in Adorno, *Negative Dialectics,* p. 20. Also see above, Chapter 4.
26. See Horkheimer's treatment of the systems of the logic of bourgeois thinkers. In particular, he repudiated Husserl's notion of systematics as representative of traditional theory ("Traditional and Critical Theory," in *Critical Theory,* pp. 189–90, 200, 210, 222).

The Exegetical Solution

is thereby contradicted, it nevertheless appears then in a new light which illuminates new aspects and elements of its object. The new situation gives new import to many demands and indices of the theory, whose changed function accords it in a more intensive sense the character of 'critical theory'.[27]

As in Adorno, Critical Theory is to rise upon the failure of philosophy to realize itself. But more than the failure of philosophy is involved; it is the failure of dialectics—that is, of system itself. The failure of system is what makes an unsystematic Critical Theory essential and what gives it significance. The absurdly rational development of the system demands an antisystematics to solve it.[28]

The need is even deeper than this, however, for as Adorno argues after Auschwitz:

> We cannot say any more that the immutable is truth, and that the mobile, transitory is appearance. The mutual indifference of temporality and eternal ideas is no longer tenable even with the bold Hegelian explanation that the temporal existence, by virtue of the destruction inherent in its concept, serves the eternal represented by the eternity of destruction.[29]

Auschwitz made the particular and the ephemeral universal. Events that previously had been transitory, and that the Hegelian could calmly wait for the eternal dialectic to annihilate, had now left the realm of mere quantity, thingness, and become quality: they had become authentic. The experience of Auschwitz demands eternity. The moment of suffering represented by it can no longer by brushed aside by history and historical systematics. To attempt to do so is a disservice to its victims, and, more importantly, it is utterly dangerous to the present and future. Now it is the particular moments that have, through technology, gained such awesome power and that constitute the threat of humanity; hence, they are the authentically significant moment.

The transhistorical systematics of a Hegel, therefore, are not enough to grasp the significance of the nomads of existence that are now not just grist for the historical mill but have become the real

---

27. Marcuse, "Philosophy and Critical Theory," in *Negations,* p. 142.
28. Adorno, *Negative Dialectics,* p. 21.
29. Ibid., p. 361.

truth of the historical moment. These ad hoc human conditions cannot be comprehended systematically. Each must be viewed in its awesome singularity. Thus the meaning of Benjamin's phrase—"An historical materialist approaches an historical subject only where he encounters it as a monad"—becomes clear; and the rest of the Frankfurt School radically expands it.[30] The 'monads' of history cannot be conjured up into a singular system. Each is too horribly unique to be viewed that way. Systems fail to grasp the monad-ness of the event. Thus Critical Theory must eschew systematics because the historical can no longer tolerate the burden of being sytematized.

The moment of Critical Theory must first move to unsystematic thought because the historical moment demands that it do so if philosophy is to become negative once more. If philosophy is to oppose the system effectively, it must eschew its form lest it be corrupted or crushed. Second and complementarily, it must move to unsystematics because the historical moment demands its undivided attention. History has become such that the particles of experience can no longer be understood if they are forced into the unnatural categories of eternally unchanging systems.

Critical Theory thsu becomes akin to guerrilla warfare, striking at the target in order to grasp its meaning but never holding the position long lest it be destroyed by the enemy and become indistinguishable from him. Worst of all, it may forget why it approached the target in the first place, in its zeal to hold a fixed position.

Furthermore, Adorno writes:

> The form of the system is adequate to the world, whose substance eluded the hegemony of the human thought; but unity and unanimity are at the same time an oblique projection of pacified, no longer antagonistic conditions upon the coordinates of supremacist, oppressive thinking. The double meaning of philosophical systematics leaves no choice but to transpose the power of thought, once delivered from the systems, into the open realm of definitions by individual moments.[31]

---

30. Benjamin, "Theses on the Philosophy of History," in *Illuminations*, p. 263. Note that Jay feels that this element of Benjamin's thought is particularly intolerable to the Frankfurt School (*Dialectical Imagination*, p. 203). Juxtapose it, however, with the above quotation from Adorno to see clearly that Jay overstates the case.
31. Adorno, *Negative Dialectics*, pp. 24–25.

The Exegetical Solution

To take a systematic stance would be to abandon the struggle against the system. Systems reconcile one to systems. In order to maintain the war, we must take a more subtle if less elegant approach (which is, after all, the nature of guerilla warfare).

This would tend to make the practice of Critical Theory seem irrelevant. As Horkheimer puts it:

> Consequently, although critical theory at no point proceeds arbitrarily and in chance fashion, it appears, to prevailing modes of thought, to be subjective and speculative, one-sided and useless. Since it runs counter to prevailing habits of thought, which contribute to the persistence of the past and carry on the business of an outdated order of things it appears to be biased and unjust.[32]

To those who support the system (in all its phases), Critical Theory seems to be arbitrary opposition to order, an opposition that refuses to stand and fight. Indeed, this is Critical Theory's tactic. It appears to lapse into subjectivity because only there does it expect to find the autonomy necessary to strike out against a reified world. And its work appears irrelevant precisely because it *is* irrelevant to the system. The system cannot take seriously anything unsystematic. But only what is unsystematic can give serious opposition to the system.

The system has presented the world with no alternatives. The complex of affirmative thought faced by the Frankfurt School left no room for an immanent transcendence. Each complex lacked the internal contradictions that would autonomously explode the system of their thought. And none (not even the apparently implacable foes of Positivism and Heideggerianism) stood in any authentic opposition to one another. Thus, the dialectic had stalled.

Critical Theory was designed to give transcendence a new moment. Inasmuch as the current moment presented no self-realized solution, Critical Theory intended to summon one. Because the thought of the moment left no space for systematic alternative formulations, the Frankfurt School chose to conjure the solution from the very essences of the systems of thought that they opposed. Their exegesis of the texts of others were this moment of theoretical

---

32. Horkheimer, "Traditional and Critical Theory," in *Critical Theory*, p. 218.

conjuring. The Frankfurt School intended to mine the depths of texts that would not autonomously dissolve themselves and force them to do so, yielding up their morsels of truth. But the structure of thought that had captured these morsels did not intend simple reconciliation, at least, not on the level of the particular particles of truth. The deadliness of culture, as taught by Spengler and Freud, was to be juxtaposed to the love of these thinkers for the highest moments of the cultural. The tension between the two positions would be allowed to stand. The ultimate truth of the Frankfurt School was negativity—the perpetual opposition of the irreconcilable—so that an authentically human and autonomous existence could be lived in the neutrality created by the tensions. It was only when the oppositions held each other in a dialectical balance, perpetually negating each other in cycles rather than in progressions, that autonomy, the choice between culture and the anticulture, was conceivable. Only in the thing and in its opposite was the possibility of freedom conceivable.

Critical Theory was, therefore, not a positive position but a methodology for conjuring negativity. As Horkheimer puts it:

> There are no general criteria for judging the critical theory as a whole, for it is always based on the recurrence of events and thus on the self-reproducing totality. Nor is there a social class by whose acceptance of the theory one could be guided. It is possible for the consciousness of every social stratum today to be limited and corrupted by ideology, however much, for its circumstances, it may be bent on truth. For all its insight into the individual steps in social change and for all the agreement of its elements with the most advanced traditional theories, the critical theory has no specific influence on its side, except concern for the abolition of social injustice. This negative formulation, if we wish to express it abstractly, is the materialist content of the idealist concept of reason.[33]

The truth of Critical Theory thus rests not in any specific formula for social change, although it knows many, but in the *concern* for social change and justice. It is not the concern for the positive, for the systematic, that grips Critical Theory but concern for the negative, for the unsystematic. It is impelled to this stance by the possibilities and demands of the historical moment, and one can imag-

---

33. Ibid., p. 242.

The Exegetical Solution

ine a moment (such as Hegel's) when dialectical negation would demand both systematics and affirmation again. Never will these be demanded for their own sake, however, but only for the sake of negating the negation. For only in the space neutralized by the force of the two negations is freedom, and thus true social justice, conceivable.

Thus, as the negation of Marxist historical practice and as a negation of the practicality of the world, Critical Theory takes a stance of fastidious abstractness. At this moment, the world's practice is polluting. Critical Theory must take place in some relationship with a system that has the power to absorb the most powerful negatives into itself. Thus, to maintain its autonomy and reality, Critical Theory couples its stance of irrelevance with the exegetical strike at the core of the system's traditions. But the theoretical moment does not intend to remain within itself but rather to move to its antipode, to radical political practice. Its ultimate concern is with the real sensual world. It mediates itself through the text because both the sacred and profane forms of the world are somehow congealed within its language and because the moment is not ripe for an unmediated approach. But the text, in both directions, is merely the mediated moment. Ultimately, the cataclysmic exegetical transfiguration performed by the Frankfurt School on the world's texts must be recapitulated in the cataclysmic revolutionary transfiguration that the Frankfurt School intends to perform on the world itself. The ultimate hope is for the transfiguration of being itself into a realm of utter negativity and autonomy.

15. The Political Solution

Just as the goal of Critical Theory in dealing with texts had been to transcend the textual material, so the goal of the Critical Theory in dealing with the world was to transcend the practical.[1] True, the Frankfurt School primarily concerned itself with textual transfigurations; this, however, was in response to the historical moment. It was in the world, sometimes in opposition to the existential mode of the exegeticists, that Critical Theory intended to work itself out.[2]

The problem of political practice was still the problem of consciousness rather than a problem of immature material conditions. To the Frankfurt School, the failure of the consciousness of the proletariat to develop became the single most significant phenomenon of contemporary history.[3] It represented the failure of the dialectical movement of consciousness. In effect, the crisis of the self-consciousness of the proletariat became the political cutting edge of the crises in the numerous other realms caused by similar dialectical failures.

The failure of the proletariat to achieve a revolutionary consciousness or to realize its objective misery did not negate the objective critique of society delivered by the Frankfurt School nor the reality of the suffering of the proletariat. As Adorno puts it:

1. Transcendence of the practical was the task of works that tended to view the world more directly, such as Adorno and Horkheimer's *Dialectic of Enlightenment* and Marcuse's *One-Dimensional Man*. It must not be forgotten that, although the object of these works was history itself, even here it was mediated through such prismatic texts as those of Homer, the Marquis de Sade, Hegel, and Marx.
2. The opposition to exegesis can be seen in the pure practice of the followers of the Frankfurt School as opposed to the pure theory of the Frankfurt School itself. The death of Adorno, following his humiliation by naked students, explicates this contradiction. See Peter Bruckner, "Und nach uns Kömmen nichts Nennenswertes," in *Die Neue Linke nach Adorno*, p. 11.
3. Horkheimer, "Traditional and Critical Theory," in *Critical Theory*, pp. 213–14.

The Political Solution

> Direct communicability to everyone is not a criterion of truth. We must resist the all but universal compulsion to confuse the communication of knowledge with knowledge itself, and to rate it higher, if possible—whereas at present each communicative step is falsifying truth and selling out. Meanwhile, whatever has to do with language suffers of this paradoxically. Truth is objective, not plausible.[4]

There exists a democratic, and implicitly nihilistic, tendency to confuse the communicability of a truth with truth itself. The failure of communication is seen today as the refutation of what is not communicated. Yet, as Adorno says, communication itself, under current circumstances, falsifies truth. The structure of communication under the aegis of the culture industry works to render communicated truths false.

Thus the crisis of consciousness is shown on one side as the crisis of communication. The truth of suffering is overwhelmed by the appearance of plentitude. Perhaps the prime example of this is the television news broadcast that juxtaposes the suffering of people with the implicitly truer reality of the commercials of plentitude. Indeed, the plentitude of communication, represented by television's mere existence, tends to deny the poverty of the communicated; the appearance of plentitude, however, leaves untouched the objective reality of the poverty.[5]

Under these circumstances, the revolutionary moment begins with the shattering of the communicative veil over truth. It is the theoretical preface to such an event that Marcuse attempted to give in his essay "Repressive Tolerance." Published in 1965, it offered a theoretical justification and framework for the intolerance of the New Left. It was criticized for being implicitly totalitarian.[6] In a sense it surely was but, before it is condemned and dismissed, it must be considered because it follows logically and reasonably from the Frankfurt School's reading of the historical situation. Their totalitarianism revealed the importance and difficulty of shattering the affirmative structure of consciousness prevalent in late capitalism.

---

4. Adorno, *Negative Dialectics*, p. 41.
5. Adorno, "Fernsehen als Ideologie," in *Eingriffe*, pp. 82–83.
6. An example of this argument can be seen in David Spitz, "On Pure Tolerance," in *Dissent*, Sept.–Oct. 1966.

Marcuse is concerned with the illusory character of modern toleration:

> This pure toleration of sense and nonsense is justified by the democratic argument that nobody ... is in possession of the truth. ... Therefore, all contesting opinions must be submitted to 'the people' for its deliberation and choice. But I have already suggested that the democratic argument implies a necessary condition, namely that the people must be capable of deliberating and choosing on the basis of knowledge ..., their evaluation must be the result of autonomous thought.[7]

Mill's utilitarian argument for toleration assumed that in the marketplace of ideas the consumer was an autonomous subject, free to discern the difference between damaged goods and choice products. Marcuse dismisses this notion:

> But with the concentration of economic and political power and the integration of opposites in a society which uses technology as an instrument of domination, effective dissent is blocked where it could freely emerge: in the formation of opinion, in information and communication, in speech and assembly. Under the rule of monopolistic media—themselves the mere instruments of economic and political power—the mentality is created for which right and wrong, true and false are pre-defined wherever they affect the vital interests of the society.[8]

The tolerance of late capitalism is revealed to be false. While giving the illusion of autonomous choice, it actually denies it because any alternative must be mediated through the same culture industry.

The tolerance of modern society, less brutal than the enforced censorship of formally totalitarian countries, is nonetheless totalitarian.[9] Under the guise of freedom, it systematically allows the expression and consideration only of ideas that are either objectively harmless or essentially irrelevant to the system. Thus radical critiques, such as those of Marcuse himself, are tolerated and indeed widely disseminated by the media, while they are rendered impotent. The possibility of their acceptance by the masses is presented as ludicrous, or the critique is allowed to enter the con-

---

7. Marcuse, "Repressive Tolerance," in *Critique of Pure Tolerance,* pp. 94–95.
8. Ibid., p. 95.
9. Ibid., p. 99.

The Political Solution

sciousness of the masses only marginally while the overwhelming power of the official ideology is maintained. Finally, when the system is actually threatened by external critiques, it demonstrates its power by adopting the *form* of the analysis while stripping away its social content, its real venom. It coopts the critique by rendering it fashionable.

The system is thus totalitarian because, despite formal rights and guarantees, it objectively denies individuals room to make autonomously negative judgments. The formal right of dissent is granted only as far as that dissent is objectively impotent. Thus the communication of the sorrow of the human condition in late capitalism is as impossible in the liberal democracies as it is in formally totalitarian regimes. This is liberal democracy's tragedy.

The only hope is to shatter the affirmative power of the culture industry. The formal toleration that is allowed must be made objectively tolerant as well. Marcuse writes:

> Liberating tolerance then, would mean intolerance against movements from the Right, and toleration of movements from the Left. As to the scope of this tolerance and intolerance: ... it would extend to the stage of action as well as of discussion and propaganda, of deed as well as of word. The traditional criterion of clear and present danger seems no longer adequate to a stage where the whole of society is in the situation of the theater audience.[10]

The only objectively liberating form of tolerance—that is, the only form of tolerance that is authentically negative—is repressive tolerance. Repressive tolerance involves the systematic repression of those whom history has rendered repressive and reactionary. True tolerance, according to Marcuse, must dialectically pass into the guise of its opposite if it is to be effective against a social order that both dehumanizes and simultaneously prevents the realization of that dehumanization. The withdrawal of legitimacy from the overwhelmingly powerful system is the only true form of toleration.

Marcuse sees a historical difference between reactionary and revolutionary violence. Both might be considered ethically inhuman and evil, but it is history's nature to be both.[11] Under these circum-

---

10. Ibid., p. 109.
11. Ibid., p. 103.

stances, the question is, Who is to judge what is revolutionary repression and what is reactionary? In effect, who shall be the censor? To this Marcuse had a radical answer:

> The question, who is qualified to make all these distinctions, definitions, identifications for the society as a whole, has now one logical answer, namely, everyone 'in the maturity of his faculties' as a human being, everyone who has learned to think rationally and autonomously. The answer to Plato's educational dictatorship is the democratic educational dictatorship of free men.... The problem is not that of an educational dictatorship, but that of breaking the tyranny of public opinion and its makers in the closed society.[12]

Marcuse tries consciously to distance himself from the "elitism" of Plato's philosopher-king by linking the practice of educational dictatorship to democracy. The quasi-Platonic roots nevertheless are clear. The judgment of the good and bad, of the human and inhuman forms of expression, action, and consciousness, will be made by those with wisdom. The wise men—that is, the rational and autonomous men—should rule. Clearly, given the power of the system, people of this description are few. If Marcuse does not argue for an absolute inegalitarianism, he argues for a historical one. At this moment, the wise should rule in the name of the many. But the argument is, in the end, only quasi-Platonic. Plato, after all, knew the rule of the wise to be impossible. It is Marcuse's Hegelianism that makes such a vision plausible.

But it must be recalled that there is no longer any dialectical certainty that the wise will emerge in history. Indeed, considering the historical circumstance—the power of the repressive mechanism of society—it appears most unlikely. Even if a wise man were to emerge, he would have to seize political power in order to use the media to promulgate his wisdom. But in order to seize political power, he would have to control the media until after he had seized power. And so on, in a historical negation of the very dialectics of history. History seems to dissolve itself into a circle.

This is the political crisis of the dialectic. What is needed to liberate repressed and oppressed men requires the seizure of politi-

---

12. Ibid., p. 106.

The Political Solution

cal power. The seizure, however, in turn depends on the prior attainment of the requirements of liberation—that is, a revolutionary consciousness. Marcuse is a Hegelian who has lost his teleological way; he is also a Platonist without Plato's sense of historical limits. He is a pessimist who takes a strangely hopeful position. He has explicated a historical circumstance without any apparent dialectical possibilities, and yet he can write such a hopeful work as *An Essay on Liberation*. What motivates him, under the circumstances, appears to be a Messianic hope. Something, it would seem, must enter from the outside in order to shatter the historical cul-de-sac that the more advanced nations of the world have entered. The rule of the wise can come about, it would appear, not dialectically but Messianically.

There seem to be two different varieties of historical eschatology. The first is the dialectical, which holds that history has an underlying rationality in regard to the whole. That is to say, the movement of history is grounded in the autonomous workings of an essential realm, to which historical phenomena are merely superstructure. Under this conception, moreover, the development of history proceeds internally. Each historical moment postulates its problematic but, as the same time, proceeds to develop the problematic's solution out of the same ground from which it developed the problematic. Thus at the same time that the underlying ground of material development was creating the problem of capitalism, according to Marx, it was also developing the solution to the problematic. The central thesis here is that mankind (and its history) does not pose problems for itself for which it does not already, at least implicitly, possess a solution. It is from the internal movement of the matter of history that the historical dialectician draws the certainty of his eschatology.

The Messianist, it would seem, shares the eschaton with the dialectician but holds a contrary notion of the *process* of history. Where the dialectician can conceive of no insoluble historical problem (from the perspective of the essential functions of man, that is, reason or production), the problem of history for the Messianist is precisely that it is insoluble from an internal perspective. History, rather than working itself out from its own material, bogs down in its own quandary. To the Kabbalist, for example, the moment of Messianic intervention was bound up with a catastrophe beyond the power of a Jew to cope with.¹³ To the Messianist, it is not the *telos* of history but, on the contrary, the catastrophe of history that shapes his vision. The awesome catastrophe for which men cannot even conceive a solution is the ground for the appearance of the Messianic force. The Messiah appears not from within human history (except, perhaps in its guise) but from outside. The Messianic hope is for an exogenous intervention into the material of history that will shatter the structure of the historical impasse. The Messiah appears when the situation is hopeless and solves its hopelessness through its temporal dissolution.

The Frankfurt School faced a time of catastrophic hopelessness. History, rather than automatically manifesting its own solution, seemed to be caught in the grip of a humanly insoluble crisis. History seemed to have lost the dialectical solubility that was the ground of the dialectician, material or otherwise. If there was hope for the abolition of the perpetually inhuman perpetuity that threatened, its source did not seem to be within the structure of history itself. If there was a hope, it would have to come from the outside.

Benjamin abandons his formal dialecticism for a Messianism in the following passage:

> A historical materialist approaches a historical subject only where he encounters it a monad. In this structure he recognizes the sign of a Messianic cessation of happening, or put differently, a revolutionary chance in the fight for the oppressed past. He takes cognizance of it in order to blast a specific era out of the homogeneous course of history—blasting a specific life out of the era or a specific work out of the lifework.¹⁴

It is not in the whole of a homogeneous time that the historical solution is encountered; rather, it is encountered as a monad that incorporates in itself the insoluble tensions of history. The revolutionary act is not living with the monad but rather reacting violently against it, a blast. In the insolubly tense monad that is the incarnation of the historical moment, there is found the catastrophe

---

13. Scholem, *Major Trends in Jewish Mysticism,* pp. 245–47. In particular, the Kabbalist drew the hope for the Messiah's coming from the Jewish catastrophe of 1492.

14. Benjamin, "Theses on the Philosophy of History," in *Illuminations,* p. 263.

The Political Solution

that is the ground of the Messianic hope. The revolutionary acts not within the monad of time that he faces but against it. He is not part of time but its excluded enemy. His intention is transcendence, a preservation of the moment, but the ground of practice is violent opposition. The Messiah preserves the world by catastrophically reshaping the very texture of its time, blasting it from the profane into the sacred. In this the profane is preserved but transfigured. So, for Benjamin, the monad is preserved but also, Messianically, transfigured. This is the ground of Benjamin's rejection of philistine optimism among the dialecticians of Social Democracy.[15]

The insoluble monads of time are the objects of the Frankfurt School's study and dilemma. The problem is finding the means for summoning up the revolutionary strong enough (in Benjamin's words, man enough[16]) to blast the historically insoluble monad out of existence. The School turned to the textual side of Critical Theory in search of a formula that would accomplish this task. On the practical side, Critical Theory's task was equally the identification and conjuring of the Messiah: the revolutionary subject. The tightening of history into a Gordian knot required that something outside of the catastrophe—more precisely, against the catastrophe—cut it, blasting history out of its continuum.

The Messiah came from outside history. So too, the revolutionary subject must come from outside history. It must be either irrelevant to history or untouched by it. The intellectual's task, like the task of the Kabbalist, was to identify the catastrophic moment and find the formula for summoning the Messianic power in order to shatter that moment. Their task was to identify the structure of history's failure and to work toward the creation of the revolutionary force that would break it apart. With the Critical Theory, the Frankfurt School identified the catastrophe. What remained was to find the pristine or irrelevant force that could shatter the structure of that historical moment. In this quest two classes seemed to have Messianic possibilities: the systemic irrelevance of students and the pristine externality of the Third World. In these two groups, the Frankfurt School put its hopes for the Messianic negation of the negation.

---

15. On Benjamin's Messianism, see Tiedmann, *Studien zur Philosophie Walter Benjamins,* pp. 146–50.
16. Benjamin, "Theses on the Philosophy of History," in *Illuminations,* p. 262.

The earlier formulations of Critical Theory offered rather traditional views of class.[17] Acknowledging the failure of the proletariat to achieve a subjective consciousness of their objective misery, the Frankfurt School (particularly Horkheimer in his earlier work) reevaluated the intellectual's role in catalyzing the proletariat. The first suggestion of how a new revolutionary class would emerge had the intellectual acting not autonomously but in a dynamic unity with the proletariat. The intellectual would supply the theoretical basis for a revivified consciousness of the proletariat, and the proletariat in turn would supply the mass base for acting out their theoretical vision in practice.[18]

The earliest formulations of Horkheimer bound the intellectual inextricably to the proletariat. It was not until the 1950s and 1960s, perhaps because of the radically increased reification of the general consciousness, that the Frankfurt School (most particularly Marcuse) identified a new revolutionary subject, more or less independent of the proletariat. Benjamin, who died in 1940, never abandoned his hope for the proletariat; to him the proletariat always remained the revolutionary agent, in some ways far more so than for the rest of the Frankfurt School. Adorno and Horkheimer, even after their estimate of the authentic revolutionary potential of the proletariat had become deeply pessimistic, rarely considered explicit historical alternatives to the proletariat. In a way, their great hope was in the proletariat and the failure of the proletariat left them with little beyond despair. In the end, even while they were caught up in the student and radical upsurge of the 1960s, they tended to distance themselves carefully. It was Marcuse who affirmed the need for an historically exogenous revolutionary force and embraced the student and Third World movements as the great historical alternatives to the proletariat.

The great upheavals of Paris in spring 1968 revealed to Marcuse the possibilities of the student movement. His *Essay on Liberation* sought a theoretical understanding of the possibilities of student rebellion:

> With respect to the student movement, a basic trend in the very structure of advanced industrial society favors the gradual development of

---

17. Horkheimer, "Traditional and Critical Theory," in *Critical Theory*, pp. 213–16.
18. Ibid., pp. 214–16.

The Political Solution

such a community of interests [a workers-student alliance, with the students taking a leading role—GF]. The long-range process which, in large areas of material production, tends to replace heavy physical labor by technical, mental energy, increases the social need for scientifically trained, intelligent workers; a considerable part of the student population is prospective working class—'new working class,' not only expendable but vital for the growth of existing society.[19]

The first aspect of Marcuse's analysis sees the students as a new proletariat. But perhaps a more accurate statement of his view would be that he sees the proletariat as being replaced in its historical function by a new proletariat. True, Marcuse argues that the students must be linked to a mass base if they are to be powerful, but he simultaneously argues that they are coming to constitute their own mass base.[20]

The development of late capitalism tends in two directions. There is a tendency toward integration; discordant elements are integrated into a single cultural and political structure. At the same time, late capitalism tends to deemphasize brute labor in favor of the more abstract forms of activity made necessary by technologized production and administration. These two developments tend to make the students both socially critical and relatively unintegrated. They are important for their acquired expertise in the more esoteric realms of social activity. At the same time, they above all others are able to be relatively less integrated because of their status in the university.

To Marcuse, the university is still the place in which true consciousness is developed.[21] The university is the concretion of the theoretical realm; if the possibility of theoretical criticism is to be taken seriously, even when it does not enter society as a whole, it must enter the university. The university, even when being encroached upon by the systems of reification, is still the only realm in society that wholeheartedly, if only formally, subscribes to the ethic of free inquiry.[22] Embedded in the university, the source of his class,

---

19. Marcuse, *An Essay on Liberation*, p. 59.
20. Ibid., p. 60.
21. Ibid., p. 61.
22. On reification in the university, see Horkheimer, "Threats to Freedom," in *Critique of Instrumental Reason*, pp. 143–46.

the student is both pivotal in the development of advanced capitalism and at the same time relatively free.

The rebellion of the student class is a moral rebellion: "To the degree to which the rebellion is directed against a functioning, prosperous, 'democratic' society, it is a moral rebellion, against hypocritical aggressive values and goals, against the blasphemous religion of this society, against everything it takes seriously, everything it professes while violating what it professes."[23] It is an idealistic rebellion, in both sense of the term. It is philosophically idealistic in that it originates not in the realization of the sensual insufficiency of the social order but in a theoretical critique of the social order's values and mores. It is this idealism that makes the student movement exogenous to the "real, sensuous development of history." That is, students constitute a class only on the most formal of levels. Their real function is to serve as a moral critique of society, made possible by their status in the university and effective through their possible future relationship with the means of production. But their power rests in the catastrophic shattering of the moral structures of the social order, not motivated by a dialectical interplay on the sensual level by a freely considered theoretical and moral critique of the social order. Their idealism is what makes the students historically exogenous. According to Marcuse, they will intervene from outside history—for the university is anomalous—and shatter the catastrophic moment of consciousness in order to create what Marcuse calls a new sensibility.

What the student movement accomplished theoretically, and began on a practical level with sabotage in the university, the black community could undertake in the United States, and the Third World could do in the world as a whole. The interest of the Third World, at least internally, is to achieve a formal revolution. Having recapitulated the American experience during their anticolonialist uprisings, the Third World now enters a second phase. They must now shake off the bonds of the past and create, in opposition to both the neocolonialism of the West and the new imperialism of the Soviet Bloc, an internal social revolution.[24]

In the Third World, however, as in the West, the experience of

---

23. Marcuse, *An Essay on Liberation*, p. 62.
24. Marcuse, *One-Dimensional Man*, pp. 45–48.

The Political Solution

the social revolution is ambiguous. Since the social revolution historically has been bound to technology, and since the impact of technology on the more advanced societies of the world has been ambiguous at best, Marcuse finds the prospect of a technologized Third World relatively unappealing. Rather than being the agent of liberation, such a development would appear, if Enlightenment's dialectic is to be taken seriously, to prepare the way for a depersonalized totalitarianism.[25]

Marcuse, however, hopes that the Third World might escape this fate. The rise of technology as the operant social principle might be opposed in these less-developed areas of the world by the indigenous cultures.[26] Unlike the West, which since Plato has been caught in the dialectic of Enlightenment, the Third World possesses a cultural framework that might contain the totalitarian impact of the technologization process. Marcuse sees a possibility of limited applications of technology, where absolutely necessary for creating a truly human life, on the bedrock of pretechnological culture. Thus the Third World might avoid the fate of the first two.

The chance that the Third World could place an internal brake on the dialectic of Enlightenment is clearly problematic. Enlightenment is imperialistic; its very nature is to deny space to anything that wishes to live outside of its hegemony. It is, however, in just such a problematic turn that whatever hope there is resides. The imperialism of Enlightenment cannot be arrested from within. Its internal machinations perpetually compel it to realize itself. Development can be blocked only by an exogenous force. Just how a society could exist under two antithetical principles—the principle of Enlightenment and the principle of tradition—when neither can, by its nature, tolerate the other, is a troublesome question. But only such an arrangement can defeat the inborn imperialism of Enlightenment.

What tradition does to restrain technology inside the Third World, the Third World must do for the technologized world as a whole. Tradition, escaping the power of Enlightenment, must use that power piecemeal to bring Enlightenment to a standstill. So the Third World, which is outside the technologized world as a whole,

25. Ibid., p. 46.
26. Ibid., p. 47.

must bring the power of that world to a standstill even while it draws on the forms of power that gave the technologized world strength.[27]

Unlike Lenin, Marcuse does not argue that imperialism is the linch-pin of late capitalist economics.[28] Although the Third World was clearly essential to capitalism at the height of industrialization and is still a residual part of the system, the less-developed countries are not now at the center of the industrialized economy's development. The Third World thus is left as essentially exogenous to the system. Just as traditional culture and technology stand opposed within the Third World, so the Third World and the industrialized world stand opposed in Marcuse's geography. The task of the underdeveloped nations is to maintain tradition; the Third World stands in opposition to the technical and social outrages of the industrialized parts of mankind. This opposition is not simply an act of reproach. The rise of the Third World as a political power signals catastrophic danger to industrial capitalism. Although Marcuse does not explicitly predict that the Third World will seize control of the natural resources that the capitalistic industries need in order to function, such a development is a distinct possibility. This is foreshadowed in the series of real and attempted Third World economic consortiums since the mid-1970s, most notably in OPEC. In the Near Eastern countries, economic self-interest and the demands of traditional culture struggle to find a balance in the face of increased wealth and growing technologization. Driven by this complex of factors, the Third World has already demonstrated its power to enter autonomously and destructively into the functioning of the industrial machine, thereby threatening to shatter the structure of capitalism. The Third World's relative freedom from technology, derived from its continued intimacy with tradition, gives it the autonomy to act as it does, even to appear at times to conventional Western wisdom as lunatic.

The Third World is outside the worldwide system of production and consumption, except for the geographic accidents of location. This frees them to intervene in the dialectical immobilism of the West, shattering its structure. The complex of wars of national liberation, the numerous embargoes, and the seeming lunacy of the

---

27. On this possibility, see Marcuse, *An Essay on Liberation,* p. 56.
28. Ibid., p. 57.

The Political Solution

Third World are the manifestations of an exogenous assault upon the rational, capitalistic Western system. Marcuse is far from certain that the attack will be sustained or will prevail; the outcome depends on an internal weakening of the metropoles.[29]

Another and more direct possibility is a revolt of America's internal Third World: the blacks in America's ghettos. The failure of the traditional American proletariat to revolt, or even to be adequately exploited, directed the attention of the Frankfurt School to the authentically oppressed group in American society, the blacks. As Marcuse put it:

> The modifications in the structure of capitalism alter the basis for the development and organization of potentially revolutionary forces. Where the traditional laboring classes cease to be the 'gravediggers' of capitalism, this function remains, as it were, suspended, and the political efforts toward change remain 'tentative', preparatory not only in a temporal but also in a structural sense.... Under total capitalist administration and introjection, the social determination of consciousness is all but complete and immediate: direct implatation of the latter into the former. Under these circumstances, radical change in consciousness is the beginning, the first step in changing social existence: emergence of the new Subject.[30]

The issue in America is, Who will the new subject be? Only the blacks offered a sufficient alternative. Their advantages were fourfold. First, even though they didn't comprise a majority in American society, they still were a mass group concentrated very near to the centers of American power. Confined in the inner cities, their violent intervention in those cities' functions could destroy the social and mechanical structure of American society. Second, like the Third World in general, the black subculture, much noted by popular sociologists in the 1960s, seemed to offer an effective defense against the technologized mass culture of the prevailing society. Their autonomous culture was a defense against their being seduced by the dominant culture. Third, their menial status kept them effectively separate from the more powerfully seductive components of technology. Although the blacks had played a critical role in the early capital accumulation, the growing sophistication to technol-

---

29. Marcuse, *One-Dimensional Man*, p. 48.
30. Marcuse, *An Essay on Liberation*, p. 53.

ogy and the decline in the need for menial labor had tended to freeze them out of the more important aspects of the industrial machine, such as communications and data processing. At the same time, the area in which they functioned, menial labor, remained relatively untouched by technology and grew more and more peripheral to the economy as a whole. Fourth, their increasing irrelevance to the industrial machine meant that they were becoming basically unnecessary to the system. To the capitalist system, cooptation of the proletariat as a whole was crucial; the cooptation of blacks was possible but unnecessary. Thus, according to Marcuse, blacks were unintegrated into the mass society. These four elements, combined with the sheer misery caused by the economic position of the blacks, conspired to give the blacks an authentic and immediate grievance against society as a whole while offering them the possibility of an autonomous consciousness necessary to execute their revenge.[31]

The power of the blacks, like that of the Third World in general, rests on their power to intervene catastrophically in the working of the system. Free of the constraints of mainstream social conditioning, they alone retain the real potential to so intervene. It must be noted that Marcuse explicitly denies that the black community or white student radicals can ultimately replace the proletariat as a revolutionary force—their function is that of catalyst[32]—but Marcuse's analysis does go far in this direction.[33]

Marcuse says that the proletariat does not retain an authentic subjectivity. It is conceivable (although he and the entire Frankfurt School, except for Benjamin, tend to vacillate on this point) that the proletariat can be catalyzed into action. Action whose origin is in exogenous catalysis, however, is primarily unfree. It originates in objectivity rather than subjectivity and its course is never freely determined. According to Benjamin, the proletariat is blasted out of its position in time and space. The complex of exogenous interventions performed by students and the domestic and foreign Third Worlds, serve to force the proletariat, against its actual subjective will, to stand in opposition to the system.

31. Ibid., pp. 52–59.
32. Ibid., pp. 51–52.
33. An accusation made against Marcuse by Leftist critics; see, for example, Graubard, "One-Dimensional Pessimism," in *Dissent,* May–June 1968, pp. 227–28.

The Political Solution

In a real sense, neither the blacks nor the students are of our space and time; and their intervention is formally a Messianic blast from outside the confines of space and time. Students, in theory, are timeless—if we are to take them seriously at all. The Third World is prior to time—in a metaphysical and practical sense, it is prehistoric. Both groups are cast into the current of history, but neither is part of its stream. Structurally they stand neither for nor against but merely apart from epoch. The current epoch is theirs merely in the sense that they have nowhere else to go.

But precisely because they are separate they retain the last vestiges of an authentic subjectivity; they are strangely archaic. It is this archaic element, this being rooted in the past or outside of time altogether, that frees them to take up the subjectivity that the proletariat lost by becoming too much a part of time. The rest of the Frankfurt School found it difficult to imagine someone else in the shoes of the proletariat. It was Marcuse who could imagine something new as a catalyst. But implicit in his argument was that the moment of history having passed, the moment of the archaic had begun. The student movement and the black movement, being archaic, were the real and last hope for a revolution. The revolution might have to be made with the body of the proletariat, but its mind would be found outside of them.

Critical Theory, therefore, had a threefold task. First, it had to identify and define the texture of the catastrophe that was the ground for the Messianic crisis. Second, it had to identify the Messianic force. Faced with historical catastrophe, the Frankfurt School had to discover, through the hermeneutics of the texts of the tradition that presaged the catastrophic epoch, the name of the force that could break the epoch apart. Once this name was discovered, they then needed, third, to discover the formulas through which the power of the Messiah could be invoked. How to force the students and the blacks to fulfill their antihistorical function was the critical issue, perhaps the crucial issue on which the politics of the Frankfurt School turned and fell. The rituals of invocation were difficult to master, and it was never certain whether the Messianic force was true currency or merely another in an ancient line of counterfeits. Still, if the Messiah would not enter in the next moment of time, perhaps a way could be found to force his coming. In a way, the Frankfurt School was willing to risk even itself in this task. More cannot be asked of any conjurer.

If, until now, the blacks and the students have not been catalysts in a proletarian revolutionary upsurge and we have not yet entered the sacred realm, the Frankfurt School still saw a certain virtue in attempting revolution for its own sake. For the Frankfurt School, the revolutionary act, like the hermeneutical one, is not merely a political exercise. Rather, revolution appears to them a metaphysical event, one touching the very essence of the human soul and shaping the very texture of the human experience.

To the Frankfurt School, the process of Enlightenment moved mythology from the sacred to the profane realm. The world was profane, and the mythology of the new world partook of profanity. This profanation of the world and of the heavens turned the world into a realm that was less than human: in it, the divine possibilities of human existence were singularly denied. The task was to reverse this process.

If the Enlightenment turned the world profane, the revolutionary act would make it divine once again—more fully than before. By remaking the world in the image of the God that man had created and then expelled, revolution would create a realm in which sacredness would premeate the being of the age. Moreover, it would do this while maintaining the unity between myth and reality that had been forged by the Enlightenment. The profanation of the world by the Enlightenment was paralleled by a denial, re-creation, and profanation of myth. First mythology was denied; it was called superstition. Then Enlightenment proceeded to recreate in itself the formal structure of mythology; Enlightenment came to constitute its own myth. Finally, rather than recapitulating the divine element of the myth, it united the myth with the world. However, instead of allowing the sacred possibility of myth to rule the world, Enlightenment forced the profane principle of the world to dominate the myth.[34]

The towering achievement of the Enlightenment was to abolish the distinction between myth and the world. What it failed to do was resolve the antinomy in favor of the sacred component of the myth. Revolution in its practical form would maintain the unity between myth and the world, but would resolve the opposition in favor of the sacred possibilities of the myth. The revolutionary act

---

34. See above, Chapter 10.

The Political Solution

would represent the triumph of the sacred possibilities of mythology over the profane reality of the world.[35]

The revolutionary act is an act of purification. It purifies not only the world and the profaned myth of the world but also the person who performs the revolutionary act. It purifies only when it succeeds. Although Horkheimer warns against activism as such and Marcuse warns against Sartre's notion of commitment, the revolutionary act is an act of purification.[36] The revolutionary act, according to Marcuse, brings man closer to authenticity. Benjamin sees the revolutionary act bringing man to experience his Messianic powers and possibilities:

> Like every other generation that preceded us, we have been endowed with a *weak* Messianic power, a power to which the past has a claim. That claim cannot be settled cheaply.

He then goes on to say:

> The class struggle, which is always present to an historian influenced by Marx, is a fight for the crude and material things without which no refined and spritual things could exist. Nevertheless, it is not in the form of the spoils which fall to the victor that the latter make their presence felt in the class struggle. They manifest themselves in this struggle as courage, humour, cunning and fortitude. They have retroactive force and will constantly call in question every victory, past and present, of the rulers.[37]

Benjamin seems to find the essence of revolution not merely in victory but rather in the "courage, humour, cunning and fortitude" of the struggle—in the sensibility of the experience. The revolutionary act brings to the fore the sensibility of the humane within the human. In a sense, revolution becomes an aesthetic experience, not in the cheap sense of Bakunin but in the profound sense of being the arena in which the more subliminal feelings of men can make themselves felt in their purest and most intense forms. The revo-

---

35. A sense of this is given in Adorno, *Negative Dialectics*, p. 404.
36. Horkheimer, *Eclipse of Reason*, p. 184; Horkheimer is, however, explicitly hesitant in rejecting activity as such. Marcuse, "Sartre's Existentialism," in *Studies in Critical Philosophy*, pp. 181–82.
37. Benjamin, "Theses on the Philosophy of History," in *Illuminations*, pp. 254–55.

lutionary experience, like Lenin's revolutionary cadre, distills the best of human qualities. What is objectified in the work of art in times of peace becomes manifest in the class struggle when it breaks into the open (that is, at the moment when the revolutionary comes face to face with his own mortality). In the souls of the revolutionary and in the aura imparted by the revolutionary to the revolution is to be found the authentic.

The revolutionary act is not cheap theatrics for two reasons. First, it is untheatrical in that it cannot settle with its creditors cheaply. The retroactivity of the sensibility is not directed simply at the object to be overthrown but also, if the first passage is to be believed, at the past that it has promised to redeem. The task is serious in that it is directed toward the past and not toward the future. Second, the act is not cheap because it brings us into contact with the "weak Messianic power" that is within us. The power is weak because it is not truly free; the past has a claim upon it. This claim is precisely what prevents the power from becoming trivial. And however unfree it might be in the present and future, it is still utterly, albeit weakly, Messianic. The revolutionary act brings us into contact with the essence of what men are endowed with.

Thus, to the extent that the revolutionary holds to his authentic power, the revolutionary act is an act of purification. From the impurities of objects and ignobility it distills the essentially human sensibility that is within us, making it utterly immaterial, utterly pure, and thus utterly real. At the same time, working from the other side, it brings us into contact with the power that given credibility to the sensibility of being human. The revolutionary act, even as it fails, and at times in spite of its success, is a profoundly human experience that is at the same time an approach to the divine by way of the Messianic. It is a fusion of the antinomies of man.

What is purification for Benjamin is seen as catharsis by Marcuse.[38] The catharsis of revolution recapitulates and recalls ancient and repressed rites. Most important, it repeats the slaying of the primal father. In Freud's metahistory, the slaying of the primal

---

38. Marcuse in "Sartre's Existentialism," in *Studies in Critical Philosophy*, p. 190, praises Sartre's preface to Fanon's *Wretched of the Earth*. The reason for this praise is unclear in view of Marcuse's critique of Sartre's notion of autonomous action. The praise, never explained by Marcuse, may concern the appreciation of Sartre for the cathartic power of the revolutionary act. See Sartre, "Preface," *Wretched of the Earth*, pp. 30–31.

The Political Solution

father by his jealous sons represented the archetypical act of revenge against the social forces that deny men gratification. From the slaying came both guilt and the beginnings of autonomy. Only with the death of the father could man ultimately be freed from his awesome presence.

The revolutionary act, the revolt of one age against the oppressions of the past, recapitulates the revolt against the primal father. Marcuse writes:

> The crime is re-enacted in the conflict of the old and new generation, in revolt and rebellion against established authority—and in the subsequent repentance: in the restoration and glorification of authority. In explaining this strange perpetual recurrence, Freud suggested the hypothesis of the return of the repressed, which he illustrated by the psychology of religion.[39]

Both revolution and its Thermidorian, counterrevolutionary, antithesis represent the acting out of an ancient drama. The power of the past is slain in order to free men from the unreasonable burdens that the past imposed on the present. With liberation, comes guilt. With guilt, comes restoration. With restoration, comes the need to repeat the act of murder.

What binds the acts together is the desperate need for the cathartic release that the act represent. It is not enough to appreciate the burden of the past intellectually. The revulsion against its burden has to be acted out; it has to be made both phylogenetically and ontogenetically real. In that way, we can be perpetually freed from the psychic burden imposed by the past. The slaying of the primal father, a symbol itself, comes to be symbolized in turn by the revolutionary outburst. This spitting up of the past frees one from it and renews the bonds to it (through guilt) in order to allow the cathartic liberation to repeat itself in perpetuity. Thus Marcuse sees the revolutionary act as cathartic because it acts out an ancient rite and allows the procrustean bed of guilt, which is the burden of man, to be shattered and renewed. The revolutionary act, therefore, takes on a psychic significance far beyond its material consequences. It allows man to return to an experience of his origins; civilization can

---

39. Marcuse, *Eros and Civilization*, p. 63.

existentially rediscover the roots of its discontents in the return of what had to be repressed.

The purification at the root of Benjamin's vision of revolution and the catharsis at the root of Marcuse's, have two things in common. In the first place, although the two concepts never succumb to the romanticism of Gracchus Babeuf, they turn revolution into a psycho-aesthetic event.[40] The revolutionary act becomes an act of primitive (more precisely, *Ur*-human) sensibility in which the consequences are, at least for a moment, secondary to the act itself. Never falling into either romanticism or pure existentialism, the revolutionary act is, nevertheless, elevated to a principle of existence; it is an experience of the essential dimensions of existence. Second, it harkens back to an archaic moment in which a thoroughly whole, or at least not yet differentiated man, could exist in pure acts. The purity of the hatred for the repressive social order and the purity of the sensibilities of the revolutionary both harken back to an epoch in which truly human existence could be experienced, in which the pristine purity of the act was not yet sullied by either history or reflection.

The revolutionary possibility has two sides for the Frankfurt School, both of them formally mythical. On one side, the revolutionary act is the Messianic act, the intrusion of something from outside the bounds of history into history in order to transform it from something profane to something sacred. On the other side, revolution becomes an ontological act; that is, an action that recreates the essence of the human being and for the moment frees him from the civilities of the moment. The revolutionary act puts man in contact once more with the roots of his being and sensibility. The revolutionary act is an act of liberation both in its becoming and in its being, both in its promise and in its reality.

But the revolutionary act is merely the penultimate moment historically, just as the Messiah is the penultimate moment eschatologically. The final moment is not simply the fleeting rediscovery of authentic sensibility but its realization in a permanent form, the abolition of the perpetual cycle of redemption of the eternally repressed, a shattering of the cycle of progress. As such, revolution is merely the doorway of the Messiah: it cannot as yet be the divine,

---

40. Marcuse rejects Babeuf; see Marcuse, "Thoughts on the Defense of Gracchus Babeuf," in *The Defense of Gracchus Babeuf*, pp. 96–104.

The Political Solution

even though it contains intimations of divinity. The final moment is not a political act but an ontological one. It is the act that transforms the very principles and experiences of being, making the divine historically as well as theologically indistinguishable from that which is.

16. The Transfiguration of Being

Toward the end of his "Theses on the Philosophy of History," Benjamin wrote:

> The soothsayers who found out from time what it had in store certainly didn't experience time as either homogeneous or empty. Anyone who keeps this in mind will perhaps get an idea of how past times were experienced in remembrance—namely, in just the same way. We know that the Jews were prohibited from investigating the future.[1]

The Jews could not know the future because the twist in time which the Messianic intervention caused constituted an ontological and epistemological abyss between the profanity of the present and the ever-possible divinity of the next. Instead, the Jews turned to remembrance out of reverent hatred. Also, the mind of the Jew turned toward the past out of fear of being impotent before the awesome power of time. The Jew could not know the future because the future was the authentically Other; it, and not the contemporaries who surrounded the Jew, was the strange force whose being was profoundly unknowable.

For the Marxist, this Jewish truth meant that the nature of the future order of existence was radically unknowable because the very texture of time would change from the impact of the revolution. The revolution was to be not merely a superficial attack on the surface of existence but rather the specific remaking of being itself. This meant, however, that there were limits to what could actually be known about the future. The nature of Communist society be-

---

1. Benjamin, "Theses on the Philosophy of History," in *Illuminations*, p. 264.

The Transfiguration of Being

came the most critical and, at the same time, the most unanswerable question of all.

Still, even if the Jew could not ultimately know the essential nature of the redeemed world, he could know some things about it. He could know that the present sensibility was somehow insufficient for the future, and he could know that the future would hold a new sensibility for man. That sensibility would change was obvious. The aura, the objective counterpart of the subjective sensibility, was dependent on a moment in time and space. The loss of the moment and place meant the loss of the aura. Hence a renewed sensibility was inevitable. Moreover, even as man could not know the precise nature of the future, he could and did know the insufficiencies of the present. The failures of the moment gnawed at him constantly. His very existences drove him to recognize the inadequacies of the sensibilities around him. Out of this, he could grasp, if never precisely, at least the outlines of a sensibility that could replace the present moment. This side of the Messianic redemption at least was dialectical. The solution arose from the problem. Thus the Frankfurt School could know what was lacking in this moment; through this knowledge they could dialectically approach an understanding of at least the formal outlines of the negation.

The injunction that the Jew should not utter the ineffable name, was, therefore, only a partial barrier to knowledge of God. By knowing the name of the Devil, the Jew could begin to get a glimpse of God. Inasmuch as man lives daily with the demons of his fallen state, man knows, through an intimate dialectical knowledge, at least the partial outlines of redemption. Even when the abyss could not be bridged through dialectics and even when the epistemological connection was utterly tenuous, rooted only in the negative, the link of sensibility remained. Touching on being itself and connected with theoretical knowledge as such, sensibility was not identical with either. It was a glimpse through prismatic images, an aesthetic feeling, a mythic possibility, that connected man, in some way, to the future. As Benjamin said, the Torah and the prayers turned the Jews to the past. But the folklore and the myths, the underlying aesthetic substance of the Jewish self-conception connected the Jew with the future, albeit under the table.

Thus, even when the Frankfurt School considered that it could not know the future as such, it could, through conceptual negations and the mythic images that they conjured up and destroyed, begin to glimpse the transformation of sensibilities that the future would bring. Through a glimpse of the transformed sensibilities, the existential aura of the future could be glimpsed as if the future were a work of art, which indeed it is. Through the glimpse of the aura of the future, a sense of the being of the future could be gleaned.

Approaching this problem from the opposite side, by beginning with being, we can see that its essence is in its sensibility. If Adorno was correct in claiming that taste is the truest seismograph of history,[2] then sensibility, merely the general category of taste, is essentially connected with the being of history: its telos. It would thus appear that, although the future is distinct from the present, it is not as hermetically sealed off as Benjamin implied. Access to the future is barred to *formal* dialectics perhaps; but the way seems to be open to the playful movement of glimpses, the dialectical sensibility of the negation of nuances. And in this way, perhaps the real dimension of historical change, the transformation of historical being, can be approached if not finally captured and subdued.

As Benjamin says, the question of the nature of the future makes no sense initially. It can in this phase be stated only in a nonsensical and shallow fashion. But there is a primitive and brutal event that can give the question some form and open the possibility of some meaning: the historical and metaphysical conquest of nature. According to Adorno:

> He who asks what is the goal of an emancipated society is given answers such as the fulfillment of human possibilities or the richness of life. Just as the inevitable question is illegitimate, so the repellent assurance of the answer is inevitable, calling to mind the social-democratic ideal of the personality expounded by heavily bearded Naturalists of the 'nineties' who were out to have a good time. There is tenderness only in the coarsest demand: that no-one shall go hungry any more.[3]

There is thus something elegant and pure in the demand to abolish suffering. But Adorno implies that this is also the only real starting point for considering the nature of the future. The tenderness of the demand to abolish hunger has its corollary in the real, and not

2. Adorno, *Minima Moralia*, p. 143.
3. Ibid., pp. 155–56.

The Transfiguration of Being 251

merely aesthetic, tenderness of any future age: no one shall go hungry any longer.

The nature of the psyche and sensibility of the future derives from this simple reality. On a psychic level it means the end of the perpetual struggle against nature and the abolition of the psychic structure entailed by that struggle.[4] The life that we have lived under the aegis of the Promethean myth can be finally abandoned. The conquest of nature finally means that a new principle of existence can be brought to the fore. The Social Democratic myths of the past, and even the current myths of self-actualization in an age of abundance, fail to express just how radical this break is. As Adorno puts it, "The conception of unfettered activity, of uninterrupted procreation, of clubby insatiability, of freedom as frantic bustle, feeds on the bourgeois conception of nature."[5] The chic and Social Democratic images of the conquest of nature are insufficient. They avoid only the outward appearance of struggle; inside they carry on conflict as insatiably as any child of Prometheus. The new moment of history has a meaning far more radical than any image of self-realization or of bustling fulfillment. It represents the rise of an entirely new principle of existence, a new existential myth, and a new structure for the human psyche.

To understand the Frankfurt School's sense of the future one must begin with Marcuse's vision of a re-created psychic structure for man:

> Beyond the performance principle, its productivity as well as its cultural values become invalid. The struggle for existence then proceeds on new grounds and with new objectives: it turns into the concerted struggle against any constraint on the free play of human faculties, against toil, disease and death. Moreover, while the rule of the performance principle was accompanied by a corresponding control of the instinctual dynamic, the reorientation of the struggle for existence would involve a decisive change in this dynamic. Indeed, such a change would appear as the prerequisite for sustaining progress. We shall presently try to show that it would affect the very structure of the psyche, alter the balance between Eros and Thanatos, reactivate tabooed realms of gratification, and pacify the conservative tenden-

---

4. See above, Chapter 12.
5. Adorno, *Minima Moralia*, p. 156. Also see Benjamin, "Theses on the Philosophy of History," in *Illuminations*, pp. 258–59.

cies of the instincts. A new basic experience of being would change the human existence in its entirety.[6]

A change in the structures of the human psyche was possible now that nature had been conquered and, at least abstractly, the performance principle could be abolished. Indeed, an entirely new principle of being was conceivable under the new historical circumstance.

Now the rule of Prometheus and of the myth of progress can be finally broken. The emphasis on becoming rather than on being as an existential principle can be shattered. The libidinous energies that had to be diverted from erotic gratification to labor can now, once more, return to their ancient quest. The perpetual distortion of the natural tendency of the human psyche can be replaced by an undistorted being of objective gratification, of authentic pleasure. This, in turn, makes the nirvana principle obsolete. The organism, now capable historically as well as potentially of enjoying positive gratification, no longer needs the neutrality of nothingness, of death, as a refuge from the painfulness of existence. At least potentially, the performance principle, which was based on surplus repression after the conquest of nature, can be replaced by a rejuvenated pleasure principle. The pain of life and the resulting logic of struggle against that pain can be replaced by a static peacefulness.

Out of peaceful state, the decline of Thanatos becomes conceivable. No longer is the death wish a reasonable response of the organism. No longer is Thanatos something that must be served if the organism is to stay alive. Thanatos becomes obsolete because the historical conditions that distorted the psyche and gave rise to the death wish have been abolished. Technology, which had come to serve the death instinct through the historic compromise between Eros and Thanatos, can turn from the task of domination to the task of gratifying and realizing the objective and true needs of men.

The Frankfurt School recognizes that the relationship of progress to gratification is the central problem. Their attack on progress centers on man's perpetual need for overcoming—man's need to be perpetually transcending what is rather than engaging in static enjoyment. As Marcuse observed, the very structure of instinct is inherently conservative. The instincts seek rest and gratification; they seek surcease from the perpetual struggle with nature. Simi-

---

6. Marcuse, *Eros and Civilization*, p. 143.

The Transfiguration of Being 253

larly, it must be assumed that they seek rest from the perpetual overcoming of the self; they seek subjective gratification, although such satisfaction may be illusory in the Hegelian sense.[7] Yet the Frankfurt School seeks not merely subjective equilibrium between the instincts and their environment; it seeks to push the instincts beyond more subjective gratification to an objective freedom in which happiness is secondary. Thus, in positing an objective happiness, the Frankfurt School seeks to end the war with nature and to cause man, despite his protestations, to be at war with himself, in order that ultimately all struggle could be abolished and life could be made peaceful, objectively and subjectively.

The mitigation of this tension between gratification and progress is part of the structure of the thought of the Frankfurt School: the overcoming of external nature must be followed by an overcoming of the self, not as reification and self-domination nor as self-realization through activity but rather as an authentic freeing of human potential, so that man can come to an authentic rest.

The vision of that rest, of a state of being that is the negation of becoming, is a return to ancient visions of existence. Just as Enlightenment ultimately returns to mythic forms, so the negation of Enlightenment is a return to the authentic core of those forms. The negation of the negation, the transcendence of the transcendent, involves a return to the ancient teachings that the Enlightenment tried to abolish. These teachings were never historically realized. Now the mythic images of the past can finally be made real: that which never was can be recollected.[8] It is in this return to mythic content that can be seen an outline of a new form of existence and of a new structure of the human psyche.

In a limited sense, the Frankfurt School really brings the theme of human existence, immanent in Western thought, to its logical conclusion. They repeat the task of Hegel and Marx by bringing becoming to rest in a mythic form of being made real. But in so doing, they also reveal an essential contradiction in the reconciliation theme of the West. Man's alienation from external reality, from the essential substrata of reality, causes existence to be defined as becoming. Hitherto existing forms of human existence have revolved

---

7. Marcuse, *Five Lectures*, p. 10.
8. Marcuse, *Counterrevolution and Revolt*, p. 99. This is also the meaning of Communism for Marx.

around activity, the concretion of becoming, rather than around rest, being. Even contemplation is, in a way, a category of becoming. Yet the motivation in becoming has been to reconcile subject and object; that is, to achieve a state of being. Even in ancient philosophy, the forms of being have revolved around forms of gratification, around the theme of the pleasures of existence.[9] Modernity did not distinguish between being and becoming; rather, becoming became a form of being. The good was to be found in activity itself. For liberalism (of which Marx was a subcategory) with its materialist conception of nature, the particular form of activity was labor. Labor itself became defined as the good life, and gratification became inextricably bound up with sheer labor. Thus, when Adorno cast a suspicious eye on Marx's notion of labor or Benjamin criticized the Social Democratic conception of life as a happily active process, their real concern was with this Marxian linkage of labor and pleasure. Marx saw labor not as a means to redemption but as redemption itself.

However, to the Frankfurt School, the objective painfulness of labor could not be denied by a subjective feeling of gratification. The Promethean myth, having attained its most powerful position as a principle of Marxism, could not deny the objective damage done by labor to the psyche. The psyche had to violate its natural proclivities in order to carry out labor. The Frankfurt School thought that the performance principle, as a form of being, was objectively false because of what it did to the psyche. The historical reality of the performance principle, its sheer historical necessity, did not transform that principle into a transcendental truth. The performance principle only defined men in an epoch, it did not define the potential reality of man.

In fully appreciating the reality of man's objective reconciliation with nature, of his conquest of it, and of the concrete meaning of the end of history, Marcuse must go backward behind Marxism, the philosophy of becoming, to pre-Modern forms that dealt with the meaning and purpose of being. Marx had considered the problem of the state[10] and the status of technology. But the attainment of being requires far more than this, for these are still considerations rooted in the realm of becoming. It is necessary to focus on the

---

9. Consider Plato's notion of the Erotic or Aristotle's Felicity.
10. The themes of Hegel's *Philosophy of Right* and of Marx's *Critique*.

The Transfiguration of Being   255

new form of man's being, a form organized not by the demands of a dynamic becoming but to serve a static existence: a being-in-itself. As Marcuse says, "Static triumphs over dynamic: but it is a static that moves in its own fullness—a productivity that is sensuousness, play and song."[11] In this way, Adorno's question about the theme of becoming as self-fulfillment and Benjamin's doubts about the busyness of the Social Democrats move toward an answer.[12]

The static reality of man, the fullness of existence, must revolve around gratification. The historical self-denial of man must give way to a form in which men seek gratification rather than deny it.[13] Thus the Frankfurt School returns to mythic forms. The progressive struggle to reconcile subject and object, man and nature, is replaced by the realized end of progress: a paradise wrought on earth, in which ancient human dreams of gratification are rendered practical and real. The labor of previous generations paves the way to being. But labor by itself cannot move beyond itself. Only through the cataclysmic intervention of the exogenous revolutionary forces can the final narrow yet impassable chasm between becoming and being be crossed. A new form of being can be created only when labor as a universal principle is cataclysmically replaced.

Nevertheless, the problem of the form of being remains. Unknowable in essence but necessary to know if one is to proceed, the theological debate on the nature of paradise is repeated by the Frankfurt School. The problem of man at the end of history, at the final abolition of becoming, is the problem of the proper form of Being. The abstract concept of self-realization must be concretized into a proper form of being human. The eternal return of the repressed—which must be repeated in the resurrection of the mythic visions of being, which alone touches on *Ur*-existence—can conjure up a path and a goal. Myth alone can comprehend the primordial humanness of true being. To negate the modern vision of being as becoming is to return cyclically to a purer vision of being.

Myth, for the Frankfurt School, represents the horizons within which men live. The new age demands a new horizon. Yet, the

---

11. Marcuse, *Eros and Civilization,* pp. 150–51.
12. Adorno, *Minima Moralia,* pp. 155–56; Benjamin, "Theses on the Philosophy of History," in *Illuminations,* pp. 258–59.
13. Self-denial is the concern of modern morality. See Adorno and Horkheimer, *Dialectic of Enlightenment,* pp. 88–89, 112–14.

demand is not simply for a new horizon, for the dream and the vision represent an ancient longing. Thus myth is critical of Marcuse in two senses. In a Nietzschean sense, myth represents horizon; it is the formal outline of being. A change of myth is critical to a change in existence. Second, myth is archaic. It represents eternal human longings. The form of the new age is to be the return of the repressed, the return of the mythical. Moreover, just as the new age is an act of cataclysmic intervention, of will, so the myth of the new age is an act of conscious choice. It too must be willed. Marcuse discusses myths when he speaks of the new form of being, because myth, history, and being are for him inextricably bound up with one another.

Marcuse, seemingly developing his thoughts out of mythic analysis of Adorno and Horkheimer's *Dialectic of Enlightenment*, returns to two antithetical, mythic forms in order to define the tension within Western thought. The forms consist of antithetical culture heroes, Prometheus and Orpheus/Narcissus:

> If Prometheus is the culture-hero of toil, productivity, and progress through repression, then the symbols of another reality principle must be sought at an opposite pole. Orpheus and Narcissus (like Dionysis to whom they are akin: the antagonist of the god who sanctions the logic of domination, the realm of reason) stands for very different reality. They have not become culture heroes of the western world: theirs is the image of joy and fulfillment; the voice which does not command but sings; the gesture which offers and receives; the deed which is peace and ends the labor of conquest; the liberation from time which unites man with god, man with nature.[14]

Prometheus, representing the progressive conquest of nature, bears as the price of his initial act of conquest the wound that the gods (the objective and external reality with which he must cope) inflict upon him. The initial purpose of the Promethean act was to bring fire (gratification and happiness) to mankind. But implicit in this act of conquest was pain. In Freudian terms, it is the perpetual repression of man in a world of scarcity. In this suffering, the original act of conquest for gratification was lost and in its place was the perpetuity of suffering that resulted from the conquest. Just as granting fire to man became an obsession to Prometheus, so labor,

---

14. Marcuse, *Eros and Civilization*, pp. 146–47.

The Transfiguration of Being 257

as an end in itself rather than as a means, has become an obsession to modern man. The performance principle, more than the Protestant ethic (since that at least was directed toward the goal of salvation), has no goal beyond its own maintenance. Thus the performance principle, implicit in the myth of Prometheus, turns becoming into the substance of being; perpetual progress becomes the form of modern existence.

The image of Prometheus is opposed by the images of Orpheus and Narcissus. They have not been the culture heroes of the Western world, yet they have been an everpresent underground longing. The return of what had been repressed is represented by their image. Where Prometheus speaks of toils, they speak of the joy of gratification. Where Prometheus seeks to dominate nature, they seek to live in harmony with its harmless and pleasant form. They represent the image of rest and the possibility of gratification. As long as man lived in a world of scarcity, as long as perpetual labor was required merely to maintain life, Orpheus and Narcissus were hidden. By exploding the horizon of Prometheus, civilization and life itself would have been destroyed. Unchecked libidinous strivings could not coexist with a perpetual struggle in which man was compelled, by gross reality, to participate. But with the coming of a new age—one in which the psychic structure represented by Prometheus was not essential for existence, one in which wealth rather than poverty defined human existence—exploding the Promethean horizon was not destructive but liberating.

Establishing a new horizon, one defined by the images of Orpheus and Narcissus, is the form of liberation; it represents a new form of being divorced from perpetual overcoming. This latter psychic form, perpetually re-creating itself under the cover of progress, now reverses its relationship to progress. Historical realities allow the underground myth to break through into consciousness. Thus both the progress of man and the cycle of repression can now be broken; the return need not be repressed any longer. A new form of existence can now manifest itself, free of historical progress and psychic cyclicism.

Marcuse derives the image of Orpheus from Rilke.[15] Orpheus is the everpresent possibility of the erotic that is within us. It sleeps, for its gratification is rooted in the unreflectiveness of sleep. Or-

---

15. Marcuse quotes Rilke in ibid., p. 147.

pheus represents the eroticization of all things. The repression of the id genitalized the erotic; it made Eros identical with reproductive sexuality. Orpheus is the image of the eroticization of the entire body. The psychic re-creation represented by Orpheus' implantation into human consciousness implies that all of the human being will be made erotic. It implies that a polymorphic sexuality, one that transcends the genitalized sexuality of the repressive era, is obtainable and will transfigure human existence into a bountiful and limitless joy. The Orphic myth also holds forth the possibility of an eroticized world in which nature itself can be made erotic. The hostile distance kept by nature before it was conquered is no longer necessary or meaningful.

The spell that Orpheus casts over man also extends to man's conception of nature. The trees are made magical. Nature itself becomes erotic. Nature, an historical object, ceases to be historical once it is conquered. It is not that nature would in and of itself become erotic. Clearly, it lacks the self-consciousness that is the prerequisite of authentic Eros. But through man, and through man under the aegis of Orpheus, nature can be viewed in an erotic light as an object of pleasure—in and of itself. The myth of Orpheus, in Marcuse's reading of Rilke's construction of it, holds open the possibility of an erotic relationship between man and nature that can replace the hostility between them that existed before the abolition of the Promethean myth by the Orphic.

The inwardness of the reflected-upon God represents the rootedness of the Orphic in the soul itself. Orpheus is itself unreflective. Man's reflection upon the Orphic expands its aura into the nooks and crannies of being. Not only nature will become a source of joy and gratification—all existence within that nature will become joyous.

The eroticization of nature has its counterpart in polymorphic sexuality. Sexuality would no longer be confined to, as Kant would have it, the mutual use of genitalia. It would expand outward so that perversion itself would become its governing principle. What is now perverse because it stands in opposition to the norms of the performance principle would become the norm. Activity would cease to be painful labor and would transform itself into joyous playfulness. Joy would not know its abolition, death, any more than did Adam before the Fall. It is this universal eroticization that, under the Orphic myth, would become the governing principle of the world.

The Transfiguration of Being

The new epoch envisioned by Marcuse is truly world historical, insofar as it involves a complete transfiguration of the subject/object relationship. From Bacon onward, nature constituted object, and man's relationship with that object was necessarily antagonistic. His triumph over nature necessarily abolished the antagonism: the relationship between slave and master, when the slave in the very roots of his being is under the control of the master, is necessarily something other than antagonistic. Thus absolute conquest dialectically implies reconciliation.

Man organizes his existence around relationships higher than himself; the conquest of nature made nature subservient to man. This nature could no longer form the antipode of the subject/object relationship. Man therefore enters into a new, reconciled relationship with nature: "The opposition between man and nature, subject and object, is overcome. Being is experienced as gratification, which unites man and nature so that the fulfillment of man is at the same time fulfillment, without violence, of nature."[16] Nature becomes more beautiful. In so doing it fulfills itself as object and at the same time becomes subject. In speaking of nature fulfilling itself, in implying a teleology, Marcuse implicitly attributes subjectivity to nature. Thus, in reconciliation, man as subject become subliminally linked to nature as subject, in the sense that both are in the process of realization. Nature is fulfilled through man and man through nature. Unity, through the parallel existences of each, becomes perfected.

There is still another dimension to this reconciliation; the objectification of man. Sensuality is necessarily linked to object, at least as a point of mediation. Sensuousness as a form of existence is the link between subject and object in the intercourse of gratification. Thus, in a sexual context, man plays the dual role of subject and object. In the autoeroticism of the myth of Narcissus (not incidentally, the other side of the Orphic) subject and object are merged practically as well as conceptually into one.

The logic of gratification compels this objectification of man. As Marcuse writes:

> When the body has completely become an object, a beautiful thing, it can foreshadow a new happiness. In suffering the most extreme reification man triumphs over reification. The artistry of the beautiful

---

16. Ibid., pp. 150–51.

body, its effortless agility and relaxation ... herald the joy to which men will attain in being liberated from the ideal once mankind, having become true subject, succeeds in the mastery of nature.[17]

As nature becomes subject, man becomes object. This is the penultimate moment of reification, for this same moment holds within itself the possibility of transcending itself. In making an object of the body, it succeeds at the same time in making it at least formally beautiful. This is the preface to making the body authentically erotic by the attainment of absolute subjectivity. It also is the preface to Narcissism.

Man turned into beautiful object is the precursor to his own eroticization. Man's eroticization liberates him, for eroticization is the practical ground upon which the logic of gratification (the negation of repressive struggle) operates. But, at the same time, it is only a moment of the process. The other side is the simultaneous subjectification, that is, self-enjoyment, which is the clearer side of liberation. Man's becoming an object represents the opening to the highest and most profound moment of liberation. To pursue the erotic, the sensual, man must become an object; total liberation dictates that man enjoy himself, perhaps most of all. If liberation ultimately means the reconciliation of subject and object, then the subjectivity of pleasure has its highest realization in itself, now as object. Practically, the reconciliation of subject and object means their merger into a single being.

Man's antagonistic relationship with nature is broken down as well. Man himself, becoming object, becomes a part of nature. He thereby splits himself into subject and object. But the schism is not centrifugal; Eros links man to himself. Instead of alienation, this split represents polymorphic self-discovery and self-pleasuring. Making man an object and nature subject reconciles the two. At the same time, in the spirit of Nietzsche turned egalitarian, it allows man to come to constitute his own horizon. Under the myth of Narcissus, man becomes his own meaning as well as his own pleasure.

In unifying subject and object, man faces a crisis. All previous forms of existence have assumed a subject/object relationship between discrete components. This relationship has been the structure

---

17. Marcuse, "Affirmative Character of Culture," in *Negations,* p. 116.

The Transfiguration of Being 261

through which man defined his being; to lose it implies the total alienation of man; man is in danger of losing his way in an utterly chaotic universe whose parts have no meaning, in which the whole has been reduced to its parts. Man confronts a most profound quandary: he must discover a new object through which his existence and activity can be defined. If man's highest activity is the search for gratification and his very being becomes erotic, then man must search for his object in the source of highest gratification: man himself becomes the object.

The Narcissus myth holds the key to the problem: Narcissus was self-gratifying. Man turns inward, finding pleasure inside of himself. He reaches into the world in order to draw pleasure from men and nature but experiences pleasure inside of his being. Indeed, as the discussion of happiness indicates, pleasure is the most profoundly subjective phenomenon in the world; to experience it (though not necessarily its source) is the most purely subjective phenomenon. It is truly not intersubjectively transmissible. Thus the objectification of man is at the same time his complete subjectification, because the Narcissistic is the least mediated and most direct and absolute pleasure knowable.

In explicating the myth of Narcissus, Marcuse and most of the Frankfurt School (Benjamin, who rooted sociality in the past, was an exception) are objectively involved in the privatization of man. It is the opposite side of Horkheimer and Adorno's bemoaning of the loss of the individual.[18] Marcuse rediscovers the individual in the age of the mass in the privacy of the erotic. In making man's self the object of being, Marcuse drives man inside himself. The process of history is the complete concretization of object; history proceeds from Spirit to political and social abstraction, to nature, and now, at the highest moment of existence, to man himself. This is not to say that the community of man is destroyed. The Frankfurt School is very much concerned to avoid annihilating the whole by the self, as they thought Nietzsche and Kierkegaard had done.[19] On the contrary, the very polymorphic nature of sexuality, the erotic role of other beings in the experience of gratification—the Orphic myth, in other words—involves the need for community.[20]

18. Horkheimer, *Eclipse of Reason*, pp. 158–60. Adorno, *Minima Moralia*, pp. 152–155.
19. Horkheimer, *Eclipse of Reason*, pp. 159–60.
20. Marcuse, *Five Lectures*, p. 14.

On the experiential level, however, the level on which the subject/object relationship is most fully realized, man is left private. The orgasm, the highest moment of the erotic, is the most intimate linking of subject and object (in either Orphic or Narcissistic moments). At the same time, on a more profound level than mere physical coupling, its pleasure is the most intensely private possible. That one cannot describe sex to a virgin or the beauty of a cloud to a blind man, that the sensuous experience, the act of gratification, cannot be transmitted from subject to subject, is proof of the private nature of gratification. In this sense, all gratificatory action is masturbatory. Orgasm is in contact with the object, but it takes place within the subject. It is in this sense that the fullness of the Narcissus myth is revealed. Narcissus is the paradigm of masturbation. It is in the self-experience of gratification that man becomes fully multidimensional, both subject and object.

This multidimensional being repeats the Jewish theme that the experience of God takes place within man. The community of worshipers at the Minyan might facilitate the relationship between man and God, not as an intermediary but rather as a conductive environment. The experience of the Day of Atonement, however, remains essentially private. Marcuse is returning with the myth of Narcissus, perhaps unconsciously, to a Jewish theme. The direct, unmediated, simultaneous experience of both subjectivity and objectivity is the highest moment of both prayer and sexuality. The concrete result is to privatize both the Jew and Marcuse's polymorphic man. The difference is that the Jew returns to the congregation; the high sacred moment passes. For Marcuse, the new moment of gratification becomes universal and permanent. Its end is to become the universal principle, one tolerating no exceptions. In becoming the universal principle, the myths of Orpheus and Narcissus serve to turn man inside himself.

Adorno, in particular, is aware of this as a problem. First, since Marcuse is really speaking of a new identity principle, he is violating Adorno's thesis that the only liberating dialectic is a perpetually negative one. Second, the other members of the Frankfurt School speak directly of Narcissism only to criticize it. Adorno associated Narcissism with defense mechanisms, claiming the Narcissism is libido that, having been thwarted in the world, ricochets inward to find a home in defeat.[21] The stakes are high. If Narcissism is

21. Adorno, *Sociology and Psychology*, 2:88.

The Transfiguration of Being

allowed to stand as a universal principle, then the species part of species-being is in danger of being lost to a discrete notion of being while the positing of any reconciliatory principle of existence threatens to become a repressive positivity. On the other hand, failing to find a mythic alternative leaves one impotent against Prometheus, that is, in danger of nihilism. The Hero-ism of Narcissism is a danger; avoiding all principle is an even graver one.

Even more seriously, the rejection of Narcissus implies a rejection of gratification as a universal principle. For Adorno or the rest of the Frankfurt School to reject Narcissism outright, therefore, would risk losing their roots in matter and threaten capitulation to the prurient bourgeoisie asceticism associated with Enlightenment and the performance principle. Marcuse, in a way, recognizes the quandary least clearly and so capitulates to Narcissus most easily. Adorno, who knows the problem perhaps best, vacillates out of intelligence. But in the end, in the realm of phantasy, he too finally capitulates to privatism as the experiential salvation of individualism.

The Frankfurt School's discussion of the new principle of being has an abstracted quality to it. The crisis of modernity is not so much the lack of principles as the lack of consciousness of principles and the further inability to actualize those principles. The myths of Orpheus and Narcissus represent the resurrection of an undamaged psyche. But given the power of surplus-repression and the continued dominance of the Promethean myth, it is not at all clear that the resurrected mythology can be realized. Here, as in other fields, the dialectic appears arrested. The only hope is for a cataclysmic intrusion that would disrupt the structure of consciousness. For the Frankfurt School, phantasy represents the possibility of such a cataclysmic intrusion from outside the confines of the administered consciousness. Phantasy is the realm to which the eternally repressed has been exiled; they see it arising, shattering the structure of the reasonable world and forcing its symbols, Orpheus and Narcissus, to become the new historical principles.

Phantasy for the Frankfurt School, as for Freud, constitutes a very real level of existence, one in which reality can be negated and a new form of experience erected. Phantasy results from schism in the pleasure ego.[22] The bulk of it formed the reality principle and, as such, joined the mainstream of the psyche. This made it power-

---

22. This is also the source of Narcissism according to Adorno, ibid., p. 88.

ful, the dominant element of the psyche. Another, much smaller, segment refused to join the reality principle; in a way, it repudiated the real. It refused to acknowledge that the real demanded such suffering. It repudiated the real as something cruelly unreal. This pleasure ego, which operates on a level preceding the contact of the psyche with reality, serves as the base of phantasy. In effect, phantasy retains the structure of the psyche before its organization by reality.[23]

In this sense, phantasy is a manifestation of the return of repressed qualities. The faculty of phantasy is important for its insistence on utopia. In its authentic form it cannot imagine destruction or horror, for both are thanatotic and phantasy exists before the thanatotic moment. As such, it is the negation of reality. In demanding utopia it insists, unreasonably, upon a reconciliation between its demands and the world. The very nature of phantasy, the reclusive and anarchistic manner in which it carries on its warfare in the psyche against the dominant reality principle, shows its longing for private gratification. It effectively reinforces, by being focused on the discrete ego of the being as well as the id, the desire of Narcissus for himself. Phantasy turns the organism inward.

Phantasy constitutes the unreasonable longing of the organism for a gratification promised by its body but which was ultimately denied. It is a return of the repressed in the form of dreams, hallucinations, and art, in an unreasoned and unreasonable demand for utopia.[24] It is unreasonable in having no concern for rationality; the dream as dream is indifferent to either the law of nature or of history. From the viewpoint of reality, however, phantasy is a constant reproach. It stands as a perpetual criticism of the insufficiency of the world. Its strength is in its cataclysmic seductiveness. By seducing the organism away from the reality principle in a Siren's Song, which may finally manifest itself in the hallucination of hashish[25] or in the politicized schizophrenia of R. D. Laing, the faculty of phantasy shatters the power of the reality principle. The organism is sucked into a vortex of rational utopianism in which the

23. Marcuse, *Eros and Civilization*, pp. 128-29.
24. Ibid., p. 130.
25. This was, I think, the reason that Benjamin wrote a series of articles on hashish, collected in a volume entitled, *Über Haschisch*, in which he records his own experience with the drug. The opposition of hashish to reality can be seen most clearly on pages 72-75. Hashish served to conjure phantasy. This is also the link between Frankfurt and its marijuana-using followers.

The Transfiguration of Being

impossible comes to constitute the reasonable. It is the Messianic intrusion of the exiled into the consciousness of the human being.

Historically, the impact of the intrusion of phantasy has been the cataclysmic destruction of the organism. The rejection of the reality principle led to the catastrophic annihilation of the individual. Having forced man to exile phantasy, nature would respond to its return, to the mad withdrawal of the individual from the rule of its principles, by destroying him. This, however, was true only in a world in which utopianism was utterly opposed to the real. Until now the world could not bear the utopian possiblities that were the substance of phantasy's reality.

A new moment has dawned, however, in which the utopian possibilities of phantasy, hitherto ridiculed, have become the most reasonable prospect.[26] Phantasy is perpetually indifferent to reason. Reason, however, need be indifferent to phantasy only under those historical conditions that render phantasy destructive. The principle of this new age is that the possibilities hitherto exiled into phantasy can now be made into principles of existence. Phantasy's vision of instant and constant gratification, its multitudinous perversions, was unthinkable under the historical conditions of scarcity. Under the circumstances of conquered nature, however, those dreams become not merely possibilities but actually the most reasonable solutions to history's problems. The Paris slogan of 1968, "Be reasonable, demand the impossible," reflects this new reality. Phantasy can now end its long exile.

Generally, there is a link between reason and phantasy. As Horkheimer puts it:

> One thing which this way of thinking [Critical Theory] has in common with fantasy is that an image of the future which springs indeed from a deep understanding of the present determines men's thoughts and actions even in periods when the course of events seem to be heading far away from such a future and seems to justify every reaction except belief in fulfillment. It is not the arbitrariness and supposed independence of fantasy that is the common bond here, but its obstinacy.[27]

---

26. See Benjamin's praise of Fourier's apparently irrational utopianism in "Theses on the Philosophy of History," p. 259. Also, see Marcuse, *Essay on Liberation*, pp. 3–6.

27. Horkheimer, "Traditional and Critical Theory," in *Critical Theory*, p. 220.

Reason, like phantasy, is a form of the eternal return of the repressed. By obstinately returning to the path of its deepest demands, by perpetually wishing for the realization of its deepest hopes, even in moments when history seems farthest away from then, reason shares with phantasy the unshaking commitment of the historically impossible. True, reason turns itself toward the demands, or the historical moment, while phantasy perpetually remains faced in one direction: toward gratification. But, although more flexible, reason in the end is as unwilling to turn away from ultimate fulfillment of its rationally determined dreams as is phantasy. In the end, it shares with phantasy a distant criticism of reality.[28] This formal linkage of phantasy and reason is doubly enforced under the current circumstances of history, in which reason and phantasy can both open themselves to the same possibilities and make the same demands upon the world.

Thus the faculty of phantasy, conjured up through dreams, narcotics,[29] or even madness, serves to shatter the psychic structure of instrumental reason. Instrumental reason ceases to be critical. Just as Freud sees the ego split between the reality and the pleasure ego, so reason splits, in this age, between affirmative and critical reason. And just as the two egos stand in opposition to each other, so do the two reasons.

Critical reason, that is, Critical Theory itself, allies itself with the other exile of the psyche: phantasy. Since the principled opposition between them has been abolished by history, they wage a joint struggle against the instrumentalized reason of late capitalism—one from the side of philosophy, the other from the side of the unrational psyche. Phantasy and reason effectively become one.

In so doing, together they forge a space between the powers of Positivism and existentialism. Armed only with reason, the opposition to these overarching systems was impotent. Critical Theory by itself was forced into pure hermeneutics. Armed with the revanchist power of phantasy, the hermeneutic of the text can be replaced by a hermeneutic of the mind. With phantasy it becomes, at least on one side, nonrational. As such, it can avoid the powerful rational seductiveness of both Positivism and Heideggerianism. In a sense, Critical

---

28. Adorno, *Minima Moralia*, p. 127.
29. On this, see Schweppenhauser, "Die Vorschule der profanen Erleuchtung," in *Über Haschisch*, pp. 13–23.

The Transfiguration of Being

Theory as phantasy is allied with both Heidegger and Positivism. Like Positivism, it is wedded to the sensual. Its only concern is with the erotic gratification of the organism. As such, it partakes of the materialism of Positivism. On the other side, it realizes what Heidegger promised but could not deliver, the abolition of fact-oriented reason. Critical Theory is, by its nature and through its wedding to phantasy, beyond the fact. Even though conjoined to sensuality and materialism (through gratification), it still is concerned with a sensuality beyond the ontically given. In a way, Critical Theory seeks to overcome the distinction between the ontic and ontological by granting to things in the world a gratificatory commitment to the ontic, while recognizing that, dialectically, such gratification can be realized only through a commitment to an authenticated ontology. Being itself must be transformed if the practical gratification is to be achieved. This gives Critical Theory's phantastic quality at least a theoretical possibility of transcendence.

It remains unclear what force could serve practically to break the hegemony of instrumental reason over the reified consciousness of man. It is unclear that there is historically any hope: if there is, it apparently resides in the congealed form of phantasy: the work of art. Adorno sees art and a critical metaphysics as inextricably linked:

> Nietzsche's work is brimful of anti-metaphysical invective, but no formula describes metaphysics as faithfully as Zarathustra's "Pure fool, pure poet." The thinking artist understood the unthought art. A thought that does not capitulate to the wretchedly ontical will founder upon its criteria; truth will turn into untruth, philosophy into folly. And yet philosophy cannot abdicate if stupidity is not to triumph in realized unreason.... Folly is truth in the form which men are stuck with as amid untruth they will not let truth go. Art is semblance even at its highest peaks; but its semblance, the irresistible part of it, is given to it by what is not semblance. What art, notably the art decried as nihilistic, says in refraining from judgments is that everything is not just nothing.[30]

To Adorno, then, art is the last refuge of the metaphysical protest against the stupidly ontical, against the reality that is not as much as

---

30. Adorno, *Negative Dialectics*, p. 404.

it could be. This is one side of art. If art is the bulwark of metaphysics, it is also the refuge of phantasy.

It is in art the phantasy first realizes itself. Sublimated in the aesthetic form, hidden within the structure of art, is the repressed harmony of sensousness and reason that is the meaning of phantasty. Phantasy contravenes those previous forms of the reality principle that have denied the possibility of sensual gratification and have made gratification irrational. Phantasy denies this division of sensuousness and reason. It insists that gratification is possible and that reason and gratification are not irreconcilable. Art, the objectification of beauty, is the intellectualized manifestation of the repressed longing of phantasy: it reconciles reason and gratification within its form. On the one hand, it takes the sensuous beauty of reality and, by abstracting it, by subjecting it to rationalized forms, by making a science of beauty, it abstractly unites (as phantasy does) gratification (beauty, sensuality) with the structure of reason (science, form). At the same time, the work of art unites phantasy and metaphysics within its existential confines.

In history, however, art, like phantasy, has remained illusory. Just as phantasy has represented a longing for liberation, for the permanent return of the repressed, so art, as the semiconcretization of phantasy, has been made utopian by the historical epochs in which it was forced to operate:

> ... for only in art has bourgeois society tolerated its own ideals and taken them seriously as a general demand. What counts as utopia, phantasy, and rebellion in the world of fact is allowed in art. There, affirmative culture has displayed the forgotten truths over which realism triumphs in daily life. The medium of beauty decontaminates truth and sets it apart from the present. What occurs in art occurs with no obligation. When this beautiful world is not completely represented as something long past, it is deprived of concrete relevance by the magic of beauty.[31]

Thus, just as phantasy is denied by the performance principle, the bourgeois epoch transforms art into illusion. It renders art fantastic, for illusion is merely phantasy from a "practical" point of view. Just as phantasy maintains its truth, its knowledge in the face of the

---

31. Marcuse, "Affirmative Character of Culture," in *Negations,* p. 114. Also see Adorno, *Ästhetische Theorie,* pp. 372–73.

The Transfiguration of Being

attacks of reality, so art, within the context of its form, in the sensuous beauty found within those forms, maintains its truth.[32] But the reality of scarcity necessarily transfigures the functioning of that truth. In reality, beauty cannot become the organizing reality of the new order, its truth cannot be perpetually realized, because of the unbeautiful nature of the world. The reality of the world, the necessary transience of the experience of beauty in a world of suffering, makes the longing for beauty particularly vehement; one wants the return of the repressed with a vengeance. Beauty in this sense has a liberating quality. The bitterness felt at the loss of a beauty that art has shown to be possible, to be real in the Hegelian sense, drives men either to despair or to struggle against the reality that denies perpetual sensual gratification.[33] The man who abstractly experiences beauty longs for its concretization in the world.

The reality of scarcity drove man to bitter despair because beauty could not be fully realized in time and in the world. It drove men to see beauty as being outside of time, to make beauty abstract, or worse, to deny beauty. When the historical moment of the end of scarcity arrives, a new form of reaction to beauty becomes possible: a longing becomes realization; one last act of becoming arrives at a perfected state of being, a state within time and upon this earth. Thus art, the representation of the repressed, can choose to be not simply illusory, need not present merely fleeting chips of beauty; but by transforming its content, it can become a real force in liberation. As Marcuse writes:

> By virtue of this transformation of the specific historical universe in the work of art—a transformation which arises in the presentation of the specific content itself—art opens the established reality to another dimension; that of possible liberation. To be sure, this is illusion, *schein*, but an illusion which another reality shows forth. And it does so only if art wills itself an illusion: as an unreal world other than the established one. And precisely in this transfiguration, art preserves and transcends its classic character. And transcends it not toward a realm of mere fiction and fantasy, but toward a universe of concrete possibilities.[34]

32. Adorno, ibid., pp. 134–39.
33. Marcuse, *Eros and Civilization*, pp. 107–9.
34. Marcuse, *Counterrevolution and Revolt*, pp. 87–88. Also see Adorno, *Ästhetische Theorie*, pp. 122–23.

By forming itself as an illusion, by demonstrating in illusion the possibility of beauty and of sensual gratification, art demonstrates that there can be a reconciliation between the pleasure principle and reality principle. Art itself could serve as a revolutionary force, as a power in becoming; at the same time, it would constitute the structure of a new form of being. This is Marcuse's view of Rilke and Benjamin's of Kafka.

What gives art its truly subversive possibility is its unity with phantasy.[35] The demands of the eternally repressed cannot be eternally denied. Pleasure's denial was rooted in the ability and need of nature to destroy men who succumbed to its seductive power. Now, however, society and not nature is what retaliates against those who would succumb. The power of phantasy is infinitely greater against society than against nature. True, society has the sophisticated weapons of philosophy, culture, and surplus repression on its side. But the phantasized metaphysics, the eroticized art, and the possibilities for gratification will inevitably rise up against each of these arms. In the end, the most powerful weapon, the last-ditch defense of the repressive social order, is brute strength, the sheer ability of the social order to destroy those who would oppose it. This is why fascism is the final form of modernity's social order; it is also why fascism will fail. Who will prevent the seduction of the oppressor? Finally, there is the possibility that the vengeful, Messianic, return of the repressed in the complex of apparent madness and art will free the mind of the oppressor as well as shatter the bonds of the oppressed. That this will happen is never certain; it is the perpetual Messianic hope.

Clearly this idea of art as redeemer is in tension with Benjamin's warning that art should never be allowed to rule politics.[36] Adorno, who sides with Marcuse against Benjamin, explicitly acknowledges and rejects Benjamin's thesis that the domination of politics by art is fascistic. Adorno held that Benjamin's thesis was true at the moment he wrote it but was untrue now in view of the overwhelming power of empirical reality: now art becomes a progressive force in liberation.[37] Even when the artist is officially a reactionary, his nostalgic reaction conjures the repressed to return. It is this aspect

---

35. Adorno, ibid., p. 55.
36. See Chapter 12.
37. Adorno, *Ästhetische Theorie*, pp. 377–80.

The Transfiguration of Being

of nostalgia that renders reaction potentially revolutionary. In a way, Benjamin acknowledged Adorno's point. Benjamin's extensive collection of fairy tales and his studies in the world of the child (which he saw repeated particularly in the work of Proust and generally in the work of art) represents his understanding, paradoxical as it may seem, that if there is hope, it resides with danger. His collection of fairy tales is a political as well as an existential statement. Bound up in the fairy tale is the repressed possibility (and dangers) that the child in his purity once knew but that the adult, now sullied, has forgotten. Childhood too may run amok, but despite the danger, the only hope is to collect, arrange, and thereby conjure up the critical powers residing in the work of childish art (the art most intimately linked to phantasy in and of itself). Benjamin feared art because of his understanding of its dangers, which were certainly clearer to him than to Marcuse.[38] But had he lived to see the rise of fascism and the humiliation of Ezra Pound, he very probably would have had to break with Brecht over the role of art. Otherwide there would have been no hope at all.

It was in art and phantasy that the Messianic hopes of all the other realms were bound up. The Messianic intrusion of the exogenous political forces depended on the emergence of a prior consciousness; this was the crisis of Marcuse's "Repressive Tolerance." Phantasy paved the way for such a transformed consciousness. It placed a foot in the philosophic camps of Heidegger and Positivism while neutralizing both through its nonphilosophic side. It shattered the walls of the culture industry by refusing to bow to its aesthetic dictates. And it breached even the most reified consciousness by breaking in, against the will of the apparent subject, from the everpresent and ultimately untouchable realms of being. Phantasy was the reality and preface to the authentic liberation of man and the basis of his realization of authentic gratification.

The emergence of gratification as the highest human principle, the objectification of man, leads to a new form of human existence. Where spirit was the object, religion was the form and prayer the activity. Where the polis was the object, the political was the form and politics the activity. Where nature was the object, economics was the form and labor the activity. But now, with the emergence of a new object, man himself, a new form of existence is required to

---

38. See Scholem, "Walter Benjamin," *Leo Baeck Yearbook,* pp. 119–20.

relate subject and object. The form is gratification; that is, it is the perpetual pursuit of pleasure in a self-realized universe. But an activity needed to concretize the new form of existence. The Frankfurt School found this form of activity in play.

In play, the sensuous and the rational are reconciled.[39] The sensuous, the demand for pleasure, seeks to turn all activity into pursuit of gratification. The rational is content, or is forced to be content, to pursue mere existence. This is an insoluble contradiction in a world of scarcity, where full gratification contradicts survival. Yet with the transformation of the universe into a place of abundance, the contradiction between reason and gratification is eradicated. The pursuit of pleasure becomes completely rational, for it does not lead to self-destruction. Further, the pursuit of anything but pleasure is fundamentally irrational. To pursue painful labor for its own sake is no longer necessary. Thus the proper activity of man in relation to the new object, himself, is play. Play embodies, in and of itself, pleasure. As Marcuse writes:

> The play impulse is the vehicle of this liberation. The impulse does not aim for playing with something: rather it is the play of life itself, beyond want and external compulsion—the manifestation of an existence without fear and anxiety, and thus, the manifestation of freedom itself.... In a genuinely humane civilization, the human existence will be play rather than toil and man will live in display rather than need.[40]

Thus existence itself, the very process of living, will be what brings man gratification.

In this sense man turns inward, into his own existence. This inwardness is made possible by the pacification of the externalities. This pacification requires a unity between man and external forces, a truce (so to speak) or a conquest. But there is an inwardness in the forms of existence—in gratification, phantasy, play—that seems to lead beyond this prior unity to a new level of existence. It is one in which the Frankfurt School seems to want to dwell only briefly in their telling of the tale. It is an existence of singularity. In this

---

39. Marcuse, *Eros and Civilization*, p. 171.
40. Ibid., p. 171. Adorno claims that intellectuals have already abolished the distinction (*Minima Moralia*, p. 84).

The Transfiguration of Being 273

existence, men live apart from other men, although they are linked by their common heritage of struggle to pacificy the external and by their continued common effort to subdue nature.

But beyond this linkage, there is a gulf between men. As each plays, as each pursues his own gratificatory existence, and as each experiences that gratification, he is separated from other men by the impossibility of communicating the meaning of the pleasures that are being experienced. Moreover, there appears to be no need to transmit that meaning. First, gratification is inherently private and requires no communication, even if communication were possible. Second, where the possibility of gratification is equally available to all, there is no need for secondhand accounts. If happiness is universal, vicariousness as a human faculty must necessarily be lost. But vicariousness is the basis of discourse. With the loss of vicariousness, discourse is uprooted. Further, the fullness of all men's pleasures would leave little to be said. The fullness of the pleasure would leave men speechless. Thus in a very real sense, communication between men, beyond that necessary to facilitate mutual masturbation, would decline. The act of giving would become meaningless in a world where all equally possessed abundance, both physiological and psychological.

Human communication, at its most meaningful deals with the highest levels of human experience. The experience of Moses with God, an experience that all could not share in equally, made the Pentateuch meaningful and necessary. Plato's dialogues dealt with significant knowledge that the many could share in only vicariously; few could create philosophical intercourse, the linking of reason and speech, on such a level. Even the discussions in a modern boardroom or factory are meaningful experiences in human existence. Yet, what form of communication is possible when the highest human activity is gratificatory? Gratification is inside of man and available to all men. What needs to be said? What could be said?

Logically, human communications, beyond the immediately sensual (that which is necessary for pleasure), would logically be broken off by universal gratification. The new man experiencing the new existence will be different from all previous men in this sense: he will be more alone than other men were. He will also be more self-sufficient than other men have been. Thus a strangely solitary figure emerges: not superman but last man, playing rather than working, experiencing the new universe, organizing his existence by the concept of play rather than that of work.

Play, in a sense, is pleasurable work. It is activity that gives pleasure in and of itself. Initially, pleasure was the motivation for work. Men worked because it gave them pleasure to do so. Thus play is a return to the most primitive form of existence possible to man. It is a return to the only form of existence where activity is not inherently painful. To quote Marcuse:

> To be sure, there is a mode of work which offers a high degree of libidinal satisfaction, which is pleasurable in its execution. And artistic work where it is genuine, seems to grow out of a non-repressive instinctual constellation and to envisage non-repressive aims—so much so that the term sublimation seems to require considerable modification if applied to this kind of work.[41]

This is precisely the point of play: it involves a desublimation and, therefore, a real transformation of the structure of the psyche. Play is the extension of art as a form of existence. In this sense, Marcuse is transfiguring Marx and, at the same time, rescuing him. Labor for Marx was both painful and essential to human existence; the end of alienated labor does not mean the end of labor itself. Thus the problem laid at Marx's feet by Arendt—the tension between the need to abolish labor and while acknowledging its necessity for human existence—is dealt with by Marcuse through the reintroduction of Schiller's notion of play. Activity remains essential to man, but that activity is not necessarily labor. The abolition of labor leads to a new form of existence, play. Thus by extending Freud's concept of instincts into a new historical epoch, the problem of Marx is resolved: the content of nonalienated labor is defined and its form is found within the realm of the aesthetic.

Through the introduction of the concept of aesthetics, the problem of the nature of liberated productivity, implicit throughout the work of early Marx and particularly salient today in non-Soviet revolutionary movements, is resolved. The aesthetic becomes the form of human productivity.[42] As we have seen, art is a manifesta-

---

41. Marcuse, *Eros and Civilization*, p. 77.
42. Marcuse, *Essay on Liberation*, p. 45.

The Transfiguration of Being

tion of phantasy; it is imaginings structured in a aesthetic form. But as long as the level of productivity is low, the possibility of realizing the beautiful utopia that the aesthetic can imagine is nil. The truth of the modern epoch is the incredible potential of the industrial machine. Thus there is the possibility of realizing phantasy concretely. The aesthetic becomes the organizing force of modern society. Material productivity and aesthetic creativity merge. Creation as an act of imaginative transcendence and production as an act of brute domination of the potential wealth of nature are no longer distinctive. Creativity is brought to earth and production is no longer exploitative. The distinctive feature of the aesthetic was its separation from reality; it shared with phantasy an unfamiliarity with the concrete. The introduction of the aesthetic into the material world causes art to lose its distance. Imagination ceases to be purely abstract and becomes concretely connotative. Just as the world form is transformed by the action of the aesthetic, the aesthetic is transformed by the impact of the world upon it.[43]

The role of the aesthetic in creating the new world is to force the creation of the new forms of production. What is needed is "the development of new modes and ends of production—new not only (and perhaps not at all) with respect to technical innovations and production relations, but with respect to the different human needs and the different human relationships in working for the satisfaction of those needs."[44] What is needed is the end of opposition between individual and social needs, not through the suppression of individual needs but through recognition of them and the altering of the social order to suit the individual. Productivity is rejected in favor of human creation; in this sense, the reconciliation of the aesthetic and the world mirrors the reconciliation between art and productivity.

The creation of a new society would revolve around the creation of a sensuous environment, one from which man could draw gratification without pain.[45] This sensualization, the eroticization of the world, parallels the subjectification of nature: nature, the environment, through acts of human creation, will become truly erotic. This eroticization of nature is paralleled in man. Scarcity

---

43. Adorno, *Ästhetische Theorie*, pp. 518–19.
44. Marcuse, *Essay on Liberation*, p. 88.
45. Ibid., p. 92; Horkheimer, *Eclipse of Reason*, pp. 100–101.

required that libido be diverted from sexuality to labor. The erotic was repressed, forced into a purely genital form, and the body deeroticized. Now, the totality of the human body must once more become erotic: "The organism in its entirety becomes the substratum of sexuality while at the same time the instincts' objective is no longer absorbed by a specialized function—mainly that of bringing one's own genitals into contact with those of someone of the opposite sex."[46]

The eroticization of the body and the sensualization of the environment means that all truly human activity will bring erotic joy to man. It is in this sense that play, this epoch's highest form of human activity, must be understood: it is a truly joyous thing in an erotic sense. The eroticization of both the subject and object of the previous epoch and their unification into a single unity (which does not negate the essential privateness of man) completes the reconciliation of man with that which hitherto has rested outside of him. In a sense, utopia has been created. This has become possible through the realization of the progress of man. This state of being is the negation of all previous becoming. It is, at the same time, its culmination. Perpetual progress has given way, because of its own success, to perpetual gratification. The Frankfurt School's own image of being gives way to what Adorno feared most: identity.

46. Marcuse, *Eros and Civilization*, p. 187.

CONCLUSION

The Frankfurt School and the Failure of Modernity: A Critique

Herbert Marcuse, speaking for the Frankfurt School, proclaimed the spirit of a new age: the age of Eros. The conquest of nature, together with the Messianic shattering of the structures of mind and polity that supported Thanatos, created a new and historical moment in which the joys of sensual pleasure triumphed over a world of suffering. Now, at this final moment in which becoming can come to rest in a self-satisfied being, history could be replaced by the perpetual enjoyment of existence. Only minimal forms of social maintenance would be necessary to perpetuate social and economic conquests, and the quantities of life so expended would be an insignificantly minuscule part of the quality of existence, or else a pleasurable diversion from the pursuit of sensual gratification.[1]

It is a problem, however, to imagine a world in which all that stands against man has been so fully conquered that all laborious activity is made insignificant. Even Proudhon saw a need to administer things even as the administration of men was abolished. The administration of things—that is, the perpetual vigilance of men to keep the things they have procured for themselves under their control—demands more than a brief part of existence. At the very least, administration would require a degree of conscious attention to the problem that could only detract from the unmediated pleasurableness of life.

Even if administration were not a problem, however, there is another problem on which Marcuse's vision of eternal gratification founders. That is the problem of time and its issue, death. The Frankfurt School deals extensively with the problem of scarcity and

1. Marcuse, *Eros and Civilization*, p. 187.

the process whereby man overcomes it. On close inspection, this problem is seen to be really a subsection of the general struggle of man against death and time. These are, jointly, the great enemies of man. Scarcity without entropy is, after all, not very threatening. Scarcity is fearsome only because of the decay and destruction with which it threatens the organism. Thus the perpetual struggle of human activity is a general struggle against death and against time.

Marcuse observed that under the bourgeois form (and indeed he might have added, in general), there was particular bitterness about art, stemming from the utter transience of the experience of its beauty. The enemy of art and its reconciliation with the world is time. The viewer experiences art and its beauty in monads of time set aside for that purpose by society and fate. The moment passes and the viewer is plunged once more into the general ugliness of the world. The experience of beauty leaves one bitter with anger at a world and society in which beauty cannot be universal. One feels a tragic nostalgia. Marcuse would blame nature for the transience of beauty before the rise of the bourgeois world and he would blame society after the triumph of man over nature. The real culprit, however, seems to be neither nature nor society but an enemy that overarches both: time. Time, even if the world were perfect, would rob the work of art of its beauty either by rendering it commonplace or by annihilating it at the end of time, at death.

Life, like the work of art, is transient both in what it can endure, even of joyous things, and in how long it can endure. Marcuse argues that bourgeois art is tragic in its transitoriness, but bourgeois life is tragic for the same reasons. The triumph of man over nature in the simple sense announced by Marcuse cannot abolish the fundamental transitoriness of existence, any more than abolishing the bourgeois epoch would avoid the tragedy of art and its loss. Life itself is transient. It is perhaps the most utterly transient form in the universe. By its nature, it is rooted in time; it is by its nature entropic. And time and death are, in the simplest sense, the abolition and negation of the erotic. The conquest of brute nature in no way touches upon the subliminal theft of pleasure by time. Each moment that passes sees the loss of another moment of time and its contents, no matter how pleasurable. With the loss of each moment, death comes closer.

Therefore, when Marcuse speaks of a new form of existence, one founded on the statics of pleasure and gratification rather than the transcendent struggles of progress, he speaks of life that has utterly exhausted the possibilities of existence. The conquest of the erotic is the end of the dialectic. The abolition of the Promethean in favor of the Orphic and Narcissistic is based on the end of the need to struggle. Yet the presence of death, the negation of life, proves that the dialectic perpetuates itself, despite Marcuse's pronouncements. Man has not come to rest and cannot come to rest, because nature, now in its ultimate guise of time, has not been reconciled to man.

It is the eternity of the universe (eternal in that it is time itself), the source of the joys of existence, that coupled with the transience of existence imbues life with the special bitterness that Marcuse assigned only to bourgeois art. The perpetual rest that he envisioned for man is not, in fact, to be man's but still belongs to the universe. Nature perpetuates itself in the face of man's death. To speak of rest in the face of death is not to find a fully liberated eros; rather, it is to abandon hope itself. To speak of the conquest of nature and of the impending abolition of struggle in the face of omnipresent death is actually an act of resignation. It resigns man to his fate, to his ultimate scarcity, all the while fraudulently proclaiming the millennium.

The tragedy of death becomes all the more intense over against the new myth of existence, the pleasures of Orpheus and Narcissus. Death in a painful world is, in a way, a reward. The abandonment of suffering is not in itself tragic. Rather, it may be seen as redemptive. But in a pleasurable life, death comes not as a relief but as a tragedy. The release of man from the sorrows of his existence calls for praise of the universe; his expulsion from a life of joy calls for imprecations. Thus death is actually made more tragic if the Orphic myth of polymorphic sexuality is realized. An utterly pleasurable world dooms man to spend his life contemplating not simply its joys but their impending loss. What can be endured in an evil world becomes a heartache that would permeate and destroy the very fabric of the erotic in a good world. Time's ally, death, negates all the claims made for life by Marcuse's Orpheus.

His Narcissus radicalizes the problem even further. Adorno writes, "Only a solipsistic philosophy could acknowledge an ontological priority to 'my' death over and against any other."[2] Aside from other problems with this passage (such as the profound and

2. Adorno, *Jargon of Authenticity*, p. 150.

unsolipsistic concern of the Christian with his death) it must be pointed out that Narcissism is basically a solipsism. Narcissism existentially proclaims the primacy of "my" pleasure over that of others. It is thus a solipsism in that the subject and the object of pleasure are identical. The Narcissist is profoundly concerned with his death—and must be, for in an existential sense the Narcissist has come to constitute his own universe. For him, death extinguishes not merely a life but the complete universe. Marcuse makes Heidegger concrete here but without Heidegger's sophistication concerning the relation of Being and becoming and without his subtlety concerning time. Thus, for Marcuse, the brute fact of death explodes the brute reality of pleasure.

Marcuse is caught in a bind. On the one hand, not only does the existence of death threatens the structure of his erotic monism, but the problem of death is actually intensified and made more tragic by the new modes and myths of existence. On the other hand, if he struggles against death or advocates the development of technology to abolish death, he repudiates Orpheus and Narcissus and proclaims the rebirth of Prometheus, the mortal enemy of peaceful gratification.

The attempt to abolish death, if it is to be at all practical, must assume the continuation and expansion of technology. Technology is necessary to hold scarcity at bay and simultaneously to make the environment conducive to long life (that is, to eliminate carcinogenic material, poisons, and the like) while still maintaining society's dominance of nature. For the individual, technology must address itself to the physiology of death in order to arrest the process of nature. To abolish death, technology would have to be so expanded that it might administer and make unnatural the body itself. In all cases, technology and the harsh struggle that is its element would have to be maintained, extended, and brought to rule in hitherto untouched areas. The struggle against death, in any practical form, would reincarnate Prometheus as a cultural form and drive Orpheus and Narcissus back underground.

Marcuse is not foolish enough to miss the threat that death and its continued existence poses to his system: "But the fatal enemy of lasting gratification is time, the inner finiteness, the brevity of all conditions. The ideal of integral human liberation, therefore, necessarily contains the vision of the struggle against time."[3] Marcuse

---

3. Marcuse, *Eros and Civilization*, p. 175.

clearly realizes that he must modify his theory to accommodate this overpowering reality. Either he must embrace perpetual struggle against death or he must make death itself erotic. The former course explodes the totality of his teleological structure; the eternal struggle against death would extinguish the possibility of gratification as an absolute principle. Under these circumstances the logic of transcendence, which he and Frankfurt School inveigh against, could not be brought to heel by the logic of gratification, which they praise.

At the same time, Marcuse cannot embrace the erotic death, because to do so would be to accept Neitzsche in the fullness of his meaning. Consider Nietzsche in *Zarathustra:* "Many die too late and a few die too early. The doctrine still sounds strange: die at the right time.... I show you the death that consummates—a spur and a promise to the survivors. He that consummates his life dies his death victoriously."[4] In this view, death is the consummation of life, the greatest and deepest act of will. To accept it as such is to accept the perpetuity and validity of Thanatos alongside Eros. To do this would also explode the erotic monism that is the motive force in Marcuse's world. To see virtue in the negation of Eros is to see virtue in the negation of gratification. The implication that meaningful life is more than perpetual joy destroys the myth of Orpheus. Existence would come to be struggle once again—not the progressive struggle of Hegel, to be sure, but the cyclical struggle of Nietzsche.

Marcuse accepts the danger to his thought represented by death. But the problem seems insoluble within the context of Marcuse's thought. Marcuse himself understands the problem and Nietzsche as well, yet he cannot make peace with any alternative. Marcuse himself writes:

> The eternal return thus includes the return of suffering, but suffering as a means for more gratification, for the aggrandizement of joy.... The doctrine of the eternal return obtains all its meaning from the central proposition that 'joy wants eternity'—wants itself and all things to be eternal.[5]

In attempting to understand Nietzsche, Marcuse founders on the heart of his problem: joy cannot have eternity. Suffering may be a

---

4. Nietzsche, "Thus Spoke Zarathustra," in *The Portable Nietzsche*, p. 183.
5. Marcuse, *Eros and Civilization*, p. 112.

means for gratification, but the end of suffering is death and the end of all sensation. Where Nietzsche, in the power of this thought, can speak of an eternal return and hence give meaning to eternity, Marcuse, having focused on gratification as the complete negation of suffering, can do no more than look longingly for affirmation in death. To fully accept the metaphysics of the eternal return would be impossible for him. If he embraced death he would abandon the very theme of his thought.

Marcuse has only two choices. He can embrace perpetual progress and the overcoming of death, or he can accept death as affirmative and offer a friendly hand to Thanatos. To do either is fatal to his thought. To do nothing would throw his system into a philosophical sterility from which it could never escape. Instead, and amazingly, Marcuse comes out trying to do both:

> Death would cease to be an instinctual goal. It remains fact, perhaps even an ultimate necessity—but a necessity against which the unrepressed energy of mankind will protest, against which it will wage its greatest struggle. In this struggle, reason and instinct would unite. Under conditions of truly human existence the difference between succumbing to disease at the age of ten, thirty, fifty or even seventy and dying a 'natural' death after a fulfilled life may well be a difference worth fighting for with all instinctual energy.[6]

Thus he implies both struggle against death and an embrace of death. Death itself is not the enemy; the enemy is the unconsummated death. Nonetheless, death must be struggled against. Both perpetual struggle and Nietzsche's free death are accepted.

This compromise, aside from being impossible, does not clearly save Marcuse. Both the admission that death is scarcity (of time) against which man must struggle and the presentation of it also as the consummation of life are not merely contradictory but dangerous to his structure of liberated being. In either case, the state of perpetual self-gratification is threatened. It is a problem on which Marcuse founders. Having made the argument for the erotic, he is forced into a position in which the erotic must either be complemented or postponed. But Marcuse's argument for the new historical possibility of the conquest of nature was that neither would be necessary. Death backs Marcuse into a corner from which he

6. Ibid., p. 120.

The Frankfurt School and the Failure of Modernity

cannot emerge and remain *simply* an advocate of the erotic. However, to become an advocate of anything beyond the erotic would be to declare the mythic forms bankrupt even as they are being proclaimed.

The problem of death makes, I would argue, the entire project of the Frankfurt School problematic. They are not simply arguing that an improvement in the human condition is now possible. Rather, they are saying that an ontological break with the struggle and repression of the past is upon us. The omnipresence of death demonstrates that such a break is impossible.

Adorno, more sensitive than Marcuse, tried to head the problem off before proclaiming the new age by attempting to demonstrate that consciousness of death as a problem is a manifestation of the distortions of bourgeois life:

> As the subject lives less, death grows more precipitous, more terrifying. The fact that it literally turns them into things makes them aware of reification, their permanent death and the form of their relations that is partly their fault. The integration of death in civilization, a process without power over death and a ridiculous cosmetic procedure in the face of death, is the shaping of a reaction to this social phenomenon, a clumsy attempt of the barter society to stop up the last holes left open by the world of merchandise.[7]

Marcuse knew what was at stake but faced it only after the proclamation of the new age, trying to integrate death into his thought as an afterthought. Adorno knew full well that that could not work. Hence, before the new order comes, death as a problem must be shown to be bourgeois and so a problem only to the old order. Death is thus terrifying only because of the poverty of our lives. The attempt of Heidegger to come to terms with death was simply the last attempt of the bourgeoisie to control what is beyond them.

This attack is as insufficient as Marcuse's. Death was a terrifying problem long before the merchants ruled (it was a problem to Plato, who faced it in Socrates' life), or even philosophers. Death is always at least the penultimate problem and frequently the ultimate one. To brush off its awesomeness is as much a disservice to its impossible grandeur as is Marcuse's formulating irreconcilable solutions to it.

7. Adorno, *Negative Dialectics*, p. 370.

Adorno, almost as if he knew that the first tack was insufficient, goes on to a second one:

> it is impossible to think of death as the last thing pure and simple. Attempts to express death in language are futile, all the way into logic, for who should be the subject of which we predicate that it is dead, here and now? Lust—which wants eternity, according to a luminous word of Nietzsche—is not the only one to balk at passing. If death were that absolute which philosophy tried in vain to conjure positively, everything is nothing; all that we think, too, is thought into the void; none of it is truly thinkable.[8]

Having first declared death to be beneath philosophy, Adorno now declares death to be beyond philosophy. It is impossible (and undesirable) to think of death because it is unthinkable, for how can one speak of that which is utterly unknowable? Joy wants eternity and so does thought. Thought that cannot conceive of its own negation must deny anything beyond itself. Death cannot be a philosophical question because death is a void, and philosophy cannot tolerate the void.

Adorno desperately tries to expel death as a problem. It is immaterial whether the problem is cast down into the brutishness of the marketplace or elevated beyond thought. Death must not be allowed to pollute the ontological, lest the re-creation of being be made impossible. But death remains the singular practical problem of existence. The realization of impending death lends urgency to man's use of time. If, as Nietzsche says, all life can be known by its rhythms, then death is the thing that conditions life, for it sets life's tempo.

For the welfare of the project of the Frankfurt School, death must be made ineffable lest it make their plans impossible. From Adorno's point of view, Marcuse, in even considering the problem seriously, seems to be endangering the project as a whole. Adorno, wiser, declares that the problem is null and void. But death can never be irrelevant, particularly when one is constructing an erotic vision—that is, a vision of life. The ultimate vision of the Frankfurt School fails; and, in a way, Adorno's treatment of death is an oblique acknowledgment of its failure, because it does not and cannot cope with death. The Frankfurt School's love of life and of

---

8. Ibid., p. 371.

life's pleasures makes it impotent against life's universal and inevitable negation. They cannot stand against the negation of existence without seriously reconsidering the problem of existence itself. Nietzsche said that optimism is shallow; and the Frankfurt School's optimism for the possibilities of life is too shallow to comprehend life's depth: death.

Adorno speaks of man in general but he might be thinking of himself and his colleagues when he writes:

> The indifference of consciousness to metaphysical questions—questions that have by no means been laid to rest by satisfaction in this world—is hardly a matter of indifference to metaphysics itself, however. Hidden in it is a horror that would take men's breath away if they did not repress it. We might be tempted to speculate anthropologically whether the turn in evolutionary history that gave the human species its open consciousness and thus the awareness of death—whether this turn does not contradict a continuing animal constitution which prohibits men to bear that consciousness.[9]

Here, Adorno puts his finger on the problem of the Frankfurt School. Consciousness of death is possible, but it is by its nature alien to the species (that is, bestial) character of man. The object of the Frankfurt School is ultimately to realize that bestial and sensual nature in an unmediated form. Consciousness of death can exist only beyond the sensual. The Orphic is the sensual. Thus the level on which the reconciliation of man and his nature is possible and desirable precludes the consideration of death. The problem is that this level is insufficient: death must be considered, and to give the organism the illusion of escaping it is to succumb to the propaganda of reification that is anathema to the Frankfurt School. If it is impossible to think about death on the level on which the Frankfurt School wishes to operate, that is by no means a refutation of death. It opens the way to a refutation of the Frankfurt School's pretensions.

The problem of death is not solved even if it is abolished as an existential dilemma. The problem of death would have to be faced even if science could somehow abolish death practically. Consider life in which the only death is accidental; the undamaged man is eternal. With the abolition of natural death, the problem of death

---

9. Ibid., p. 395.

would be intensified, and all existence would be ruled by fear. The root of courage was, in a real way, to be found in the inevitability of death. Whether one died at this moment or in years to come, death remained total, inevitable, and utterly democratic. In its inevitability and in the infinitesimal distinction between two or seventy years from the perspective of eternity, man could find the courage to face death at any given moment. The inevitability of death was man's great solace upon encountering it. Death would come; if it had to be faced sometime, it could be faced now. This courage would be impossible if all but accidental death were abolished. The accidental death of an eternal being would be so tragic and so unnecessary that no one would be capable of the courage required to face death. Moreover, all creativity, rooted on the deepest level in courage and in the risks that flesh is heir to, would be rendered impossible. Who could bear to face the abyss when the abyss no longer loomed as fate? Fate and creativity are bound up, for fate is solace to the creator. In other words, the abolition of death would not solve the problem of perpetual gratification; it would only intensify it, for through the portals of practical immortality could walk only the last man, the man who knew only comfort and fear.

Even if the problem of death did not stand as a refutation of the Frankfurt School's proclamation of the operant principles of the new age, even if men were to become immortal, or if some philosophical finesse could be discovered to deal with the problem, there is yet another issue that endangers the Frankfurt School's solutions. Ironically, it is Adorno, speaking of the problem of affluence in bourgeois society, who points out this problem most graphically:

> What keeps all living things occupied and in motion, is the striving for existence. With existence, however, once secured, they do not know what to do: thus, the second force that sets them in motion is the striving to be rid of the burden of existence, to make it imperceptible, to 'kill time', i.e., to escape boredom. But this concept of boredom raised to such unsuspected dignity, is—and this is the last thing that Schopenhauer's anti-historical mind would admit—bourgeois through and through. It is the complement of alienated labour, being the experience of antithetically 'free time', whether because this latter is intended only to restore the energy expended, or because the appropriation of alien labour weighs on it like a mortgage.[10]

10. Adorno, *Minima Moralia*, p. 175.

The Frankfurt School and the Failure of Modernity

Adorno raises the problem in order to dismiss it, but the problem does not go away so easily. The problem is the problem of Nietzsche's last man, the man late to the feast of tasks, who has nothing left to think of but himself and his comfort in blinking satiety.

Adorno in acknowledging the problem tries to make the last man into a uniquely bourgeois matter by arguing that the emptiness of satiety is the result of the form in which comfort is achieved rather than a transhistorical problem involving the nature of man. What Adorno never answers is how satiety in socialist society would be less boring and less troublesome. Benjamin, almost as if attempting to answer this question—or rather, defuse it—had argued that the ontological character of socialist society was inherently unknowable; hence the issue was moot. But if Adorno has proposed that bourgeois fears of boredom are unique to a bourgeois epoch, it is not at all unreasonable to raise at least the formal problem: in what way would the bloated sensuality of a life predicated solely on the logic of gratification be less tedious and less meaningless than the life of Nietzsche's last man or than a similar life in a bourgeois epoch?

Quite simply, the issue is whether the Frankfurt School's erotic man is fully human. Aristotle, I would argue, would not think him human. From the Aristotelian point of view, man's erotic being is utterly private. As previously argued, the elevation of the sensual to the highest level of consideration privatizes man. In the first place, man's concerns are primarily sensual, in that they are practically concerned with organic gratification, both in the minimal sense of the survival of the organism and in the higher sense of the achievement of the greatest erotic satisfaction conceivable. As such, the sensually erotic man is concerned with things of the household, of the family, and not with things of the city. Marx and Lenin themselves had argued that the abolition of the political would be the confirmation of the end of history. The concern of the Frankfurt School for the erotic is simply the radicalization of the privatization implied by the universalization of the household (into a thing coterminus with society as a whole), which Marxism traditionally argued for.

It is a privatization in a more personal and radical sense, however. Elevating pleasure to the highest end privatizes man in the absolute sense of turning him inward to search for gratification for himself and from himself. The reduction of the polis to the household is ontogenetically recapitulated in the reduction of man from social and political concerns to personal and sensual ones. True, the search for erotic gratification might be mediated outward to incorporate others (although even this is unclear, considering the nature of Narcissistic perversion). But the starting point is the self and, more importantly, the self is also the end point. Thus, society as a whole becomes merely the context for private existence and the personal experience of life is turned inward.

Aristotle argued that the man who is not of the polis—that is, the truly private man—is not man but a beast or a god. If we are to believe the Book of Genesis, the prerequisite to Godhood is immortality, something beyond the Frankfurt School's power to bestow. Thus Aristotle sees something bestial about the eroticism of the Orphic and Narcissistic.

One can see this bestiality most clearly when one considers the qualities that Aristotle argues are the most fully human. Virtue in the highest and most fully human sense is both meaningless and impossible for the Frankfurt School. Either virtue would be too threatening to the erotic well-being of the organism or else it would have no function, those things to which virtue would be juxtaposed having been banished from the world.

Courage would be impossible. What, after all, would there be to be courageous about? Courage has meaning only when existence (or the organism's highest principle) is threatened. The nature of the world after its millennial transformation would make those dangers impossible. One could not be courageous, for there could be no danger. Moreover, the nature of transformed existence would make any dangers that existed impossible to face. As I have previously argued, the tragedy of death would be singularly intensified by the pleasurability of the world. The comfort to be taken from the cessation of pain would be gone. With it, also, would go the solace behind the truly courageous act, the solace of knowing that in a fundamental sense life as a coward would be practically unbearable. To live as a slave, the outcome of cowardice, would be an impossible consequence if the Frankfurt School's hopes were taken seriously. Even if there were an object to stand against, the price of courage would be so enormous and the rewards so limited, that the reasonable and prudent man could not risk the consequences of courage. Hence, if being human means having courage, the erotic man is not fully human, since he is incapable of being truly courageous.

The Frankfurt School and the Failure of Modernity 291

Perhaps there could be a false courage, the bravado of the imprudent man, for prudence would also be impossible. Prudence is meaningful only in a dangerous world where there are penalties for choosing badly. The prudence of Aristotle and of Machiavelli coincide only on this point: that prudence is necessary in a world of dangers. Only there is the imprudent forced to face the price of his excesses. The world of the Frankfurt School's vision is radically different from this. Without danger, nothing is to be gained from prudence and, hence, prudence has no meaning.

Moreover, there is much about which to be imprudent. Eros is, by its nature, excessive. It cannot and will not limit itself but meets its limits either in the world or in other parts of the soul, from repression. Above all else, however, the Frankfurt School wishes to abolish repression. Their argument is thus an argument for the immoderate man. Marcuse's argument for the pleasures of perversion is simply the most extreme manifestation of immoderation. A beast, at least, has the world to limit him. The Frankfurt School's man seems to wallow, with neither internal nor external limitation, in his own voluptuousness.

There would seem to be something singularly disgusting about such bestiality. It goes beyond bestiality. There is something unjust to it—that is, until one considers the problematic status of justice itself. Justice, by its nature, is political; it is logically and practically inconceivable without a political problematic to condition and necessitate it. Herein lies a problem, one that is small theoretically but one that is a major issue practically: the mode of political administration. To the Frankfurt School, politics, being predicated upon alienation and classes, cannot exist at the end of history. Even if politics were reduced to the administration of things—that is, to the household—the requirements of administration, reifying by their nature (because they focus on things and recipients of things), would to some extent cause alienation.

Even if politics and reification could be practically abolished, there would remain the theoretical issue of the apolitical life, the life without justice. Upon what basis would relations among men be regulated? Within the practical household, practical considerations concerning the strength of the father condition the structure, if not the justice, of relationships. In the Frankfurt School's theoretical and universal household, a household comprising men of equal stature and strength, there is no such basis for structuring relationships. Without politics, the excesses of perversion would (even without its thanatotic components of sadomasochism) involve choices that might cause disagreement. These could be adjudicated only by brute force, which would be a primordial reentry into politics. Justice, theory designed to regulate relationships, would be unacceptable, because it would mean a return to politics. And politics would be unthinkable, since by its nature it demands some repression. Thus justice could not logically be introduced; and at the same time, the household, even without the more brutal demands of nature, could not conceivably be administered without some form of authority and, hence, some concept of justice.

Set aside the practical problem, however, and consider justice as theoretically unnecessary. There still remains the existential question of a life without considerations of justice. What sort of existence is possible if only the solipsistic considerations of pleasure rule the person's relationship with other beings? What pleasure would there be in gratification through an object that never sees you as yourself but only, in turn, as an object for its gratification? Justice is the art that recognizes men as men. To speak of justice is to speak of human things. But to speak of justice is to speak of limits. The unlimitedness of the Frankfurt School, the immoderation that leads it to ban considerations of politics and hence of justice, would seem the most extreme moment of reification. It objectifies man most radically because it hermetically seals off others except through the mediation of pleasure.

Similarly, wisdom as a virtue would be banned by the conquest of natural death. If the just man could not exist because the just man is by nature the repressed and the alienated man, the wise man also would be inconceivable, for what, after all, would there be to be wise about? Wisdom was most consequential in considering things human—that is, in considering matters of justice. This is true even when wisdom (as in Plato) demonstrated its distance from justice. Political philosophy is conceivable, as Marx himself knew better than perhaps anyone, only in a less than perfect world. Perfection needs only the science of public administration; imperfection is what requires philosophic reflection on the nature of the good. In an utterly good world, however, there would be no point to wisdom, to *logos*. *Phronesis* would perhaps be useful; not for Plato's reasons (being for things beneath the unattainable) but rather for the rule of things perfect and obtained. The wise man would here be the fool, it would be unutterably foolish to contemplate the good as a distant thing when it was in fact all around you. *Logos,* and

The Frankfurt School and the Failure of Modernity

even dialogue about high things, would be pointless. As I have previously argued, dialogue considers things that are naturally the most important. In the world of Frankfurt School pleasure is both most significant and least communicable. Thus, not only would *logos* have no high object but what object it had would be outside its reach; the object, in its bestiality, would be beneath *logos*.

Even the practical ambitions of modern science would no longer be possible. The Frankfurt School argued that the task of modern science was to subjugate nature. Marcuse declared, and the rest of the Frankfurt School did not dispute him, that the Promethean task of modern science, the conquest of nature, had been accomplished. Thus modern science would have no great tasks left. The would-be epigone would be reduced to picking at the crumbs left over after the great scientists had actually solved the root problems of nature and had abolished scarcity. Modern science would be impossible, first, because it would have no great tasks left to perform, and second, because its continuance would be an anachronism, a throwback to the principles of an age that had been surpassed. Science involves struggle and the practical task of the Frankfurt School was to abolish struggle.

For all these reasons, I believe that Aristotle would have seen the private man of the Frankfurt School as a beast and not as a god. Gods are immortal. Greek gods possess virtues. The erotic life envisioned by the Frankfurt School is a life of vice. The ennobling virtues are to be banished by rendering them impossible. With the virutes banished, the issue of the meaning of existence becomes paramount. Existence in the face of struggle had at least a little moment of meaning: one struggled in order to win. But now, even struggle for a more noble existence, struggle for even the most brutish virtue of courage, would be rendered meaningless. There appears to be something singularly beneath man in the Frankfurt School's vision of man.

It seems to me that the Frankfurt School's vision of life is radically childlike. Aristotle thought that men left childhood not merely out of need, but in order to be human. Man realized himself in the self-alienation of the life of virtue. To be human was to live in the complexities of adulthood. The Frankfurt School attempts to replace the suffering inevitably present in complexity with the pleasures of singularity: the self-indulgence of childhood. They find ends where we must see beginnings.

It could be argued, of course, that it is unfair to judge the

Frankfurt School by the standards of antiquity. I doubt that this is true, but let us judge the life they advocate through the eyes of one most radically modern: Nietzsche. Nietzsche ends Part One of *Zarathustra* with a consideration of virtue. After appropriately considering death (for virtue might explain the freedom of his notion of death), Zarathustra says: "Uncommon is the highest virtue and useless; it is gleaming and gentle in its splendor: a gift-giving virtue is the highest virtue."[11]

What gifts are there to bestow? The gift-giving virtue demands courage. What threatens? The last man, the man who knows nothing of courage because the world had for him abolished fear. The gift-giving virtue is possible only where men still fear the last man. The Frankfurt School, as Adorno acknowledged, did not fear the last man. Rather, in the stupid voluptuousness praised by Marcuse, too petty even to be called Dionysian, they welcomed the last man. They had abolished the gift-giving virtue because they had given man all that he needed. There were no presents that man lacked, therefore the virtue of giving a gift, even for the selfish reason of which Nietzsche speaks, had no meaning. Even from a radically modern view, the Frankfurt School's vision of the possibilities open to man is beneath humanity. It is subhuman in the same sense that the last man is beneath his own humanity.

When Aristotle and Nietzsche agree on the sterility of an existential form, we must suspect that something about it is indeed deformed. This deformation perhaps is equally and even more fully apparent in Marx, but the Frankfurt School builds radically upon it. It is the deformation of the unalienated life for, it must ultimately be argued, life is by its nature alienated; or more precisely, life is alienation and must remain that. The separateness, man's sense of being estranged from something he does not know but feels to be beyond him, something torn from him and lost, is the essence of being human. The human being is the being who gains sufficiency from a sense of insufficiency. True, it is fully human to struggle against one's suffering and alienation. The issue is, however, whether it is human to abolish suffering and live in gratification. Aristotle and Nietzsche would agree that it is not. It might be divine or superhuman or it might be bestial or it might possess elements of both, but in the end it is not simply nor truly human. This may be

---

11. Nietzsche, "Thus Spoke Zarathustra," in *The Portable Nietzsche*, p. 186.

the profound tragedy that the Frankfurt School and Marxism in general must face: that what is most fully human—to struggle—succeeds and turns itself into something utterly inhuman and unbearable—success. Surely they knew the problem, for they had read both Aristotle and Nietzsche. Yet they chose to wallow in it.

Or let us say that they wallowed on one level. There is a tension in their thought. They praised the last man, prepared for his coming, and tried to make the world safe for him. Yet strangely, and despite their criticisms of those who praised alienation, they also tried to abolish his coming. Adorno's *Negative Dialectics* was the attempt to annihilate, through a resuscitation of negation (and hence of alienation), the last man. This was the true and insoluble tension in their thought: they feared more than anything the coming of the man whom they had proclaimed.

There is ultimately an unbearable tension between Marcuse's proclamation of the erotic man and Adorno's attack on affirmation. It is represented most clearly in the split between *Eros and Civilization* and *Negative Dialectics;* but the split is not ultimately between two thinkers of the Frankfurt School. It is a tension that cuts through the thoughts of all thinkers associated with the School. Adorno, after all, had spoken of a form of being comparable to Marcuse's vision, and Marcuse himself had criticized the logic of affirmation.[12] The tension resulted from the Frankfurt School's inability to commit themselves either to the logic of negation and the perpetuation of alienation that it implied or to a vision of utopia realized and the solution of negation that utopia entailed. To choose the former courted the danger of returning to the bourgeois logic of Prometheus and the latter involved the danger of sterile and meaningless existence in a world that no longer needed the truly human, the ability to transcend the given.

On the surface the problem is quite simple. The Frankfurt School both wants something and does not want it. On the one hand, they desire the creation of a social order in which men could and would realize their true intentions. On the other hand, the realization of such a society would mean the end of dialectics, in the simplest sense that a social order would have been created that didn't need to be transcended. However desirable such a social order might be

12. Adorno, "Spätkapitalismus oder Industriegesellschaft?" in *Gesellschaftstheorie und Kulturkritik;* Marcuse, "Philosophy and Critical Theory," in *Negations,* pp. 135–36.

in the abstract, it is alienated as well. It is alienated from the possibility of transcending itself. If the envisioned form of being is accepted, the last man is proclaimed in the literal sense; if it is perpetually denied, then dialectics loses its meaning as it loses its *telos*. This problem, even if distant, is not insignificant, for realizing that the solution is no solution—that indeed there may be no solution—must and should color the practice of all of our lives. The realization teaches us what is and is not important.

The problem of the Frankfurt School is by no means a stupid error. Rather, it is a problem that cuts to the heart of Hegelianism and Marxism. In both cases, the issue is whether or what meaning life could have when history had realized itself. For the Frankfurt School, since their notion of the end is even more radical than the one hinted at by Marx in the *German Ideology*, the problem of the end in their case is also more radical. The problem is compounded when one remembers that much of their criticism of bourgeois society revolved around its satiety, its affluence, and its resulting stupid lack of tension. True, the Frankfurt School considered that the satiety of a truly socialist society would not lead to the stupidity of the bourgeois, since it would be accompanied by a meaningful existence. But that would be merely rhetoric unless they could demonstrate concretely how socialism would solve the problem of satiety. On this they must, like Benjamin, fall silent with metaphysical protestations or else resort to empty polemics.

Adorno alone realized that more was needed. *Negative Dialectics* was his attempt to criticize both Hegelian affirmation and Heidegger's apparent negation while somehow retaining both the affirmative vision of a teleology and the negative power of dialectics. Adorno's attempt is brilliant in its realization of the problem, but it fails because it simply cannot logically or historically reconcile the two criteria that are set. They are mutually exclusive. One cannot simultaneously speak of being and becoming. In a way, the Frankfurt School attempted to do metaphysically what Trotsky and Mao attempted politically: to institutionalize revolution by making it permanent. The attempt to reconcile institutionalization with revolution, is, however, logically and historically doomed to failure. One cannot both be and become. Even Hegel's logic excluded the two possibilities, which is what made him both historical and teleological.

The tension within the Frankfurt School's politics stems from this contradiction. They are men without a country. They cannot have a country because their enemy is anything that is; the very fact of being is their enemy. Only the *concept* of being is tolerable. The Frankfurt School could tolerate neither the Soviet Union nor Social Democratic Europe, not because they had faults, but because they existed. Existence ipso facto demonstrated their failure. China and Cuba, being both distant (and hence merely symbols) and unformed, were tolerable—but only until they were formed. At that point, negativity would demand that they be criticized. The criticism would always be from the perspective of an unachieved being.

No existent form could ever be acceptable, because nothing that was could also not be. Observers of the young followers of the Frankfurt School were often puzzled by protesters who apparently never wanted what they had and achieved things only in order to demand other, sometimes contradictory things. What was merely youthful foolishness among their followers was an enshrined metaphysical principle for the Frankfurt School. And what may perhaps have been understandable among the young was an outrage among philosophical thinkers of the stature of the Frankfurt School.

Their thought led them into impossible contradictions. The grossest of these was Marcuse's praise of repressive tolerance[13] when directed toward revolutionary goals. Tolerance is formally desired by Marcuse and the Frankfurt School. The formal right to believe is by no means insignificant to them. It is significant, however, only when the formal right to be tolerated does not exist. One might assume that they would argue (as do their survivors) that the Chilean regime's lack of tolerance for opponents is repulsive. But, when a regime is tolerant, it is by definition institutionalizing toleration and also, by definition, is surviving it. By surviving, the regime is rendering the tolerated dissent inauthentic. A tolerant regime can be negated only by being abolished. Logically, this leads to the conclusion that intolerance is the only outcome of toleration. Otherwise, the toleration is false. One cannot conceive of a regime that is truly tolerant by Marcuse's standards. A regime that survives while tolerating is, by definition, not allowing itself to be touched by what it only formally tolerates. One that evolves under the impact of dissent can be accused of only coopting dissent while not changing its

---

13. See Chapter 15.

essential form. And a regime that radically transforms itself under the impact of dissent is guiltless only until the point that it tolerates a new form of being. A new being by its nature excludes other forms, and so in accepting it the regime returns to intolerance, even if it is formally tolerant. Thus no regime is tolerant except one perpetually negating itself. Such a regime is no regime. It is not that Marcuse is an anarchist, for even nothing must be something that excludes somethingness. The problem is that, in attempting to maintain dialectics, he is forced to oppose the antipode to dialectics, the object, the thing that is. He thus embraces the irrationalism of perpetual dialectics, for he cannot allow the object to become rationally grounded, that is, rooted in anything that is. He is always forced not to be, and his vacillations on this score indicate that he finds even this too affirmative.

Marcuse's call for repressive tolerance is a call for intolerance as the only effective way to transcend (by definition) inauthentic tolerance. Intolerance, alone, would render the abolished regime authentic, while allowing the ground to be laid for the abolition of the new unauthentic intolerance in favor of true tolerance. Negative dialectics, the need both to be and not be, has led Marcuse into the most peculiar convolutions of thought. It has also led to the most barbaric practices. The intolerance of the New Left was by no means accidental. It was rooted in the logic of negation. It would have been humorous if it had all not been so painful.

The Frankfurt School cannot avoid problems of this sort. They wish to resurrect the virtues of the past. Their notion of being human does, at root, involve being courageous, prudent, just, and wise. It does involve giving gifts. This is the basis of their nostalgia. They long for a world of virtue. At the same time, however, their notion of alienation leads them to argue against being alienated, and hence, against the virtues that are, at bottom, the product and essence of alienation. They chose for their formal position the abolition of alienation. In their underlying sensibilities, they could not tolerate the vision of the unalienated life, the life without virtue. They chose the illogic of negative dialectics precisely because their position was untenable. They were trying to have the world while being lost in it. The intention was, in a way, touching. But the thought was murky and the practice potentially unforgivable. They wished art to be both a mode of being and perpetual criticism. It could never be both unless they could accept perpetual alienation,

The Frankfurt School and the Failure of Modernity   299

the notion that to live was to be alienated. Their inability to do so threw into jeopardy their mode of thought and their politics.

In a final sense, the fault of the Frankfurt School was a too faithful adherence to modern philosophy. Modernity has always sought to abolish the distance between being and becoming by somehow rooting being in the practice of becoming. Marx, the most radically modern (uniting both Hegel's historical practice and end with Hobbes's ontology of practice), was also ultimately the most resolutely mysterious. He wished becoming to culminate in a being that allowed the universalization of the practice of becoming. This is why the abolition of the division of labor was necessary. The problem of Marx was, simply put, whether there was any point in becoming when one could simply be, and whether simply being was sufficiently human. Marx left the issue a mystery, probably because he himself could not unscramble the philosophical and historical problem. The Frankfurt School tried to unscramble it but failed, and had to fail, because the problem as formulated is ultimately insoluble. One cannot simply reconcile being and becoming historically. The historical insolubility of the problem is what makes it tolerable; it allows the ontological distinction to be bearable, if not made clear. In the *Republic* Plato was able to show the distinction, and the permanence of the distinction, between perfect existence and mere existence by showing the relationship between being and becoming and by never forcing an identity between the two. The point of the *Republic* was the permanent distinction between the two. This was the transhistorical power of Plato and the Ancients.

The Frankfurt School attempted to explicate the unwritten passages of Marx by means of the thought of Freud, Nietzsche, and Heidegger and thereby to devise a being that was not only reconciled to becoming but allowed becoming (negation) to continue to function. They attempted to do this, however, without embracing the fullness of Freud's, Heidegger's, or Nietzsche's thought. Rather they attempted to get Marx off the hook by partial purchases of a non-Marxist ontology. They could never of course, make the final payments.

That they felt compelled to reach outside of Marx to solve his problem indicated a fatal weakness in Marx. That they never solved the problem and, as we have seen, logically could never solve it, was Marx's death notice. The Frankfurt School played Marxism out to its end and gave it its *coup de grâce*. The problem of being in time was too awesome to deal with while being faithful to Marx's dream of abolishing alienation. The Frankfurt School marks the close of his system.

The reaching outward to purchase parts of alien thought in order to salvage Marx is nowhere clearer than in the Frankfurt School's concession to antiquity: Judaism. They became too Jewish without being nearly Jewish enough. They went back to Genesis to discover a motif for labor that would be concurrent with play. They spoke of a sensuality unmediated by reason, like the nature of the sensual before man's fall. They saw a realm in which man was utterly unalienated. They became too Jewish, for they sought, like Messianic Judaism, to abolish all that was human through a return to preternatural bliss. This was the basis of their problem for, in the end, this world of gratification held forth no human meaning. It was pure playfulness without the meaning that play is given by the omnipresence of suffering. And they were not Jewish enough, because for them, the playful world was both desirable and meaningless. To the true Jew, the meaning of such a redemption was received through God and not man. They were Jewish enough for a Jewish hope, but only Jewish enough to allow the hope to create an insoluble and unbearable dilemma for them. They were never Jewish enough to allow the fullness of the Jewish solution to render the problem of meaninglessness meaningless in and of itself. They were also too Heideggerian without being Heideggerian enough, and too Nietzschean without being Nietzschean enough. They had to be all these things, for they were too Marxist and Marxism was simply not enough.

In the end their radically modern return to Jerusalem could not stand up. It could not stand up because modernity cannot stand. The tension between the things that modernity's most extreme proponents wanted is too powerful to offer a ground on which to construct a life. The tension between sensual gratification and desirability of struggling for that gratification, the tension between history moving toward an end and the end of history, the tension between life as alienation and the unalienated life, and, ultimately, the tension within modern dialectics between ends as a mode of existence and means as ends in themselves—all this proves insurmountable. The Frankfurt School is most notable precisely because they radicalized the problem.

By posing the problems of being and becoming, which ultimately was their major task, and by attempting to relate them, the Frankfurt School posited the problematic of modernity most radically. By radicalizing the problem, they demonstrated, and manifested in their nostalgic dissonance, that modernity could not stand. Their foray into the motif of Jerusalem ratified the impossibility of modernity. The Frankfurt School is, in the end, most praiseworthy for the thing that they failed to accomplish, for by failing, they demonstrated the bankruptcy of modernity. Their brave foolishness kept them moving forward. But, in their deepest thoughts, they knew they would fail. Thus did they look longingly at the past.

Bibliography of Cited Works

Adorno, Theodor W. *Ästhetische Theorie.* Frankfurt, 1970.
———, E. Frankel-Brunswik, D. J. Levinson, and R. N. Sanford. *The Authoritarian Personality.* New York, 1950.
———. *Drei Studien zu Hegel.* Frankfurt, 1963.
———. *Eingriffe.* Frankfurt, 1973.
———. "Erinnerungen an Walter Benjamin." In *Über Walter Benjamin.* Frankfurt, 1968.
———. *Erziehung zur Mündigkeit.* Frankfurt, 1975.
———. *Gesellschaftstheorie und Kulturkritik.* Frankfurt, 1975.
———. *Introduction to the Sociology of Music.* Trans. E. B. Ashton. New York, 1976. (First published Suhrkamp Verlag, Frankfurt, 1962.)
———. *The Jargon of Authenticity.* Trans. K. Tarnowski and F. Will. Evanston, 1973. (First published Suhrkamp Verlag, Frankfurt, 1964.)
———. *Kritik, Kleine Schriften zur Gesellschaft.* Frankfurt, 1971.
———. *Zur Metakritik der Erkenntnistheorie.* Frankfurt, 1970.
———. *Minima Moralia.* London, 1975. (First published Suhrkamp Verlag, Frankfurt, 1951.)
———. *Negative Dialectics.* Trans. E. B. Ashton. New York, 1973. (First published Suhrkamp Verlag, Frankfurt, 1966.)
———. *Philosophy of Modern Music.* Trans. A. C. Mitchell and W. V. Blomster. New York, 1973. (First published Suhrkamp Verlag, Frankfurt, 1949.)
———. *Prisms.* Trans. S. Weber and S. Weber. London, 1967. (First published Suhrkamp Verlag, Frankfurt, 1955.)
———. "Sociology and Psychology." *New Left Review* 46 (Nov./Dec. 1967).
———, and Max Horkheimer. *Dialectic of Enlightenment.* Trans. John Cumming. New York, 1972.
Arendt, Hannah. *The Human Condition,* Chicago, 1958.
Avineri, Shlomo. *The Social and Political Thought of Karl Marx.* Cambridge, 1970.
Benjamin, Walter. *Briefe.* 2 vols. Frankfurt, 1966.
———. *Illuminations: Essays and Reflections.* Ed. Hannah Arendt. New York, 1968. (First published Suhrkamp Verlag, Frankfurt, 1953.)

———. *Reflections*. New York, 1978. (Essays were published by Suhrkamp Verlag, Frankfurt, between 1955 and 1972.)
———. *Schriften*. Ed. T. W. Adorno and G. Scholem. 2 vols. Frankfurt, 1955.
———. *Der Stratege im Literaturkampf*. Frankfurt, 1974.
———. *Über Haschisch*. Frankfurt, 1972.
———. *Versuche über Brecht*. Frankfurt, 1966.
———. "Zur Kritik der Gewalt und andere Aufsätze." Frankfurt, 1971.
Bernstein, Edward. *Evolutionary Socialism*. New York, 1961.
Bernstein, Richard. "Herbert Marcuse: An Immanent Critique." *Social Theory and Practice* 2 (Fall 1971).
Brazill, William J. *The Young Hegelians*. New Haven, 1970.
Brenner, Hildergaard. "Theodor W. Adorno als Sachwalter des Benjaminschen Werkes." In *Die neue Linke nach Adorno*, ed. W. F. Schoeller. Munich, 1969.
Bruckner, Peter. "Und nach uns Kömmens nichts Nennenswertes." In *Die neue Linke nach Adorno*, ed. W. F. Schoeller. Munich, 1969.
Buck-Morss, Susan. *The Origins of Negative Dialectics*. New York, 1977.
Cohen, Jerry. "Critical Theory: The Philosophy of Marcuse." *New Left Review* 57 (Sept.-Oct. 1969).
Deutscher, Isaac. *The Prophet Armed*. New York, 1965.
Fleming, Donald, and Bernard Bailyn. *The Intellectual Migration*. Cambridge, 1969.
Freud, Sigmund. *Beyond the Pleasure Principle*. Trans. J. Strachey. New York, 1950.
———. *Civilization and Its Discontents*. Trans. J. Strachey. New York, 1962.
———. *An Outline of Psychoanalysis*. Trans. J. Strachey. New York, 1949.
———. *Three Contributions to the Theory of Sex*. Trans. A. A. Brill. New York, 1962.
Fromm, Erich. *Beyond the Chains of Illusion*. New York, 1962.
Gay, Peter. *The Enlightenment: An Interpretation*. New York, 1966.
———. *Weimar Culture*. New York, 1968.
Goldmann, Lucien. *Lukács and Heidegger*. Trans. W. Q. Boelhower. London, 1977.
———. "Understanding Marcuse." *Partisan Review* 38:3 (1971).
Graubard, Allen. "Herbert Marcuse—One-Dimensional Pessimism." *Dissent* (May-June 1968).
Grünberg, Carl. "Festrede gehalten zur Einweihung des Instituts für Sozialforschung an der Universität Frankfurt." *Frankfurten Universitätreden* 20. Frankfurt, 1924.
Habermas, Jurgen. "Bewusstmachende oder rettende Kritik–die Aktualität Walter Benjamins." In *Zur Aktualität Walter Benjamins*, ed. S. Unseld. Frankfurt, 1972.

Hegel, Georg F. W. *Phenomenology of Mind.* Trans. J. B. Baillie. New York, 1967.
——. *Philosophy of Fine Art,* 1. Trans. F. P. B. Osmaston. New York, 1975.
——. *Philosophy of History.* Trans. J. Sibree. New York, 1956.
——. *Philosophy of Right.* Trans. T. M. Knox. Oxford, 1967.
Heidegger, Martin. *Being and Time.* Trans. J. Macquarrie and E. Robinson. New York, 1962.
——. *The End of Philosophy.* Trans. J. Stambaugh. New York, 1973.
——. "Letter on Humanism." In *Phenomenology and Existentialism,* ed. Richard Zaner and Don Ihde. New York, 1973.
Horkheimer, Max. *Anfänge der bürgerlichen Geschichtsphilosophe.* Frankfurt, 1971.
——. *Critical Theory.* Trans. M. J. O'Connell and others. New York, 1972. (First published S. Fischer Verlag, Frankfurt, 1968.)
——. *Critique of Instrumental Reason.* Trans. M. J. O'Connell and others. New York, 1974. (First published S. Fischer Verlag, Frankfurt, 1967.)
——. (Pseud. Heinrich Regius). *Dämmerung.* Zurich, 1934.
——. *Eclipse of Reason.* New York, 1974.
——. "Geschichte und Psychologie." *Zeitschrift für Sozialforschung* 1 (No. 1/2), 1932.
——. *Hegel und das Problem der Metaphysik.* Frankfurt, 1971.
——. "Schopenhauer Today." In *The Critical Spirit,* eds. K. H. Wolff and B. Moore. Boston, 1967.
——. *Zum Begriff der Vernunft.* Frankfurt, 1952.
——. "Zum Rationalmusstreit in der gegenwärtigen Philosophie." *Zeitschrift für Sozialforschung* 3 (No. 1), 1934.
Jameson, Fredric. *Marxism and Form.* Princeton, 1971.
Jay, Martin. *The Dialectical Imagination.* Boston, 1973.
Kant, Immanuel. *Prolegomena to Any Future Metaphysics.* New York, 1950.
Kojève, Alexandre. *Introduction to the Reading of Hegel.* Trans. J. H. Nichols. New York, 1969.
Lasswell, Harold. "Collective Autism as a Consequence of Cultural Conduct." *Zeitschrift für Sozialforschung* 4 (1935).
Lenin, V. I. *Selected Writings.* Ed. J. E. Connor. New York, 1968.
Lichtheim, George. *From Marx to Hegel.* New York, 1971.
Löwith, Karl. "Book Review." *Zeitschrift für Sozialforschung* 3 (1934).
——. *From Hegel to Nietzsche.* Trans. D. E. Green. Garden City, 1967.
Lukács, Georg. *History and Class Consciousness.* Trans. R. Livingstone. Cambridge, 1968.
MacIntyre, Alasdair. *Herbert Marcuse.* New York, 1970.
Mandelbaum, Kurt, and Gerhard Meyer. "Zur Theorie der Planwirtschaft." *Zeitschrift für Sozialforschung* 3 (1934).

Mann, Thomas. *Story of a Novel*. Trans. R. and C. Winston. New York, 1961.
Marcuse, Herbert. *Counterrevolution and Revolt*. Boston, 1972.
———. *Eros and Civilization*. New York, 1962.
———. *An Essay on Liberation*. Boston, 1969.
———. *Five Lectures*. Boston, 1970.
———. *Kultur und Gesellschaft*. 2 vols. Frankfurt, 1965.
———. *Negations: Essays in Critical Theory*. Trans. J. J. Shapiro. Boston, 1969. (First published Suhrkamp Verlag, Frankfurt, 1965.)
———. "Neue Quellen zur Grundlegung des historischen Materialismus." *Die Gesellschaft* 11 (August 1932).
———. *One-Dimensional Man*. Boston, 1964.
———. *Reason and Revolution: Hegel and the Rise of Social Theory*. 2d ed. Boston, 1968.
———. "Repressive Tolerance." In *A Critique of Pure Tolerance*. With R. P. Wolf and B. Moore. Boston, 1970.
———. *Soviet Marxism: A Critical Analysis*. New York, 1961.
———. *Studies in Critical Philosophy*. Trans. J. DeBres. Boston, 1972.
———. "Thoughts on the Defense of Gracchus Babeuf." In *The Defense of Gracchus Babeuf*, ed. and trans. J. A. Scott. New York, 1972.
Marks, Robert W. *The Meaning of Marcuse*. New York, 1970.
Marx, Karl. *Capital*. 3 vols. New York, 1967.
———. *Critique of Hegel's "Philosophy of Right."* Trans. A. Jolin and J. O'Malley. Cambridge, 1970.
———. *The Economic and Philosophic Manuscripts of 1844*. Ed. P. J. Struik. Trans. M. Milligan. New York, 1964.
———. *The 18th Brumaire of Louis Napoleon*. New York, 1963.
———. *The German Ideology*. New York, 1947.
———. *The Poverty of Philosophy*. New York, 1963.
Marx, Karl, and Friedrich Engels. *Basic Writings*. Ed. L. Feuer. Garden City, 1959.
———. *Marx and Engels on Literature and Art*. Trans. L. Baxandall and S. Morawski. St. Louis, 1973.
———. *The Marx-Engels Reader*. Ed. R. C. Tucker. New York, 1972.
Mead, Margaret. "On the Institutional Role of Women in Character Formation." *Zeitschrift für Sozialforschung*, 5 (1937).
Meyer, Gerhard. "Krisenpolitik und Planwirtschaft." *Zeitschrift für Sozialforschung* 4 (1935).
Neumann, Franz. *Behemoth*. New York, 1944.
Nietzsche, Friedrich W. *The Gay Science and the Case of Wagner*. Trans. W. Kaufmann. New York, 1967.
———. "Thus Spoke Zarathustra." In *The Portable Nietzsche*, trans. W. Kaufmann. New York, 1954.

Bibliography of Cited Works 307

———. "Twilight of the Idols." In *The Portable Nietzsche,* trans. W. Kaufmann. New York, 1954.
———. *The Use and Abuse of History.* Trans. A. Collins. New York, 1957.
Pachter, Henry. "On Being an Exile." In *The Legacy of the German Refugee Intellectuals,* ed. R. Boyers. New York, 1972.
Piccone, Paul, and Alexander, Delfini. "Herbert Marcuse's Heideggerian Marxism." *Telos* 6 (Fall 1970).
Plekhanov, George V. *In Defense of Materialism.* Trans. Andrew Rothstein. London, 1947.
Rosen, Stanley. *G. W. F. Hegel.* New Haven, 1974.
Rousseau, Jean-Jacques. *The First and Second Discourses.* Trans. R. D. and J. R. Masters. New York, 1964.
Sartre, Jean-Paul. Preface to *The Wretched of the Earth* by Franz Fanon. New York, 1963.
Scholem, Gershom. *Major Trends in Jewish Mysticism.* New York, 1971.
———. "Walter Benjamin." In *The Leo Baeck Institute Yearbook.* New York, 1965.
Spengler, Oswald. *The Decline of the West.* New York, 1926.
Stace, W. T. *The Philosophy of Hegel.* New York, 1955.
Therborn, Goran. "The Frankfurt School." *New Left Review* 63 (Sept.-Oct. 1970).
Tiedemann, Rolf. *Studien zur Philosophie Walter Benjamins.* Frankfurt, 1973.
Tillich, Paul. "Book Review." *Zeitschrift für Sozialforschung* 5 (1936).
Tönnies, Ferdinand. "Das Recht auf Arbeit." *Zeitschrift für Sozialforschung* 4 (1936).
Trotsky, Leon. *On Literature and Art.* Ed. P. N. Siegel. New York, 1970.
Unseld, Siegfried, ed. *Zur Aktualität Walter Benjamins.* Frankfurt, 1972.
Weber, Shierry. "Walter Benjamin: Commodity Fetishism, the Modern and the Experience of History." In *The Unknown Dimension,* ed. D. Howard and K. B. Klare. New York, 1972.
Wittfogel, Karl. *Das Erwachende China.* Vienna, 1926.
———. *Geschichte der bürgerlichen Gesellschaft.* Vienna, 1924.

Index

Adorno, Theodor W.: on art, 151–158, 267, 270; on authenticity, 72, 124; on Benjamin, 151–152, 154–159, 201–202; on boredom, 288; on Brecht, 151–152, 154–155, 157; on culture, 139–140, 150–153, 154–157, 166; on death, 281, 285–287; on Freud and psychoanalysis, 87, 89, 132, 172; on Heidegger, 71, 73, 76, 125–126; on history, 47; on identity, 115–116, 122; Insitut für Sozialforschung, relations with, 21–24; on jazz, 150–151; on Judaism, 92, 94; on language, 125–126, 227; on Marx, 199; on Narcissism, 262–263; on negativity, 52–53; on Nietzsche, 70, 267 on philosophy, 207; on Positivism, 120; on Spengler, 56–57, 59, 79, 84–85, 214–219; on suffering, 250; on system, 69, 222; on taste, 138, 250; on texts, 212

Arendt, Hannah, 274

Aristotle, 289–291, 293–295

Arnold, Matthew, 41, 196

Art, 280–281, 298; as end in itself, 141–142; and Eros, 185; and jazz, 150–151, 156; and Marxism, 136–138; and mechanical reproduction, 144–148, 166–167; and negativity, 161–164, 166–167; and phantasy, 267–271, 274–275; and politics, 147–150, 155–159, 270–271; radio and television as, 151, 161, 164; as realism, 142–144; in the Soviet Union, 198

Auschwitz, 15–16, 25, 58, 100, 102, 113, 139–140, 221

Austen, Jane, 176

Benjamin, Walter: on art, 144–150, 271; and Brecht, 141, 151–152, 154–155, 210; and Critical Theory, 210; and Heidegger, 71; on history, 38–39, 45–46, 199, 249–250; Institut für Sozialforschung, relation to, 24–26; on Kafka, 270; on language, 153–154, 211; on Messiah and Messianism, 95–98, 158–159, 232–233; on proletariat, 234, 240; on revolution, 116, 243–244; on Social Democrats, 193, 199; on texts, 210–213

Bergson, Henri, 31

Bernstein, Eduard, 34

Blacks, 239–242

Blum, Leon, 19, 30, 187

Bourgeosie, 17–19, 191–193, 198–199, 268, 283, 289, 295

Brecht, Bertolt, 103, 149, 151–152, 154–155, 157, 159

Brenner, Hildegaard, 94

Buck-Morss, Susan, 151

Bureaucracy, 55, 190, 193, 199

Calvin, John, 163

Capitalism, 40–41, 44, 61, 117, 143, 185, 192–194, 200, 227, 229, 235

Carlyle, Thomas, 196

Conquest of Nature, 48, 90, 115, 117, 129, 170, 180, 184, 194–195, 200–202, 250, 253, 279, 281, 293

Critical Theory, 207–209, 213–217, 219, 222–225, 234, 241, 266–267
Culture industry, 95, 160–166, 170, 195, 227

Death, 77–78, 90, 175, 177, 279–288, 294–295
Dostoevsky, Feodor, 14, 31

Enlightenment, 31, 59, 103, 120–121, 126–129, 185, 200–203, 237; and capitalism, 143; and Judaism, 94; and modernity, 111–114; and myth, 131–135, 253; and Nietzsche, 62–63, 68–69; and passions, 183; and scarcity, 172; and Soviet Union, 198; and Spengler, 80–81
Eros, 88, 90, 163, 172, 174, 177–180, 201, 252, 260–262, 275–276, 279–280, 283–285, 289–291

Fascism, 79, 84–85, 104, 135, 166, 184, 270; relation to art, 154–159; and technology, 148–149, 189–190
Feuerbach, Ludwig, 59
Flaubert, Gustave, 17, 41
Frankfurt Institut für Sozialforschung: founding, 13; naming, 33–37
Freud, Sigmund, 19, 24, 31, 37, 87–91, 104, 123, 132, 170–175, 177, 179, 181, 244
Fromm, Erich, 23–24, 72

Gay, Peter, 31, 33, 111
George, Stefan, 67
God, 62, 130, 212, 242, 249, 273, 290
Grünberg, Carl, 33

Hegel, Georg W. F., 14–15, 50, 51, 181, 208, 225, 296, 299; on civil service, 54, 119; on history, 72, 106, 111–112; on identity, 52, 56–57; on reason, 53, 114–116, 221; and Young Hegelians, 57, 59
Heidegger, Martin, 19, 30–31, 37, 91, 135, 137, 141; on death, 77–78, 285; on Marx, 71–72; ontology, 73–75; and Positivism, 124–127

Hobbes, Thomas, 171, 299
Horkheimer, Max: on activism, 243; on art, 141; and Critical Theory, 209, 214, 223–224; on determinism, 38; on Freud and psychoanalysis, 89, 132; on history, 68; on intellectuals, 234; Institut für Sozialforschung, relations with, 21–24; on Judaism, 94; on labor, 118; on phantasy, 265; on Plato, 118; on privacy, 163; on proletariat, 39–40, 42–43, 191; on reason, 55–56, 117, 121; on spirituality, 188

Intellectuals, 17–19, 234

Jay, Martin, 23–24, 94, 222
Judaism, 19, 32, 74, 106, 150, 153, 197, 232, 263, 300–301; Marx's view of, 92–94; and Messianism, 96–102; and parents, honoring, 94–95; and texts, 211–212; and time, 248–249
Kafka, Franz, 155, 270
Kant, Immanuel, 112, 119
Kautsky, Karl, 29, 34
Kierkegaard, Soren, 50, 59–60, 261

Labor, 173–179, 184, 199–201, 252, 254–258, 272, 274
Laing, R. D., 264
Language, 96–97, 153–154, 211
Lenin, V. I., 29, 36–37, 88, 136, 168, 195, 199, 244
Lichtheim, George, 34
Löwith, Karl, 50
Lukács, Georg, 88, 103, 143, 168

Machiavelli, Niccolo, 14, 291
Mannheim, Karl, 23
Mao tse-Tung, 136, 296
Marcuse, Herbert: on art, 140–141, 156–159, 165, 268–269, 274; on blacks, 240; on bureaucracy, 193–194; on capitalism, 40, 193; and Critical Theory, 220–221; on death, 282–289; on Freud, 88–91, 174–175, 179–181; and Heidegger, 71, 73, 76–78; on history, 44–48, 186; on

Index

Marcuse (*cont.*)
human body, 259–260; on imperialism, 237–238; Institut für Sozialforschung, relation to, 21–23; on labor, 174; on materialism, 37; on negativity, 53; on Narcissus, 263; and Nietzsche, 3, 76; on play, 272; on privacy, 189; on proletariat, 240; on Prometheus, 130; on psyche, 252–253; on reality principle, 171; on reason, 118–119; on repressive tolerance, 228–229, 236; on revolution, 116, 244–246; on Rilke, 270; on Sartre, 243; on Soviet Union, 197–198; on students, 234–235; on third world, 236–238; on time, 282; on universities, 235–236; on war, 196

Marx, Karl, 14, 19, 25–26, 30–37, 58, 60, 68, 70, 85, 91, 103–104, 121, 160, 168–170, 191, 194, 208, 296, 299–300; on bureaucracy, 54–55; on class, 39; on culture, 136–139; on determinism, 38–39; and Heidegger, 71–72; on history, 45, 48, 331; on Judaism, 92–93; on proletariat, 39, 42, 191–192, 254, 274; on psychology, 87–89; on reason, 48, 114–116; on sensibility, 41; on technology, 83, 200

Mass culture, 65, 82–83
Messiah, 25, 95–98, 150, 158–159, 219, 231–233, 241–244, 248–249, 265, 270, 279
Mill, John Stuart, 228
Myth, 60, 66, 111, 127–128, 130–135, 164, 242, 246, 253, 255

Narcissus, 77, 256–257, 259–264, 281–282, 290
Nazi. *See* Fascism
Neo-Freudians, 123
Nietzsche, Friedrich, 14, 19, 30, 37, 58, 73, 76, 104, 113, 256, 261, 286–287, 294–295; on culture, 66, 137; on death, 283–284; on metaphysics, 63, on reaction, 67–68; on systematic philosophy, 68, 220
Nirvana, 177–180, 252

Odysseus, 111–112, 130–131
Orpheus, 256–259, 261–263, 281–283, 287, 290

Performance principle, 179–181, 251–252, 254, 256, 258, 263
Phantasy, 58, 263–268, 270–274
Philosophy, 207–209, 212–214
Plato, 64, 66, 73, 75, 111–112, 118–119, 208, 212, 230–231, 273, 285, 292, 299
Play, 173, 272, 274
Pleasure principle, 171–175, 266
Plekhanov, G. V., 136–137
Positivism, 65, 69, 75, 118–124, 132, 152, 164
Pound, Ezra, 141
Poverty, 41–42, 88–89
Privatization, 261–263, 273–274, 276, 289
Proletariat, 39–40, 42–44, 137, 150, 154, 191–196, 202, 226, 234–235, 249
Prometheus, myth of, 130, 251–252, 254–258, 263, 282, 293–295
Proudhon, Pierre, 279
Proust, Marcel, 271
Psyche, 49, 87–88, 91, 190, 200–201, 251–254, 263; Freud's view of, 163–167, 170–173; critique of Freud's view of, 173–174; and labor, 175–179; and repression, 180–185

Radicalism, 17–19
Reality principle, 175, 179–180, 264–265
Reason, 60, 122, 134; crisis of, 112–118; Hegel's view of, 48, 55–57; Nietzsche's critique of, 62–66
Repressive tolerance, 227–229, 297–298
Revolution, 97, 183, 191–192, 194, 219, 232–233, 236, 242–247
Rilke, Rainer, 257–258, 270
Romanticism, 67–68, 70, 246
Rousseau, Henri, 141
Rousseau, Jean-Jacques, 112–113

de Sade, the Marquis, 176
Sartre, Jean-Paul, 243–244
Scholem, Gershom, 22, 153, 211
Schopenhauer, Artur, 56, 59, 60
Sex, 175, 179, 198, 258–259, 261, 276, 281
Social Democrats, 18, 34, 37, 41, 88, 103, 136, 152, 193, 233, 297
Soviet Union, 18, 41, 136, 154, 197–199, 297
Spengler, Oswald, 19, 30–31, 56–57, 59, 79–85, 214–217
Stalin, Joseph, 19, 30, 34, 37, 103, 159, 199
Stirner, Max, 59
Strauss, David, 58
Strauss, Leo, 14
Strauss, Richard, 141
Students, 200, 203, 233–236, 240–242
Surplus repression, 252, 180–181
System, 68–69, 220–224

Technology, 14, 254, 282; and art, 144, 156, 160, 162, 164–166; and reifica-

Technology (*cont.*)
 tion, 188–190, 192, 195, 198–201; and scarcity, 172; and science, 129; Spengler, on, 83–84; and Thanatos, 178–179; and third world, 237–239
Terror, 189, 196–197
Text, 153–154, 210–214, 216, 219, 241
Thanatos, 70, 173–174, 177–180, 198, 201, 252, 279, 283–284
Third world, 200, 233, 236–238, 240
Tocqueville, Alexis, 164
Totalitarianism, 189, 227–228, 237
Trotsky, Leon, 29, 136, 140, 296

Virtue, 290–295, 298

War, 177, 184, 196, 202, 216
Warhol, Andy, 142
Weimar Germany, 31
Wittfogel, Karl, 23

Young Hegelians, 57–61

*The Political Philosophy
of the Frankfurt School*

Designed by Richard E. Rosenbaum.
Composed by The Composing Room of Michigan, Inc.
in 10 point Sabon V.I.P., 2 points leaded,
with display lines in Sabon.
Printed offset by Thomson/Shore, Inc. on
Warren's Number 66 Antique Offset, 50 pound basis.
Bound by John H. Dekker & Sons, Inc.
in Holliston book cloth
and stamped in Kurz-Hastings foil.

Library of Congress Cataloging in Publication Data

Friedman, George.
 The political philosophy of the Frankfurt School.

 Bibliography: p.
 Includes index.
 1. Frankfurt am Main. Institut für Sozialforschung. 2. Political science—Philosophy. 3. Philosophy, Modern—20th century. 4. Frankfurt School of sociology. I. Title.
 HM47.G72F743   301′.07′114341   80-66890
 ISBN 0-8014-1279-X